American Book Company

THE STANDARDS EXPERTS

Common Core Online Testing is now available!

On your computer: 4 Easy Steps!

1. Ask your teacher for your username and password
2. Visit coursewave.com
3. Enter your username and password and click "Sign In"
4. Select Grade 5 ELA Online Test

On your mobile device: 4 Easy Steps!

1. Ask your teacher for your username and password
2. Scan the QR code below
3. Enter your username and password and click "Sign In"
4. Select Grade 5 ELA Online Test

5 ELA
Common Core
2014-2015 Edition

Scan this QR code with your smart device to jump to coursewave.com

Online testing available through:
August 1, 2015

American Book Company
The Standards Experts

Common Core in Grade 5

English Language Arts

2014-2015 Edition

Authors

Jennifer Navarre

Brittany Rowland

Curriculum Designer

Stephanie Castleberry

AMERICAN BOOK COMPANY

P. O. BOX 2638

WOODSTOCK, GEORGIA 30188-1383

TOLL FREE 1 (888) 264-5877 PHONE (770) 928-2834

TOLL FREE FAX 1 (866) 827-3240

WEB SITE: www.americanbookcompany.com

ACKNOWLEDGEMENTS

The authors would like to gratefully acknowledge the technical contributions of Becky Wright, the editing expertise of Mallory Holder, and the proofreading expertise of Billie Stewart, Tabatha Martin, and Joshua Tompkins.
We also want to thank Lauren Anderson and Ryan Guyer for their expertise in developing many of the graphics for this book.

American Book Company is not held responsible for any content, questionable or otherwise, in the links or videos provided in this book. The views and opinions expressed on said links and videos are those of the original authors and contributors. They do not necessarily the represent the views and opinions of the authors of this book or American Book Company as a whole.

Please use safe Internet viewing practices and adult supervision when visiting the sites linked in this book.

The audio in chapter 7 is used with permission granted from Loreena McKennitt. Visit her website http://www.quinlanroad.com/ for more information.

TABLE OF CONTENTS

Preface

Common Core in Grade 5 English Language Arts will help students who are learning or reviewing the Common Core State Standards (CCSS). The materials in this book are based 100 percent on the CCSS (www.corestandards.org) and were written to the 5th grade Lexile level: 830L to 1010L.

This book contains four sections:
1) General information about the book
2) A pretest and evaluation chart
3) Eleven chapters that review the concepts and skills of the Common Core Standards
4) A post test

Standards are posted at the beginning of each chapter and at the beginning of each practice. Standards taught directly in the content of the chapter are in **bold** typeface. The standards that are indirectly covered through practice exercises or chapter reviews are in regular typeface.

Teachers: See the "Teacher Guide for *Common Core in Grade 5 English Language Arts*" to access additional material for classroom and one-on-one use.

We welcome comments and suggestions about the book. Please contact the authors at

American Book Company
PO Box 2638
Woodstock, GA 30188-1383

Toll Free: 1 (888) 264-5877
Phone: (770) 928-2834
Fax: (770) 928-7483
Website: www.americanbookcompany.com

DOK Levels

Level 1: Recall and Reproduction (DOK 1)

DOK level 1 questions include recalling information such as facts, definitions, or simple procedures, pointing out key details of a text or narrative, identifying the sequence of events, and identifying characters, plot, setting, and so on. A few example DOK level 1 questions are listed below.

- This passage best fits into which genre?

- Which words best describe the main character?

- What best describes the setting of the passage?

- Based on the passage, what is the meaning of the word <u>serene</u>?

Level 2: Skills and Concepts/Basic Reasoning (DOK 2)

DOK level 2 questions involve some mental processing beyond a habitual response. These questions require students to make some decisions about how to approach the question, make inferences, understand the organization of a text, use context clues, summarize, and make predictions. A few example DOK level 2 level questions are listed below.

- Which transitional phrases show that this passage is organized using comparison and contrast?

- What is the best way to revise this sentence?

- What is the best summary for this passage?

- How does the narrator's point of view affect the outcome of the passage?

Level 3: Strategic Thinking/Complex Reasoning (DOK 3)

DOK level 3 questions require reasoning, planning, using evidence, and higher levels of thinking beyond what was required in DOK levels 1 and 2. This level requires students to explain their thinking, and cognitive demands are more complex and abstract. DOK 3 questions demand that students use reasoning skills to draw conclusions from observations and make conjectures. Some examples of DOK level 3 questions are listed below.

- After reading the passage and viewing the chart, which of the following is true?

- How do these two different passages address the same topic?

- How does the author of one passage present information differently than the author of another passage? (when comparing two or more passages on the same topic)

- Describe how the theme of this story relates to the universal themes of other stories from different cultures.

Level 4: Extended Thinking/Reasoning (DOK 4)
DOK level 4 questions cover concepts such as complex reasoning, planning, and developing. Student thinking will most likely take place over an extended period of time, and that will include synthesizing and analyzing a number of resources. Students should be required to make several connections and relate ideas within the content area or among other content areas. Level 4 questions investigate real-world problems. A few example tasks are presented below.

- Analyze the given sources to prepare a research paper on the topic covered.

- Collaborate with a group of classmates to research a topic and complete a project.

- Write a persuasive speech on a given topic to present in front of your teacher and classmates.

About the Authors

Jennifer Navarre has a Bachelor of Arts in English and a Master of Arts in Liberal Studies with an English emphasis from Clayton State University. She has worked extensively as a tutor for high school and college students and presented at conferences including the Southeastern Writing Center Association.

Brittany Rowland graduated from Kennesaw State University with a master's degree in professional writing. As a substitute teacher, she has taught English and literature to high school students. Additionally, Brittany has written short fiction and worked as a content writer for developing websites.

About the Curriculum Designer

Stephanie Castleberry has a Bachelor of Arts in English from Kennesaw State University and a Master of Arts in Educational Leadership from The University of North Florida. She has over a decade of experience in the education field, with roles including a high school English teacher, a children's librarian, an SAT tutor, a college writing instructor, and an instructional designer.

Charts of Standards

Common Core English Language Arts Standards for Grade 5

Reading Literature
Key Ideas and Details
1. Quote accurately from a text when explaining what the text says explicitly and when drawing inferences from the text.
2. Determine a theme of a story, drama, or poem from details in the text, including how characters in a story or drama respond to challenges or how the speaker in a poem reflects upon a topic; summarize the text.
3. Compare and contrast two or more characters, settings, or events in a story or drama, drawing on specific details in the text (e.g., how characters interact).

Craft and Structure
4. Determine the meaning of words and phrases as they are used in a text, including figurative language such as metaphors and similes.
5. Explain how a series of chapters, scenes, or stanzas fits together to provide the overall structure of a particular story, drama, or poem.
6. Describe how a narrator's or speaker's point of view influences how events are described.

Integration of Knowledge and Ideas
7. Analyze how visual and multimedia elements contribute to the meaning, tone, or beauty of a text (e.g., graphic novel, multimedia presentation of fiction, folktale, myth, poem).
8. (Not applicable to literature)
9. Compare and contrast stories in the same genre (e.g., mysteries and adventure stories) on their approaches to similar themes and topics.

Range of Reading and Complexity of Text
10. By the end of the year, read and comprehend literature, including stories, dramas, and poetry, at the high end of the grades 4–5 text complexity band independently and proficiently.

Reading Informational Texts
Key Ideas and Details
1. Quote accurately from a text when explaining what the text says explicitly and when drawing inferences from the text.
2. Determine two or more main ideas of a text and explain how they are supported by key details; summarize the text.
3. Explain the relationships or interactions between two or more individuals, events, ideas, or concepts in a historical, scientific, or technical text based on specific information in the text.

Craft and Structure
4. Determine the meaning of general academic and domain-specific words and phrases in a text relevant to a *grade 5 topic or subject area*.
5. Compare and contrast the overall structure (e.g., chronology, comparison, cause/effect, problem/solution) of events, ideas, concepts, or information in two or more texts.
6. Analyze multiple accounts of the same event or topic, noting important similarities and differences in the point of view they represent.

Integration of Knowledge and Ideas
7. Draw on information from multiple print or digital sources, demonstrating the ability to locate an answer to a question quickly or to solve a problem efficiently.

8. Explain how an author uses reasons and evidence to support particular points in a text, identifying which reasons and evidence support which point(s).
9. Integrate information from several texts on the same topic in order to write or speak about the subject knowledgeably.

Range of Reading and Level of Text Complexity
10. By the end of the year, read and comprehend informational texts, including history/social studies, science, and technical texts, at the high end of the grades 4–5 text complexity band independently and proficiently.

Reading Foundational Skills
Phonics and Word Recognition
3. Know and apply grade-level phonics and word analysis skills in decoding words.
   a. Use combined knowledge of all letter-sound correspondences, syllabication patterns, and morphology (e.g., roots and affixes) to read accurately unfamiliar multisyllabic words in context and out of context.

Fluency
4. Read with sufficient accuracy and fluency to support comprehension.
   a. Read grade-level text with purpose and understanding.
   b. Read grade-level prose and poetry orally with accuracy, appropriate rate, and expression.
   c. Use context to confirm or self-correct word recognition and understanding, rereading as necessary.

Writing
Text Types and Purposes
1. Write opinion pieces on topics or texts, supporting a point of view with reasons and information.
   a. Introduce a topic or text clearly, state an opinion, and create an organizational structure in which ideas are logically grouped to support the writer's purpose.
   b. Provide logically ordered reasons that are supported by facts and details.
   c. Link opinion and reasons using words, phrases, and clauses (e.g., *consequently*, *specifically*).
   d. Provide a concluding statement or section related to the opinion presented.
2. Write informative/explanatory texts to examine a topic and convey ideas and information clearly.
   a. Introduce a topic clearly, provide a general observation and focus, and group related information logically; include formatting (e.g., headings), illustrations, and multimedia when useful to aiding comprehension.
   b. Develop the topic with facts, definitions, concrete details, quotations, or other information and examples related to the topic.
   c. Link ideas within and across categories of information using words, phrases, and clauses (e.g., *in contrast*, *especially*).
   d. Use precise language and domain-specific vocabulary to inform about or explain the topic.
   e. Provide a concluding statement or section related to the information or explanation presented.
3. Write narratives to develop real or imagined experiences or events using effective technique, descriptive details, and clear event sequences.
   a. Orient the reader by establishing a situation and introducing a narrator and/or characters; organize an event sequence that unfolds naturally.
   b. Use narrative techniques, such as dialogue, description, and pacing, to develop experiences and events or show the responses of characters to situations.
   c. Use a variety of transitional words, phrases, and clauses to manage the sequence of events.
   d. Use concrete words and phrases and sensory details to convey experiences and events precisely.
   e. Provide a conclusion that follows from the narrated experiences or events.

Production and Distribution of Writing
4. Produce clear and coherent writing in which the development and organization are appropriate to task, purpose, and audience. (Grade-specific expectations for writing types are defined in standards 1–3 above.)
5. With guidance and support from peers and adults, develop and strengthen writing as needed by planning, revising, editing, rewriting, or trying a new approach.
6. With some guidance and support from adults, use technology, including the Internet, to produce and publish writing as well as to interact and collaborate with others; demonstrate sufficient command of keyboarding skills to type a minimum of two pages in a single sitting.

Research to Build and Present Knowledge

7. Conduct short research projects that use several sources to build knowledge through investigation of different aspects of a topic.

8. Recall relevant information from experiences or gather relevant information from print and digital sources; summarize or paraphrase information in notes and finished work, and provide a list of sources.

9. Draw evidence from literary or informational texts to support analysis, reflection, and research.

   a. Apply *grade 5 Reading standards* to literature (e.g., "Compare and contrast two or more characters, settings, or events in a story or a drama, drawing on specific details in the text [e.g., how characters interact]").

   b. Apply *grade 5 Reading standards* to informational texts (e.g., "Explain how an author uses reasons and evidence to support particular points in a text, identifying which reasons and evidence support which point[s]").

Range of Writing

10. Write routinely over extended time frames (time for research, reflection, and revision) and shorter time frames (a single sitting or a day or two) for a range of discipline-specific tasks, purposes, and audiences.

Speaking and Listening

Comprehension and Collaboration

1. Engage effectively in a range of collaborative discussions (one-on-one, in groups, and teacher-led) with diverse partners on *grade 5 topics and texts*, building on others' ideas and expressing their own clearly.

   a. Come to discussions prepared, having read or studied required material; explicitly draw on that preparation and other information known about the topic to explore ideas under discussion.

   b. Follow agreed-upon rules for discussions and carry out assigned roles.

   c. Pose and respond to specific questions by making comments that contribute to the discussion and elaborate on the remarks of others.

   d. Review the key ideas expressed and draw conclusions in light of information and knowledge gained from the discussions.

2. Summarize a written text read aloud or information presented in diverse media and formats, including visually, quantitatively, and orally.

3. Summarize the points a speaker makes and explain how each claim is supported by reasons and evidence.

Presentation of Knowledge and Ideas

4. Report on a topic or text or present an opinion, sequencing ideas logically and using appropriate facts and relevant, descriptive details to support main ideas or themes; speak clearly at an understandable pace.

5. Include multimedia components (e.g., graphics, sound) and visual displays in presentations when appropriate to enhance the development of main ideas or themes.

6. Adapt speech to a variety of contexts and tasks, using formal English when appropriate to task and situation.

Language

Conventions of Standard English

1. Demonstrate command of the conventions of standard English grammar and usage when writing or speaking.

   a. Explain the function of conjunctions, prepositions, and interjections in general and their function in particular sentences.

   b. Form and use the perfect (e.g., *I had walked; I have walked; I will have walked*) verb tenses.

   c. Use verb tense to convey various times, sequences, states, and conditions.

   d. Recognize and correct inappropriate shifts in verb tense.*

   e. Use correlative conjunctions (e.g., *either/or, neither/nor*).

2. Demonstrate command of the conventions of standard English capitalization, punctuation, and spelling when writing.

   a. Use punctuation to separate items in a series.*

   b. Use a comma to separate an introductory element from the rest of the sentence.

   c. Use a comma to set off the words *yes* and *no* (e.g., *Yes, thank you*), to set off a tag question from the rest of the sentence (e.g., *It's true, isn't it?*), and to indicate direct address (e.g., *Is that you, Steve?*).

   d. Use underlining, quotation marks, or italics to indicate titles of works.

   e. Spell grade-appropriate words correctly, consulting references as needed.

Knowledge of Language

3. Use knowledge of language and its conventions when writing, speaking, reading, or listening.

    a. Expand, combine, and reduce sentences for meaning, reader/listener interest, and style.

    b. Compare and contrast the varieties of English (e.g., *dialects, registers*) used in stories, dramas, or poems.

Vocabulary Acquisition and Use

4. Determine or clarify the meaning of unknown and multiple-meaning words and phrases based on grade 5 reading and content, choosing flexibly from a range of strategies.

    a. Use context (e.g., cause/effect relationships and comparisons in text) as a clue to the meaning of a word or phrase.

    b. Use common, grade-appropriate Greek and Latin affixes and roots as clues to the meaning of a word (e.g., *photograph, photosynthesis*).

    c. Consult reference materials (e.g., dictionaries, glossaries, thesauruses), both print and digital, to find the pronunciation and determine or clarify the precise meaning of key words and phrases.

5. Demonstrate understanding of figurative language, word relationships, and nuances in word meanings.

    a. Interpret figurative language, including similes and metaphors, in context.

    b. Recognize and explain the meaning of common idioms, adages, and proverbs.

    c. Use the relationship between particular words (e.g., synonyms, antonyms, homographs) to better understand each of the words.

6. Acquire and use accurately grade-appropriate general academic and domain-specific words and phrases, including those that signal contrast, addition, and other logical relationships (e.g., *however, although, nevertheless, similarly, moreover, in addition*).

[NOTE: Beginning in grade 3, skills and understandings that are particularly likely to require continued attention in higher grades as they are applied to increasingly sophisticated writing and speaking are marked with an asterisk (*).]

Common Core Chart

The following chart correlates the questions in each part of the pretest, the post test, and the online test to the Common Core State Standards. Note: Some question numbers appear under multiple standards if the questions cover more than one claim or assessment target.

Note: The chapters in **bold** typeface cover standards in content of chapter. The chapters in regular typeface include practice exercises that evaluate student's grasp of standard.

Common Core Standard	Chapter	Pretest	Post Test	Online Test
RL 1	**1, 2, 3,** 5, 6, 7, 11	1, 7	9, 14	7
RL 2	2, **6,** 7, 11	2	–	–
RL 3	**7**	6	10	1
RL 4	**4,** 5, 7, **10**	5	–	2, 8
RL 5	3, 5, **7**	–	12	4
RL 6	3, **6,** 7	4	13, 15	–
RL 7	5, **6,** 7	–	11	6
RL 9	5, **7**	3	–	3, 5
RL 10	3, **5,** 6, 7	–	–	–
RI 1	**1, 2, 3, 8,** 11	15	5	–
RI 2	**2, 3,** 6, **8,** 11	8	–	12, 15
RI 3	**2, 3, 8**	–	7	–
RI 4	**4, 8**	–	1	10
RI 5	**3, 8**	–	3	9
RI 6	**3, 8**	11	4	14
RI 7	**8**	12	6	–
RI 8	**3, 8**	9	2	13
RI 9	**3, 8**	13	–	–
RI 10	**8**	–	–	–
RF 3	**4**	–	–	–
RF 4	2, **4,** 5, 6, 12	–	–	–
W 1	**10**	29, 40	17	16, 21
W 2	8, **10**	28, 31	16, 19, 21	17, 22, 40
W 3	**10**	27	22, 23, 40	20
W 4	**1, 10**	30, 40	40	40
W 5	**10**	40	40	40
W 6	**1, 10**	40	40	40

Common Core Standard	Chapter	Pretest	Post Test	Online Test
W 7	10, **11**	35, 37, 40	33, 34, 38, 40	38, 40
W 8	8, 10, **11**	32, 33, 36, 38, 40	32, 36, 39, 40	32, 33, 36, 37, 40
W 9	**1**, 8, 10, **11**	34, 39, 40	35, 37, 40	34, 35, 39, 40
W 10	**10, 11**	40	40	40
SL 1	**12**	18, 22	25	25
SL 2	**12**	16, 20, 23	24	29, 31
SL 3	**12**	17, 19, 21	27, 28, 29	26, 28, 30
SL 4	**12**	–	26	24
SL 5	**12**	–	30	27
SL 6	**12**	–	31	–
L 1	**9**	24, 25, 40	18, 40	19, 40
L 2	**9**	24, 25, 40	18, 20, 40	18, 23, 40
L 3	7, **9**	26, 40	40	40
L 4	**4**	10, 40	40	11, 40
L 5	**4, 5**, 7	14, 40	8, 40	40
L 6	3, **4**	40	40	40

DOK Chart

The following chart shows the correlation of all test questions to the Depth of Knowledge levels. The abbreviation DOK is used to denote the level on each test question.

	DOK 1	DOK 2	DOK 3	DOK 4
Pretest	1, 15, 21, 24, 25, 26	2, 5, 8, 10, 12, 13, 14, 16, 17, 19, 20, 22, 23, 27, 28, 29, 30, 31, 32, 35, 36	3, 4, 6, 7, 9, 11, 18, 33, 34	37–40
Post Test	18, 19, 20, 25	1, 3, 7, 8, 9, 12, 16, 17, 21, 22, 23, 24, 26, 27, 28, 31, 32, 33, 34, 36	2, 4, 5, 6, 10, 11, 13, 14, 15, 29, 30, 35	37–40
Online Test	8, 11, 18, 19, 22, 23, 24, 28	2, 4, 5, 6, 10, 12, 15, 16, 17, 20, 21, 26, 27, 29, 31, 32, 33, 36	1, 3, 7, 9, 13, 14, 25, 30, 34, 35	37–40

Pretest

Excerpt from *Anne of Green Gables*
by Lucy Maud Montgomery

Matthew Cuthbert and the sorrel mare jogged comfortably over the eight miles to Bright River … When he reached Bright River there was no sign of any train … The long platform was almost deserted; the only living creature in sight being a girl who was sitting on a pile of shingles at the extreme end. Matthew, barely noting that it *was* a girl, sidled past her as quickly as possible without looking at her. Had he looked he could hardly have failed to notice the tense rigidity and expectation of her attitude and expression. She was sitting there waiting for something or somebody and, since sitting and waiting was the only thing to do just then, she sat and waited with all her might and main. Matthew encountered the stationmaster … and asked him if the five-thirty train would soon be along.

"The five-thirty train has been in and gone half an hour ago," answered that brisk official. "But there was a passenger dropped off for you—a little girl … I asked her to go into the ladies' waiting room, but she informed me … she preferred to stay outside. 'There was more scope for imagination,' she said. She's a case, I should say."

"I'm not expecting a girl," said Matthew blankly. "It's a boy I've come for. He should be here …"

The stationmaster whistled.

"Guess there's some mistake," he said. "Mrs. Spencer came off the train with that girl … Said you and your sister were adopting her from an orphan asylum and that you would be along for her presently. That's all I know about it—and I haven't got any more orphans concealed hereabouts."

"I don't understand," said Matthew helplessly …

"Well, you'd better question the girl," said the stationmaster carelessly. "I dare say she'll be able to explain—she's got a tongue of her own, that's certain … Maybe they were out of boys of the brand you wanted."

Matthew groaned in spirit as he turned about and shuffled gently down the platform towards her.

She had been watching him ever since he had passed her and she had her eyes on him now … She wore a faded brown sailor hat and extending down her back were two braids of very thick, decidedly red hair. Her face was small, white and thin, also much freckled; her mouth was large and so were her eyes, which looked green in some lights and gray in others.

An extraordinary observer might have seen that the chin was very pointed and pronounced; that the big eyes were full of spirit and vivacity; that the mouth was sweet-lipped and expressive; that the forehead was broad and full; in short, our discerning extraordinary observer might have concluded that no commonplace soul inhabited the body of this stray woman-child of whom shy Matthew Cuthbert was so ludicrously afraid.

Matthew … was spared the ordeal of speaking first, for as soon as she concluded that he was coming to her she stood up, with one thin brown hand grasping the handle of a shabby, old-fashioned carpetbag; the other she held out to him. "I suppose you are Mr. Matthew Cuthbert of Green Gables?" she said in a peculiarly clear, sweet voice. "I'm very glad to see you. I was beginning to be afraid you weren't coming for me and I was imagining all the things that might have happened to prevent you … And I was quite sure you would come for me in the morning, if you didn't to-night." Matthew had taken the scrawny little hand awkwardly in his; then and there he decided what to do …

"I'm sorry I was late," he said shyly.

1 According to the text, what mistake had been made?   RL.5.1
                                                                             DOK 1

A) The orphanage sent a girl instead of a boy.

B) The five-thirty train was late.

C) Matthew went to the wrong train station.

D) The stationmaster didn't know anything about trains.

                                                                             RL.5.2

2 What is the theme of this story? Include details from the text that support your   DOK 2
answer.

_____

_____

_____

                                                                             RL.5.9

3 How would this story **most likely** differ if it were a mystery instead of   DOK 3
historical fiction?

A) Matthew would investigate how the orphanage made a mistake.

B) The train would be able to travel through time.

C) The stationmaster would explain the lesson of the story.

D) Matthew's horse would be able to speak.

4 The author has the stationmaster say to Matthew, "I haven't got any more orphans concealed hereabouts." Why did the author choose to include this sentence in the text?

RL.5.6
DOK 3

A) to give a clue that the stationmaster is hiding something

B) to illustrate how much control the stationmaster has over the station

C) to show that the stationmaster is nervous about making a mistake

D) to reveal that the stationmaster has a sense of humor

(E) to suggest that the train brings orphans all the time

5 Read the sentences from the text on the left. Then, match the underlined word in each sentence to its closest definition on the right.

RL.5.4
DOK 2

Had he looked he could hardly have failed to notice the tense <u>rigidity</u> and expectation of her attitude and expression.	perceptive
	in sequence
An <u>extraordinary</u> observer might have seen that the chin was very pointed and pronounced.	difficult experience
	stiffness
In short, our <u>discerning</u> extraordinary observer might have concluded that no commonplace soul inhabited the body of this stray woman-child of whom shy Matthew Cuthbert was so ludicrously afraid.	unfair
	beyond the usual
Matthew … was spared the <u>ordeal</u> of speaking first, for as soon as she concluded that he was coming to her she stood up.	defiance

6 How are Matthew and the girl **most** different? Include details from the text to support your answer.

RL.5.3
DOK 3

_____

_____

_____

7 Select **three** sentences that support the idea that Matthew feels apprehensive about approaching the girl.

RL.5.1
DOK 3

A) Matthew Cuthbert and the sorrel mare jogged comfortably over the eight miles to Bright River.

B) Matthew, barely noting that it *was* a girl, sidled past her as quickly as possible without looking at her.

C) "I'm not expecting a girl," said Matthew blankly. "It's a boy I've come for."

D) Matthew groaned in spirit as he turned about and shuffled gently down the platform towards her.

E) Matthew … was spared the ordeal of speaking first, for as soon as she concluded that he was coming to her she stood up, with one thin brown hand grasping the handle of a shabby, old-fashioned carpetbag; the other she held out to him.

F) Matthew had taken the scrawny little hand awkwardly in his; then and there he decided what to do …

Teams, Clubs, and Groups

Good afternoon. For those of you who don't know me, I'm Mrs. Roberts. I'm the assistant principal here at Ridgefield School. I asked Principal Walker for a chance to speak to all of you today. Next week, I will speak to the school board about a matter that concerns you, the students of Ridgefield School. Because I believe all students should participate in at least one extracurricular activity, I am going to ask that it become a school requirement. After you hear my reasons for this, I would like to know what you think.

As a lot of you know, our school offers many different sports teams. We have various instrumental music groups and singing groups to take part in. In addition, we offer many clubs for student interest and service projects. Students are lucky to have so many options; however, only about one-third of our students take part in these programs. This saddens me. Recent studies have shown that when students are involved in school groups, it benefits both the student and the school as a whole.

Belonging to a school team, group, or club gives a student a social circle. He or she is connected to peers who share an interest. Everyone likes to belong to something. As a member of a group, you will have a chance to learn more about the people around you, and you might discover there are many things you have in common. You might discover a peer is facing a challenge you knew nothing about. You might learn from the way that person deals with those challenges. You will make friends and learn to respect others' differences.

Belonging to a school group also builds self-confidence. Joining a group can be a chance to try something new—you may have talents you have not yet discovered. You might have a gift for a sport, the arts, organization, or leadership. Extracurricular activities give students a chance to get out of the classroom and discover and develop those gifts. Once you find your feet in a club or team, you will see these talents in yourself and become a more confident person.

Participating in school activities also helps you build skills for the future. As a member of a group, you will need to learn to work with others; thus, you'll learn how to express your opinions in an effective way. You will learn to listen to and respect the opinions of others. You will learn the importance of showing up and doing your part. Middle school will offer many opportunities to become a part of a team or club. Finding out your interests now will help you to not be overwhelmed come next year.

Not only do these activities benefit the individual, but they also benefit the school as a whole. More than one study shows that students who belong to school clubs, teams, and organizations miss less school than students who do not belong. The less school a student misses, the greater the chances of school success. In addition, students who belong to these groups have a greater sense of being part of the school community. Members of a community will work together to keep their school in good shape. They are less likely to cause damage to the building or the grounds. These students also tend to look out for other members of the community, which can cut down on bullying. Finally, these activities provide added adult supervision for students; this extra guidance helps students avoid dangerous behaviors, cutting down the amount of trouble a school needs to deal with.

I've mentioned many of the findings of researchers who have studied participation in extracurricular groups. These studies are important and do highlight many of the benefits. I also would like to simplify the matter for all of you today. Join a team, group, or club because it is fun. It is fun to belong. It is fun to try new things. It is fun to get better at or learn more about what interests you. Join a team, club, or group because it will be better and stronger with you as a part of it.

Next week, I will talk to the school board about requiring students to join a team, club, or group. My hope is that once you experience the benefits of participating in an extracurricular activity, it will no longer be necessary to make it a requirement. Until then, I think you will agree that the rule is needed.

8 This question has two parts. First, answer part A. Then, answer part B. RI.5.2

Part A DOK 2

Which statement **best** summarizes the main idea of the text?

A) Participating in clubs benefits both the students and the school.

B) Only the most popular students should sign up for clubs.

C) Teams, clubs, and groups will interfere with studying time.

D) Signing up for clubs costs students too much money.

Part B

Which sentences support this main idea? Select **all** that apply.

A) Next week, I will speak to the school board about a matter that concerns you, the students of Ridgefield School.

B) Belonging to a school team, group, or club gives a student a social circle.

C) Joining a group can be a chance to try something new—you may have talents you have not yet discovered.

D) Middle school will offer many opportunities to become a part of a team or club.

E) More than one study shows that students who belong to school clubs, teams, and organizations miss less school than students who do not belong.

9 What are the reasons the speaker gives to explain why students' participating in activities benefits the school? Select **all** that apply.

RI.5.8
DOK 3

A) Participation cuts down on student absences.

B) Participation increases a sense of community.

C) Participation gives teachers a break from teaching.

D) Participation keeps students out of trouble.

E) Participation increases the number of popular kids.

10 Read these sentences from the text and the directions that follow.

L.5.4
DOK 2

> Joining a group can be a chance to try something new—you may have talents you have not yet discovered. You might have a gift for a sport, the arts, organization, or leadership. <u>Extracurricular</u> activities give students a chance to get out of the classroom and discover and develop those gifts.

Underline the phrase in the text that helps you understand what the word <u>extracurricular</u> means.

11 How would a speech written by the captain of the basketball team **most** differ from this text?

RI.5.
DOK 3

_____

_____

RI.5.7
DOK 2

12 Which graphic feature would **best** help a student understand the information in this text?

A) a map showing the locations of each club

B) a slideshow listing the benefits of clubs

C) a picture of the members of the science club

D) a timeline showing the history of school clubs

13 Read this sentence from the text and the question that follows.

L.5.5
DOK 2

> Once you <u>find your feet</u> in a club or team, you will see these talents in yourself and become a more confident person.

What does the phrase <u>find your feet</u> mean as it is used in the text?

A) to learn a new dance step

B) to adjust to something new

C) to stay physically active

D) to take on a leadership role

14 Read the information in this graph and the question that follows.

RI.5.9
DOK 2

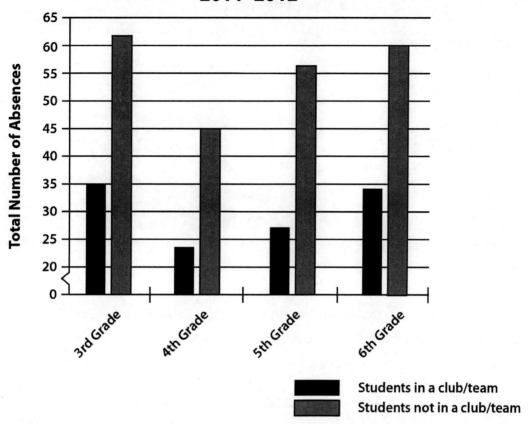

Total Student Absences at Ridgefield School, 2011–2012

The information in the graph supports which idea from the text?

A) More than one study shows that students who belong to school clubs, teams, and organizations miss less school than students who do not belong to any school-sponsored group.

B) The less school a student misses the greater the chances of school success.

C) In addition, students who belong to these groups have a greater sense of being part of the school community.

D) Members of a community will work together to keep their school in good shape. They are less likely to cause damage to the building or the grounds.

15 Why is Mrs. Roberts making it a requirement that all students must join a club, team, or group?

RI.5.1
DOK 1

A) The school board has demanded that the rule be set.

B) The arts and music groups do not have enough members.

C) Students do not know what to do in their free time.

D) Only one-third of students currently participate in the programs.

Listen to this presentation, and answer the questions that follow.

Excerpt from *Rikki-tikki-tavi*
by Rudyard Kipling

http://americanbookcompany.com/media/rikki-tikki-tavi

---

16 What is the narrator's point of view toward mongooses?

SL.5.2
DOK 2

   A) The narrator thinks mongooses are dangerous animals.

   B) The narrator thinks mongooses are brave because they are hard to frighten.

   C) The narrator thinks mongooses make better pets than dogs or cats.

   D) The narrator thinks mongooses need a lot of supervision and discipline.

17 How can you tell Rikki-tikki is curious? Use **at least two** details from the presentation to support your answer.

SL.5.3
DOK 2

_____

_____

18 In the story, Rikki-tikki and Teddy become friends. From the way Rikki-tikki behaves, what is one thing he would **most likely** do?

SL.5.1
DOK 3

   A) protect the boy from dangerous animals

   B) run away the first chance he gets

   C) hide behind the boy at any sign of danger

   D) bite the boy's hand

19 Read this sentence from the presentation and the question that follows.

SL.5.3
DOK 2

   It is the hardest thing in the world to frighten a mongoose because he is eaten up from nose to tail with curiosity.

The author uses figurative language in this sentence for what purpose?

   A) to foreshadow that Rikki-tikki will be scared

   B) to explain that many predators eat mongooses

   D) to emphasize how inquisitive mongooses are

   E) to assure readers that he has tried to scare a mongoose

Listen to this presentation, and answer the questions that follow.

Wilma Mankiller, an Inspirational American

http://americanbookcompany.com/media/wilma-mankiller

20 What happened after Wilma Mankiller moved back to Oklahoma in 1977?

A) She lived in housing provided by the government for Native Americans.

B) She became the principal chief of the Cherokee Nation.

C) She married her husband and raised two daughters.

D) She attended Dartmouth College.

SL.5.2
DOK 2

21 According to the presentation, what were **three** ways that Wilma Mankiller brought about positive change for the Cherokee Nation?

SL.5.3
DOK 1

_____

_____

_____

22 Which of the following events would **most likely** "give your spine a chill" in the same way hearing the name *Mankiller* in the presentation did?

A) hearing a strange noise in the basement when you're home alone

B) stepping outside on a windy day when you're not wearing a coat

C) opening a present and seeing that it's exactly what you wished for

D) curling up under a blanket in front of a warm fire

SL.5.1
DOK 2

23 Which **best** summarizes the information in the presentation?

A) Wilma Mankiller lived a life of luxury.

B) Wilma Mankiller dedicated her life to politics.

C) Wilma Mankiller had many responsibilities and duties.

D) Wilma Mankiller made history and brought about change.

SL.5.2
DOK 2

Pretest

Read and answer the following questions.

24 Select the **one** sentence that does **not** contain any errors.

   A) The refrigerator had neither eggs or milk, so we had to go to the store.

   B) Mrs. Clemens said, "Please close the blinds Jake so we can start the movie."

   C) Elvis Presley had a hit with the song Hound Dog in the 1950s.

   D) By the end of this year, I will have collected over sixty new stamps.

L.5.1, L.5.2
DOK 1

25 Gregory is writing an essay about llamas. Read a paragraph from his essay and the directions that follow.

L.5.1, L.5.2
DOK 1

> Llamas are a type of camelid found mainly in the Andes. They are in the same animal family as camels and alpacas. Unlike camels however llamas don't have a hump. People using llamas to carry goods and people for hundreds of years. Llamas are intelligent, friendly creatures that are easy to train.

Rewrite **two** sentences from the paragraph that contain errors in grammar.

Unlike camels, llamas don't have a hump. People use llamas to carry goods and people for hundreds of years.

26 Katya is writing a report on an American president. Read a paragraph from her report and the directions that follow.

L.5.3
DOK 1

> Many people believe that Franklin D. Roosevelt was one of our nation's ~~bossest~~ leaders. He took over our country during the Great Depression. This was a period when many people had lost their homes and their jobs. With this in mind, Roosevelt told Americans that "the only thing we have to fear is fear itself" during his first <u>inaugural</u> address. Real quick-like, Roosevelt took action to get America back on track.

Underline **two** words or phrases that are too informal or inappropriate to use in this report.

27 Francine is writing instructions on how to swim the freestyle stroke. She wants to organize her instructions clearly. Read these sentences from her instructions and the directions that follow.

W.5.4
DOK 2

2 Once you rise to the surface, bring one arm out of the water with the elbow bent.
3 Repeat the same motion with the other arm.
6 Turn your head to the side to breathe on every third stroke.
1 Push off from the wall, facing forward and lying on your stomach.
4 Begin flutter kicking right away to propel your body forward.
5 Reach forward with the same arm and, cupping your hand, pull it back through the water.

What is the **best** order for these sentences? Number them from 1 to 6, with 1 being first and 6 being last.

Page 10
Copyright © American Book Company

28 Which of the following is the **best** source to use for an assignment on the invention of film?

W.5.8
DOK 2

(A) the movie *Hugo*, which features an early filmmaker

C) the book *Cinema through the Ages*

B) an article about a new digital camera

D) a biography of Walt Disney

29 Jaden is writing a narrative about his first day at a new school. His teacher suggests that he add a conclusion to improve the narrative. Read these paragraphs from Jaden's narrative and the directions that follow.

W.5.3
DOK 2

It was my first day at the new school, and I was as nervous as could be. I wondered if I would have friends and if my teachers would like me. I wondered if I had the right clothes on and if I would say the right things. As I sat in language arts class waiting for Mrs. Reid to say it was time for lunch, a terrifying thought occurred to me in a sudden flash—I had forgotten to bring my lunch!

Yes, it was packed and sitting on the counter when I left this morning. Yes, I had brought it in the car; I remembered seeing it on the seat beside me as I had told my toddler brother not to drop his gooey, baby-wet Pop-Tart crumbs on top of it. But, where was it now?

In less than five minutes, I would be going to lunch, and I would have no lunch. At least a lunch in front of me could distract me from the fact that I had no one to talk to. Now, however, I would just have to sit and look quite silly with nothing on the table in front of me.

Write a conclusion that follows from the narrated events and matches the tone and style of the narrative.

That is the reason I was nervous as could be.

30 Danielle is writing a problem/solution essay about the duties of pet owners. Her teacher says her paragraph is missing an introduction. Read this paragraph from her essay and the directions that follow.

W.5.2
DOK 2

Our neighbors who have dogs need to remember the town ordinance: dog owners must pick up and throw away dog waste. I know that owners occasionally forget to bring baggies with them when they walk their dogs. That's why I'm proposing that the town install waste-disposal stands on various streets. These stands will have a supply of bags and a special container where dog owners can dispose of their pet's waste.

Which is the **best** topic sentence to introduce this paragraph?

(A) Our town has created certain rules for responsible pet owners to follow.

B) I personally do not own a dog because my dad is allergic to pet dander.

C) While many Americans own dogs, even more have cats as pets.

D) Our town makes a lot of rules for us to follow.

31 Farhad is writing a persuasive essay about keeping arts programs in schools. He wants to add another supporting detail to his essay. Read these paragraphs from his essay and the question that follows.

W.5.1
DOK 2

> Do you like arts classes? Have you ever studied drama, music, or dance? What if these were not part of the curriculum? Arts classes are sometimes seen as extras on top of the core classes like English, math, science, and social studies. Some people say that students shouldn't be wasting time in public school with anything but the core subjects, but these classes are just as important and should be supported in the same way.
>
> These classes promote expression, creativity, and ways of using core knowledge that open up student minds. For example, you can apply math in music when determining the number of beats per measure in a song. In fine art, geometry comes into use because it helps artists create perspective. One study found that students active in arts curricula did better in core subjects than those who were not. So, where's the waste of time in that?

Which of the following sentences would be **best** to add to the essay?

A) It's not fair that sports programs get all the attention.

B) Core subjects should be students' highest priority.

C) Our elementary school is putting on a production of *Annie*.

D) Studies have found that arts classes promote higher attendance.

32 Gonzalo is writing an essay on a scientific theory. Read this paragraph from his essay and the directions that follow.

W.5.2
DOK 2

> Approximately 186 million years ago, there was a mass extinction of aquatic life. Scientists have been trying to figure out why. They have a new theory to explain this mass extinction. Dinosaurs became extinct around 65 million years ago for mysterious reasons too. They used a process called chemical analysis to help their research. They were able to determine that sediment on the ocean floor let off a great amount of methane gas. The methane combined with oxygen in the ocean and formed carbon dioxide, which is harmful for animals to breathe.

What revision should Gonzalo make to his essay? Explain your answer.

_____

_____

33 Simon wants to use the following book entry in the bibliography of his report. Look at the entry and the directions that follow.

W.5.8
DOK 3

Curtis, Christopher Paul. "The Watsons Go to Birmingham—1963." New York: Delacorte Press, 1995. Print.

This entry has **one** error. Rewrite the entry below, correcting the error.

Curtis Christopher Paul. "The Watsons
Go the Birmingham—1963." New York.
Delacorte Pres, 1995 Print

34 Wembley is researching the American war effort during World War I. He finds these sources: an article and a graphic. Read the sources and the question that follows.

W.5.9
DOK 3

Source 1

Source 2

History for Kids

Wartime in America

The battles of World War I took place overseas. Still, the war had a great effect on the lives of American citizens at home. President Woodrow Wilson set up federal agencies to oversee the nation's wartime economy and to encourage public support for the war. The government used propaganda to influence people's attitudes toward the war effort. For example, the government used movies, pamphlets, and newspapers to paint a picture of the Germans as villains and the Americans as having a duty to fight and defeat them. In 1917, Wilson chose Herbert Hoover (the future president) to head the Food Administration. Hoover's job was to encourage the American people to conserve food that could be used in the war effort. The government also attempted to conserve fuel across the nation. This led to the idea of daylight savings time.

By having citizens turn their clocks ahead one hour during certain months, people would have more daylight and burn less fuel.

Woodrow Wilson

According to the text and the graphic, which of the following is true?

A) The US government used propaganda to encourage citizens to conserve food for the troops.

B) Daylights savings time is no longer necessary to conserve fuel and should be discontinued.

C) Americans during WWI viewed the Germans with tolerance and sympathy.

D) Food was always plentiful for American soldiers fighting in WWI.

35 Nancy is researching the characteristics of a successful student for a report. Read this paragraph from her research and the directions that follow.

W.5.7
DOK 2

> A successful student has several distinct characteristics. For one, he or she works hard. Effort matters just as much as intelligence—if not more than. A student could be very smart, but if he or she does not put in great effort studying and doing homework, he or she won't succeed. Also, a good student takes school seriously. Successful students do not procrastinate on major assignments or skip homework just because they don't feel like completing it. Finally, a successful student is organized. He or she writes down assignments in a planner and schedules regular study time. Staying organized helps these students to stay on top of assignment requirements and due dates. These specific characteristics help good students succeed in academics.

Nancy wants to include support for the claim that hard work leads to school success. Which of the following statements from the text are **most** useful for this purpose? Select **all** that apply.

A) A successful student has several distinct characteristics.

B) Effort matters just as much as intelligence—if not more than.

C) A student could be very smart, but if he or she does not put in great effort studying and doing homework, he or she won't succeed.

D) Successful students do not procrastinate on major assignments or skip homework just because they don't feel like completing it.

E) He or she writes down assignments in a planner and schedules regular study time.

36 Jae Won is researching the transition from childhood to adulthood for an essay. Read this paragraph from his research and the directions that follow.

W.4.8
DOK 2

> When someone is too old for some childhood games, yet not old enough to be a part of adult activities, the time is young adolescence. The world is fun and exciting yet still large and looming. As they enter middle school and leave behind the comfort and security of elementary hallways, ten-year-olds learn to change classes and memorize locker combinations. Outside of school, there are new interests, such as social, rather than family, circles. They become aware of personal style and begin the struggle of finding their places in the world. Young adolescence is a time of change.

Underline **at least two** reasons that **best** support Jae Won's claim that adolescence is a challenging time for some young people.

Performance Task

Your social studies class is studying important events in US history. Your social studies teacher has given you an assignment. It is your job to research the topic of the Louisiana Purchase. Below are four sources you have found in your research.

After you have looked over the sources, you will answer some questions. Take a look at the sources and the questions. Remember, you'll need to scan every source to gain information to answer the questions and write a persuasive essay.

In Part 2, you will write your essay using information from the sources.

Steps to Follow:

In order to plan and write your article, you will do the following:

1. Examine four sources.

2. Make notes about the information from the sources.

3. Answer three questions about the sources.

Directions for Beginning:

Now you will study the different sources. Take notes because you may want to refer to your notes while writing your essay. You will be allowed to come back to any of the sources as many times as you like.

Research Questions:

After studying all of the resources, use the rest of your time in Part 1 to answer three questions about them. Your answers will be scored. Also, your answers will help you think about what you have researched, which should help you in your writing assignment.

Part 1

Source #1

An article in the magazine *Louisiana History Lives*

The Purchase that Doubled the United States

By Angela Chase

Did you know that Louisiana was once owned by the French? The story of how the United States bought Louisiana is fascinating history. Thomas Jefferson was the US president in 1803 when Napoleon offered to sell the large Louisiana territory to the United States. The final price was $15 million. While that is a lot of money even today, this was a great investment.

In addition to Louisiana, the purchase included land that today makes up all or parts of Arkansas, Missouri, Iowa, Minnesota, North Dakota, South Dakota, Nebraska, Oklahoma, Kansas, Montana, Wyoming and Colorado. Think of it this way: the United States bought all this land for less than three cents an acre!

When he decided to purchase the Louisiana territory, Jefferson was thinking about farmers. Many farmers needed to pass through New Orleans to send crops all over the United States. Owning New Orleans would benefit the farming and trading industries in the United States. Thus, it was a welcome surprise when Napoleon offered to sell this large territory. The purchase doubled the size of the United States.

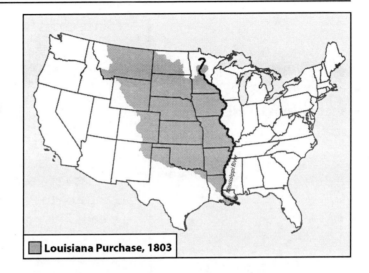

Louisiana Purchase, 1803

Jefferson did have some deep thinking to do. Some aspects of the purchase troubled him. One issue was the way the US Constitution provided for such purchases by the president. Did the laws of the Constitution give him the right to make the Louisiana Purchase? In doing so, would he hurt the power held by the states? Jefferson believed in following the Constitution.

One faction in the United States that opposed the purchase was the Federalists. The Federalists believed the government should follow the Constitution. They feared the president would take power from the states if he overstepped his bounds. However, other politicians argued that the Constitution allowed the president to negotiate treaties with other countries. They considered the Louisiana Purchase a treaty with France.

Jefferson and other members of the government decided to go ahead with the purchase. The Louisiana Purchase became one of the greatest real estate deals in history.

Source #2

An excerpt from the book *The Louisiana Purchase*

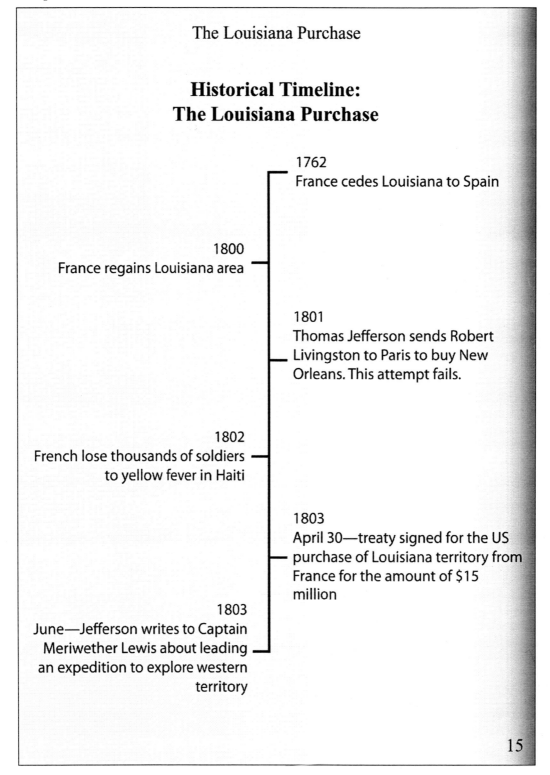

The Louisiana Purchase

**Historical Timeline:
The Louisiana Purchase**

1762
France cedes Louisiana to Spain

1800
France regains Louisiana area

1801
Thomas Jefferson sends Robert Livingston to Paris to buy New Orleans. This attempt fails.

1802
French lose thousands of soldiers to yellow fever in Haiti

1803
April 30—treaty signed for the US purchase of Louisiana territory from France for the amount of $15 million

1803
June—Jefferson writes to Captain Meriwether Lewis about leading an expedition to explore western territory

15

Source #3

A newspaper editorial written by a Federalist for a newspaper in 1803

THE GAZETTE

| No. 234 | *THURSDAY EVENING, MAY 5, 1803* | Vol XXV |

I am troubled that President Jefferson is considering purchasing the Louisiana territory from France. If he believes in following the Constitution as he claims he does, then he will not go through with this decision! Nowhere in the Constitution does it say the executive branch can acquire territory like this. Jefferson knows it too; he hastily tried to amend the Constitution giving him this power. But since he is anxious to seize this land before the offer is taken away, he abandoned this idea.

Moreover, buying such a large amount of land introduces new and varied problems. Adding this new territory will certainly disrupt the balance between slave states and free states. This will only lead to increased conflict between the northern and southern states. What about the people already living in this territory—the French and the Spanish? Are they to become American citizens? Do they understand the principles of democracy that our nation is founded on? Can we really afford this purchase? It is a lot of money for a vast wilderness. We should focus on helping our factories and merchants in the East, not farming in the West.

Jefferson is like a child gazing longingly at a large dessert. His eyes are bigger than his stomach. He needs to rethink this Louisiana Purchase and consider the problems it will introduce.

Source #4

A graphic showing the causes and effects of the Louisiana Purchase

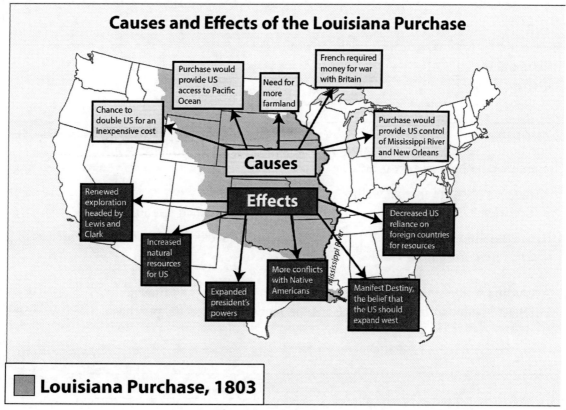

Notes

Whom did the Louisiana Purchase benefit?	
Why did Jefferson want the purchase?	
How did the purchase take place?	
Where does the organization help?	
What opposition did the purchase face?	
When did the purchase take place?	

37 For a quick reference of dates important to the Louisiana Purchase, which source would be the **most** useful?

    W.5.7
    DOK 4

  A) the excerpt from the magazine *Louisiana History Lives*

  C) the newspaper editorial published in 1803

  B) the timeline from the book *The Louisiana Purchase*

  D) the cause and effect graphic

38 According to the sources, which political group opposed the Louisiana Purchase? Name **at least three** reasons the faction disliked the purchase.

    W.5.9
    DOK 4

_____

_____

_____

39 According to the sources, which of the following statements are true? Select **all** that apply.

W.5.8
DOK 4

A) Jefferson attempted to buy Louisiana before 1803.

B) The United States hesitated to buy Louisiana because it was expensive.

C) The Louisiana Purchase benefited the Native Americans.

C) The US Constitution did not directly grant the president the power to purchase land.

E) Jefferson wanted to use the land to build big cities.

F) US trading along the Mississippi River increased after the purchase.

Part 2

You will now have time to review your notes and sources. Use this time efficiently to plan, draft, and revise your essay. You may use your notes and refer to the sources. Remember, you may also use the answers you wrote to questions in Part 1, but you cannot change those answers. Now read your assignment. Review the information about how your essay will be scored. Then, begin your work.

Your Assignment

Your assignment for your social studies class is to write a persuasive essay in the voice of an American at the time of the Louisiana Purchase. Imagine you are going to deliver this essay in the form of a public speech. Do you support or oppose the Louisiana Purchase? Explain who you are and why you feel the way you do. Use facts and details from the sources you have researched to give your essay real facts and examples. The audience for your essay will be your imaginary fellow townspeople.

REMEMBER: A well-written persuasive essay:

- has a clear organization
- stays on the topic
- has an introduction, body, and conclusion
- uses transitions
- uses details from the sources to support your ideas
- develops ideas clearly
- uses clear language
- follows rules of writing (spelling, punctuation, and grammar)

Now, begin work on your essay. Manage your time carefully so that you can do the following:

- plan your essay

- write your essay

- revise and edit for a final draft

Writing Checklist Questions

- ☐ Did I respond to the prompt?

- ☐ Is my main idea clear?

- ☐ Do my details all support the main idea?

- ☐ Did I make the best word choices?

- ☐ Are my points all in a logical order?

- ☐ Are all my sentences complete?

- ☐ Are there any errors in usage, grammar, punctuation, and spelling?

Planning

Use this outline to help plan your speech. Don't forget to review your notes for part 1.

Which side do you take in the Louisiana Purchase debate? _____

Reason 1: _____

Detail: _____

Detail: _____

Detail: _____

Reason 2: _____

Detail: _____

Detail: _____

Detail: _____

Reason 3: _____

Detail: _____

Detail: _____

Detail: _____

W.5.1, 4–10
L.5.1–6
DOK 4

40 For Part 2, you are being asked to write a persuasive essay that is several paragraphs long. Use your own paper for this assignment. Remember to check your notes and your prewriting and planning as you write, then revise and edit your essay.

End of Test

EVALUATION CHART

Directions: On the following chart, circle the question numbers that you answered incorrectly, and evaluate the results. Turn to the appropriate chapters, read the explanations, and complete the exercises. Review other chapters as needed. Finally, complete the post test to assess your progress and to continue mastering the Common Core Standards.

Note: Some questions may appear under multiple chapters as they test multiple skills.

Chapter	Question Number
Chapter 1: How to Write Your Answers	1, 7, 15, 30, 34, 39, 40
Chapter 2: Reading Strategies	1, 2, 7, 8, 15
Chapter 3: Exploring the Text	1, 7, 8, 9, 13, 15
Chapter 4: Vocabulary	5, 10, 14, 40
Chapter 5: Literary Genres	14, 40
Chapter 6: Elements of Literature	2, 4, 8
Chapter 7: Understanding Literature	3, 6, 14, 26, 40
Chapter 8: Informational Texts	9, 11, 12, 13, 40
Chapter 9: Grammar	24, 25, 26, 40
Chapter 10: Writing	5, 27, 28, 29, 30, 31, 40
Chapter 11: Research	32, 33, 34, 35, 36, 37, 38, 39, 40
Chapter 12: Speaking and Listening	16, 17, 18, 19, 20, 21, 22, 23

Chapter 1
How to Write Your Answers

 This chapter covers DOK levels 1–3 and the following fifth grade strands and standards (for full standards, please see page x):

> **Reading Literature 1**
> **Reading Informational Texts 1**
> **Writing 4, 6, 9**

In this chapter...

- You will learn how to properly construct written responses for standardized assessments.

- You will learn to use quotations from a text to support your answers.

- You will use and improve your keyboarding skills.

Welcome to *Common Core in Grade 5 English Language Arts*! This book will help you review the skills you use in school. It also will help you learn the standards for English Language Arts.

Answering questions is always good practice for future tests. As you read this book, you will see many practices with questions for you to answer. Many of the questions you will see will be multiple choice ones. This means a question will ask you to choose an answer from answer A, answer B, answer C, or answer D. But some other questions will ask you to write out your answer. This chapter will help you get ready to answer those questions that ask you to give written answers.

1.1 READ CAREFULLY

When you see a prompt, there are a few steps for you to take. First of all, read the question carefully. Make sure you understand exactly what the prompt is asking. If you need help, ask your teacher.

1.2 FILL IN THE BLANK

Some questions will tell you to **fill in the blank**. This means you will not get any choices; you will have to think of the answer on your own. Look at the sample text and question that follows.

Why the Vulture Is Bald
a Burmese Folktale

The vulture was a humble bird. His plumage was not beautiful, but it was good enough. One day, he noticed his feathers were falling off. He consulted other birds, who told him new feathers would grow later.

But he was pessimistic and worried himself sick. The other birds took pity, and each gave him a feather. After they gave him new feathers, he had vibrant plumage of many colors.

The vulture became astounded by his own beauty. He swaggered in his borrowed feathers and declared himself the most beautiful bird of all time. Young birds followed him everywhere. Birds from other flocks flew to take a look at him. He started charging them admission to gaze on his plumage.

He requested that the birds in his flock recognize him as their king. He set up an elaborate nest worthy of his glory and decided his flock should pay him for the wonder of his presence. With the money, he paid poor birds to maintain the splendor of his plumage.

Outraged, his flock stormed his nest. They plucked off the feathers that they had given him. They kept plucking. They plucked off the vulture's own feathers. By the time they were finished with him, the vulture was bald. That is why even today, the vulture is a sour and ugly bird.

Why did the other birds give their feathers to the vulture?

The other birds took pitty.

This question asks you why something happened. All you need to do is think about the events in the story. If you need to, look back at the story. Find the places where it tells you that the birds gave up their feathers. Then write down your answer on the blank line that appears after the question.

What did you write? You could write something like this:

The vulture's feathers were coming off. He worried so much that the other birds felt sorry for him and gave him their feathers.

Remember to write your answers in complete sentences.

1.3 LONGER ANSWERS

At times, you will need to do more than just fill in blanks or make lists. Some questions ask you to show a deeper understanding of what you have read. You may need to write a few sentences or even a short paragraph to explain your response. Whatever the question asks you, be sure you answer it clearly and in an organized way. Also, make sure you stick to what the prompt asks. Look at this example of a question about the same story.

What lesson can a reader learn from reading "Why the Vulture Is Bald"? Use facts from the story to support your answer.

This type of question is a little different. It asks for more than just a word or two. Often, you will not find the answer clearly written out in the text. You will have to think about the text in the way the question asks. Again, look back at the story if you need to. Once you know the answer, think of how to say it. Use complete sentences. Tell what lesson you think the story teaches. For example, here is what Lennie wrote. See how he uses part of the question in the first sentence of his answer.

> I think the lesson is not to worry so much. If the vulture had not worried, then the other birds would not have given him their feathers. Then he would not have gotten proud. If he had just listened to the other birds, he would still have some feathers. And the birds would like him better because he would not make them pay to see his pretty feathers.

Notice how Lennie used complete sentences in his answers. He also answered the question clearly. He wrote out what the lesson was. He also used facts from the story to support his answer.

1.4 WRITING ESSAYS

Sometimes you will need to do some longer writing than just a few sentences. These might be reports or essays. They might also be stories.

When you need to write an essay or story, you will see a prompt. A prompt is a question or statement that tells you what to write about. It also might give some guidelines for what to include.

Now that we've looked at what kind of answers you might be writing, let's look at how those answers will be scored. When you take an actual test, trained readers will score what you write. Here are the score points they will most likely use. The chart of score points is called a **rubric**. Your teacher might have a different rubric to use, but this one gives you an idea how answers might be scored.

Rubric for 4-Point Scoring of Writing	
4 points	The response shows that the student has a good understanding of the task. The student has provided a response that is accurate, complete, and addresses the prompt. Support or examples are included. The writing is clearly based on the text. The response contains few or no errors in grammar, capitalization, or punctuation.
3 points	The response shows that the student has an understanding of the task. The response is accurate and addresses the prompt. But support or details may not be complete or clear. The response contains some errors in grammar, capitalization, or punctuation, but they do not affect the reader's understanding.

2 points	The response shows that the student has some understanding of the task. The response may be too general or too simple. Some of the support or examples may be incomplete or left out. The response contains many errors that may harm the reader's understanding.
1 point	The response shows that the student has very little understanding of the task. The response is incomplete, has many mistakes, and might not address the prompt. The response contains many serious errors that harm the reader's understanding.
0 points	The response is not correct. It might be confused or not address the prompt. It may contain so many serious errors that it is difficult to understand.

Now you know what the readers look for when they grade your writing. You want to get the highest score possible when you write. Read this text, and look at the sample student responses. You will see what each scored answer looks like.

The Fisherman and His Wife
Adapted from the folktale as told by the Brothers Grimm

Once there was a poor fisherman who lived with his wife in a tiny hut by the sea. One day, the fisherman caught a fish that could speak.

"Please let me go," said the fish.

"I would not eat a fish that could talk!" said the fisherman. He let the fish go. The fisherman went home and told his wife what had happened.

"You foolish man!" she shouted. "That was a magic fish. Go back, and ask him to change this hut into a cottage."

The fisherman did not want to go, but his wife made him. He went back to the sea, called the fish, and told him what he wanted.

"Go home," said the fish. "It is done."

The man went home and saw that his hut was now a nice cottage. His wife was happy but not for long. She wanted a bigger house. She made her husband go back to the fish and ask for a castle.

Again, he did not want to go, but she made him. He went back to the sea, called the fish, and told him what he wanted.

"Go home," said the fish. "It is done."

The man went home and saw that the cottage was now a magnificent castle. His wife was happy but not for long. Now, she wanted to be a queen. She made her husband go back to the fish and ask the fish to make her a queen.

Again, he did not want to go, but she made him. He went back to the sea, called the fish, and told him what he wanted.

"Go home," said the fish. The man went home and saw that the castle was now his old hut. And there they live to this day.

Writing Task

Write a paragraph about the woman in this story. What traits does this character show? Are they helpful or mean traits? Use examples from the text to support your idea. Use your own paper to write your response. Make sure your writing is clear and has a beginning, middle, and end.

What would your response be? Practice writing an essay that answers this prompt. Then, when you're done, look at the sample responses from other students. Study how each response might score.

Model Student Response: 4-Point Score

The woman in this story is the wife of the fisherman. She is a greedy lady she is never happy with house she has. She controls the man and asks for more things from the magic fish. Being Greedy is a bad trait. It can get you in truble. She wanted a bigger house. That is selfish. She is also mean to her husband. She yells a lot. That is not nice either. Soon the fish got tired of her wanting more all the time. So he turned the castle back to the hut. The lady had to learn a big lesson.

Scoring Notes

This response would probably score 4 points. The student clearly answers the prompt about the female character of the story. The response begins by stating who the woman is and what she does. The student also gives two main traits of the character. The obvious trait is that the woman is greedy. But the more in-depth trait is that woman is acting selfish and mean toward her husband. The other sentences support the student's ideas. Examples include that the woman controls the man by asking for a bigger house (which shows she is greedy) and that she yells a lot (which shows she is not nice). The details show that the student read the text carefully and understood its meaning. There is a clear conclusion.

There are a few errors. The second sentence is a run-on ("She is a greedy lady she is never happy with house she has"). It should be split up into two sentences. It could also be joined by a semicolon or a comma and conjunction. The word *Greedy* in the sentence "Being Greedy is a bad trait" should not be capitalized. Also, *truble* should be *trouble*. However, these errors do not affect understanding.

Model Student Response: 3-Point Score

The woman is a main karcter in the story. She tells the fisherman that she needs a bigger house. She should be happy the house she has. she justs wants more and more. And she yells at her husbend. That is a mean trait.

Scoring Notes

This response would score 3 points. The student answers the prompt by telling the woman's character traits. The student gives support for this idea. But the answer is not as complete as a 4-point response. The ideas do not go far enough. The student writes that the woman wants bigger houses, but does not say she was greedy. The answer also has mistakes. Misspelled words include *karcter* (should be *character*) and *husbend* (should be *husband*). In the last sentence, *she* should have a capital letter and *justs* should be *just*. These mistakes do not prevent understanding.

Model Student Response: 2-Point Score

The lady in the story is bad. She asks fore a big house. She gets it but she does not like it. So she asks for a nother. And another. the woman should not do that.

Scoring Notes

This response would score 2 points. The response shows some understanding of the question. But the student's answer is too general. There is not enough support for the trait given. However, some details show that the student read the text and has a slight understanding of it. Even though the response is short, there are several mistakes. There is a run-on ("She gets it but she does not like it.) that needs to be fixed. There is also a fragment ("And another.") that needs to be fixed. In the last sentence, *the* should be capitalized. The word *fore* should be *for*, and *a nother* should be *another*.

Model Student Response: 1-Point Score

The lady dus not like the fish. That is not nice she is meen.

Scoring Notes

This response would score 1 point. This response does not answer the question in the prompt. It is not a complete paragraph. The response shows the student either did not read or understand the text. It also contains many mistakes. Only the first sentence is a complete sentence. The second is a run-on sentence. And it has two misspelled words ("dus" should be "does" and "meen" should be "mean").

Model Student Response: 0-Point Score

i lyk the fis betr than the grl.

Scoring Notes

This response would score 0 points.

Practice 1: Scoring Essays

W 4, 5 (DOK 2)

Now you can practice scoring some essays. Read this text and the prompt after it. Then read the responses that students wrote. Decide what score each answer should get. Discuss with your teacher or tutor the score you give each answer and why.

> What is your favorite type of book to read? Literature is classified into categories called genres. There are many genres of literature to choose from. In fact, some people fear there are too many literary genres. Whether you are a reader of only serious nonfiction work or a playful fan of comic books, you have endless choices. Some people enjoy reading about the lives of others, so the well-written biography or autobiography is of interest. Autobiographies are stories that people write about their own lives. Biographies are stories that people write about others' lives. Some people mistakenly think that nonfiction books are boring. But many others enjoy taking a trip back in time with historical-fiction texts. Historical fiction is a great genre for young readers. Another genre that offers intrigue for readers is the mystery and suspense-thriller category. Mystery thrillers have readers tingling with suspense. Graphic novels combine pictures and words like movies in book form. So the options are there. Do yourself a favor—pick your genre, and curl up with a good book today.

> The text tells about many types of literature. Now that you have read the text, list three types of literature the author mentions. Then tell what kinds of books you like to read.

Answer 1

The pasage talked about grafic novels and mysterys. Grafic novels have both pitcures and words. Mysterys have a lot of suspense. I like those books too. Comics are my favrit they have pictures just like graphic novels. i do not like real life stories. those are just boring.

1   What score would you give this answer? Give the reasons you chose that score. When you are finished scoring this essay, discuss your score with your teacher or tutor.

3 point because the reader didn't capitalize the "i" and spelled grafic to graphic.

Answer 2

This author gives all sorts of genres. There are biographies which are about real people. They tell all about these peoples lives. Mystery books are eciting because you never know what is going to happen. Mysteries are full of suspense that keeps you hanging on the edge of your seat. Graphic novels have drawings and neat stories. They are illustrated, like comics. There are many things to read. My favorite books are ones with intresting people and places. Usully I read fiction books because I like to use my imaginashon. I especially like fantasy and sci fi books. Still, any book is a good book because I love to read.

2   What score would you give this answer? Give reasons for your score. When you are finished, discuss the score with your teacher or tutor.

_____

_____

Answer 3

i like story books. stories are the most exciting kinds of books not biographies. my mom reeds to me every nite.

3   What score would you give this answer? Give reasons for your score. When you are finished, discuss the score with your teacher or tutor.

_____

_____

1.5 QUOTING FROM THE TEXT

When you answer a question or write an essay, it is important to support your answer using quotations and details. These details show your understanding of the text. They also help you share your thought process with others.

When you quote from literary texts, you might use characters' descriptions, words, or actions to support your ideas about them. When you quote from informational texts, you can quote the author's claims or evidence. No matter why you choose to quote, always put the author's exact words inside quotation marks.

Read this paragraph and the question that follows.

> One afternoon a fox was walking through the forest and spotted a bunch of grapes hanging from over a lofty branch. "Just the thing to quench my thirst," quoth he. Taking a few steps back, the fox jumped and just missed the hanging grapes. Again the fox took a few paces back and tried to reach them but still failed. Finally, giving up, the fox turned up his nose and said, "They're probably sour anyway," and proceeded to walk away. It's easy to despise what you cannot have.

Based on the paragraph, do you think the fox is a good problem-solver? Why or why not?

How would you answer this question? You might notice that the fox clearly wants the grapes. When he sees the grapes, he says, "Just the thing to quench my thirst." You might also see that his problem is that he cannot reach the grapes. What did he do when he saw this problem? He "turned up his nose." If you wrote an answer using quotations from the text, it might look like this.

> I do not think the fox is a good problem-solver. His problem is that he wants the grapes but he cannot reach them. He tries to reach them, but he "jumped and just missed the hanging grapes." After his second try, he gives up. He "turned up his nose" at the grapes instead of trying to get them a different way.

Do you see how this response uses quotations to support the answer? Now look at this paragraph from an informational text and the question that follows.

> Although they have earned the reputation of being scary forces of nature, volcanoes are not always destructive. They have proven to hold cures for the sick and offer beautifying qualities. Sick people take baths in hot springs warmed by volcanoes to feel better. Hardened lava, or pumice, can smooth the rough skin on your feet. Farmers use soil with volcanic rock and ash to help plants grow.

How are volcanoes different from many people's expectations about them? Explain your answer.

What do you think? The text says that volcanoes "have earned a reputation of being scary forces of nature." But volcanoes have given people many benefits. Look at this sample response that uses quotations from the text.

> Volcanoes are different from their "reputation of being scary forces of nature." Volcanoes actually do wonderful things. The warm water from volcano hot springs "hold cures for the sick." They even help us grow food because "farmers use soil with volcanic rock and ash."

This response also uses quotations and details to support the answer. Notice that the author's exact words are inside quotation marks. But the student uses her own words to explain her ideas. She selects only the most important quotations to support her answer.

Practice 2: Quoting from the Text

RI 1, RL 1, W 4, 9 (DOK 3)

Read the texts and answer the questions. Remember to use quotations from the texts to support your answers.

A Thief's Surprise

Andrea and her older brother, Dan, made it a point to get up early on that Saturday and drive downtown to get as close as they could to the route for the annual Lake City Christmas Parade. Many shops had closed along the parade route. Dan watched the parade eagerly. His girlfriend was in the marching band, and he wanted to hear the band perform the music she had worked so hard on this summer. Andrea went window shopping along the glass storefronts nearby. Andrea noticed a flash of light to her left. It came from the reflection of a man's watch. Standing with his back to the parade, he was looking intensely into the music store window.

Meanwhile, Dan listened attentively as the band marched by. The music was loud and overwhelmed all of the other sounds of the crowd. As the band was passing by, Andrea glanced to the left and noticed the same man pulling a carpenter's hammer out of his overcoat and swinging it to break the glass door of the music store. Feeling a rush of energy, Andrea ran to get her brother.

"Dan!" she shouted. But Dan couldn't hear her above the sounds of the marching band. Bolting the last several yards, she grabbed Dan from behind. "Dan, come here!" she screamed. "A man down the street is robbing a music store!" Dan was a star wrestler on his school team and was ready to put his talents to good use. He followed Andrea, running as fast as he could.

Dan traveled down the street. At the same time, the thief came out of the store. He was clutching an expensive-looking electric guitar. Dan quickly put the thief into a headlock and forced him to the sidewalk. By then, Andrea had sprinted back to the parade and found a police officer, who then arrested the would-be thief.

1   What do Andrea's actions tell you about her personality? Explain your answer using details from the text.

Andrea is smart because ran together brother and police officer to stop the theif.

2   How does Dan feel about his girlfriend? How can you tell?

Dan loves his girlfriend because he watched the parade eagerly.

3   How did Andrea first notice the thief?

Andrea noticed the theif when she noticed a flash of light to her left.

Circadian Rhythm

Human beings have an internal "clock" called the *circadian rhythm*. This clock tells us when it's time to sleep and when it's time to wake up and be active. Usually, this rhythm is tuned to the rising and setting of the sun. But in teenagers, sleep scientists have found that the rhythm is somewhat skewed. That is why teens often feel energetic at night and tired in the morning. Because of this change in the circadian rhythm, teenagers often suffer from sleep deprivation. Studies show that a lack of sleep can influence personality. It produces frequent bad moods and could hinder learning. Sufficient sleep is important for teenagers. In response to the unique sleep rhythm of adolescents, some American high schools have changed the start time of the school day from 8 a.m. to 9 a.m.

4   How are teenagers' circadian rhythms different from adults' circadian rhythms?

5   Why is sleep so important for teenagers?

_____

_____

1.6 WRITING CLEARLY

Answer each question in a clear way. If a question asks you when something happened, be sure to describe the order of events. If it asks you to compare two things, be sure to explain how they are similar.

Being clear also means that your writing must be correct. Be sure to check your spelling. Also look for any other mistakes you may have made. If you find an error, erase it completely or cross it out. Write the correct words right above it or next to it.

USE NEAT HANDWRITING

Make sure that the people who are reading your answer can tell what it says. When you write your essay, use neat handwriting so that others can read it.

1.7 KEYBOARDING

At times, your teacher may ask you to complete some assignments on the computer. One way to make such tasks much easier is to learn **keyboarding** skills. Keyboarding means using a computer keyboard to type. As you gain more practice at keyboarding, your speed and accuracy will improve. Eventually, you may find typing your answers is easier and faster than writing them by hand.

Technology is becoming more important every day, so you must learn how to use it. Ask your parents or your teacher how often they submit handwritten documents at work. Most likely, they rarely turn in anything handwritten. Typing is faster, allows files to be e-mailed, and is easy to read. Handwriting, on the other hand, can be difficult to read and easy to misunderstand. For these reasons, most businesses and organizations rely on typed communication. It is very important that you learn how to type accurately and quickly.

There are many ways to improve your typing skills. One way is to find out how quickly and accurately you can type already. You can find free typing tests online. These tests will tell you how many words per minute you type. They will also tell you how many errors you have.

Visit the website below to take a typing test. Remember, the more you practice typing, the faster and more accurate you will become.

http://www.learninggamesforkids.com/keyboarding_games/
keyboarding_games_typing_speed_test.html

Practice 3: Keyboarding

W 4 (DOK 1)

Now you will practice your keyboard skills. Fill out the mad lib below. Then, type the whole story in a single sitting. Try to type as quickly and accurately as you can.

1. Description
2. Place
3. Name
4. Animal
5. Description
6. Action verb+ ing
7. Feeling
8. Food
9. Object
10. Animal from #4
11. Object
12. Feeling
13. Description
14. Description
15. Action verb + ed
16. Feeling
17. Animal from #4
18. School subject
19. Object
20. Name from #3
21. Object from #19
22. Animal from #4
23. Description
24. Action verb + er

On one bright, Sunny day, I was walking past the mall . I had been on my way
                    1   2

to Carl's Swirl Shop, which is a place I like to go for ice cream. I was strolling along with

Maddie who is my best friend. Then, out of nowhere, came a lion ! It was big, hairy, and
   3   4

so very Scary I almost didn't know what to do!
         5

It came running toward us. It was clear this thing was up to no good. I looked deep into
         6

its eyes and I could sense madness. It showed its feelings by charging directly at us! My best
                           7

friend froze. I began to think we might not get to the ice cream shop on time. It was a shame

because I could have really gone for some chocolate at that point.
                                          8

"What do we do?" I whispered. My best friend pointed toward the box laying on the
                                                                   9

sidewalk.

"Perfect!" I shouted. "We can hide under that!" We shuffled toward it, hoping the

lion wouldn't notice. Somehow, as we huddled underneath, the animal seemed to forget
10

about us. Instead of charging, it started playfully kicking a ball around.
                                                          11

"Would you look at that!" I exclaimed. "Who would have thought the creature

would play with one of those?" It kept knocking its new toy from one side of the sidewalk,

_____ as a clam. Until my friend sneezed.
  12

To be fair, it was a really _____ sneeze. But I wish my friend hadn't sneezed just at
                            13

that moment. Because all of a sudden, the animal was no longer playing with its toy. It was

looking back at us again! And of course, this time it looked even more _____ than before. I
                                                                        14

couldn't believe my eyes when it stood up and _____!
                                            15

"Good gracious!" I cried. "What do we do now? " Suddenly, my friend darted away.

"Hey! Where are you going?" It was clear my friend was feeling too _____ to deal with this
                                                                   16

right now. I had to take care of it myself.

I looked around frantically, hoping to find something to distract the _____ with
                                                                      17

again. I didn't see a thing. But luckily, I remembered what I had learned in _____ yesterday.
                                                                            18

Those creatures are afraid of _____! Fortunately, I remembered to bring mine that day. I
                               19

jammed my hand into my pocket, only to find a gaping hole in it! My last chance was ruined!

I groaned and settled into my fate, ready for the worst day of my life. But to my shock,

as the animal crouched down to pounce, something incredible happened! From behind me

came my best friend! And _____ brought reinforcements! Half of our class was running up
                         20

behind me, each with a _____ in hand. That silly _____ had no chance now!
                       21   22

With new confidence, I roared, "Turn back, beast! Do not trouble us any more!" My friends

were all behind me, shouting in agreement. The creature turned on its haunches, look

ing much more scared than before. It ran off, never to be seen by anyone again! And all
               23

because my dear friend was such a fast runner.✓
                                        24

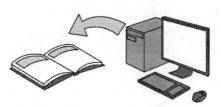

Research Connection

The modern keyboard layout is called the QWERTY keyboard. It was named after the first six letters on the top row of alphabet keys. Research the history of the keyboard. Create a timeline that shows how the keyboard has evolved throughout its history.

1.8 PERFORMANCE TASK

Your state's testing program might include a **performance task**. These tasks will give you a real-life situation to work with. Performance tasks test how well you can combine many things you know into a long, written answer. This kind of answer is called an extended response.

In your performance task, you will do some **research**. You will use sources that are given to you. Then, you will answer a few questions. Finally, you will use your research to write a story, essay, speech, or other long work.

PART 1

The performance task may be in two parts. In Part 1, you will look at many sources and use them to answer questions. These questions will get you thinking about the second part of the task before you get there. You should take notes as you read and answer these questions. Your notes will help you when you reach Part 2.

Make sure to check your answers before you turn them in. Once you have moved on to Part 2, you cannot change your answers to Part 1.

PART 2

In Part 2 of the performance task, you may use your research to create something new. It may be a story of some kind. It may be an article to explain something. Or you might be asked to persuade your readers. It may even be a speech or presentation. You will still have access to the research sources from Part 1, and you may look at them whenever you need to.

Part 2 of the performance task may take much longer to complete than Part 1. You should carefully plan, write, and edit your response. Remember, the questions you answered in Part 1 will help you with Part 2. You may look back at your answers, but you may not change them.

GRADING

Part 2 will also give you information about how your writing will be graded. As you edit your work, you should make sure your writing covers each graded element. Here are some elements to think about when you write.

1 **Statement of purpose, focus, and organization**—This measures how well you make your purpose clear, stay on task, and organize your ideas. Ask yourself these questions as you write and revise:

   a. *Argumentative and Informational/Explanatory writing*: Did I clearly write my central idea or claim? Can I point to a sentence that tells exactly what my point is?

   b. *Narrative writing*: Did I use a clear and effective plot?

   c. Did I include only sentences that are important to my main point? Did I show how each detail is related to my overall point?

   d. Do my ideas flow in a good order? Did I use transition words to connect my sentences and paragraphs? Did I include an introduction and a conclusion?

2 **Elaboration and evidence**—This measures how well you support your claim. It measures how you explain your topic or add relevant details to your narrative. Ask yourself these questions as you write and revise:

   a. Did I use information from my sources? Did I remember to cite my sources?

   b. *Argumentative writing*: Does the evidence I use support my claim? Did I show how the evidence relates to my claim?

   c. *Informational/Explanatory writing*: Did I provide everything my reader needs to understand my topic?

   d. *Narrative writing*: Did I use details and imagery in my story? Did I include dialogue where appropriate? Did I use the knowledge from my sources into my story?

3 **Conventions**—This measures how well you use conventions of Standard English. This includes grammar, spelling, and punctuation. Ask yourself these questions as you write and revise:

   a. Are all of my sentences complete? Do they make sense? Do they sound right?

   b. Did I spell any difficult words correctly? Did I mix up any words that sound the same, like *to/too/two* or *there/their/they're*?

   c. Have I used commas, periods, quotation marks, and other punctuation correctly?

The directions in Part 2 will provide a short list of questions. Ask yourself those questions as you write and revise. Make sure to use the list as you review your work.

The writing and research chapters will help you review the skills you need to complete the performance task.

CHAPTER 1 SUMMARY

Fill in the blank questions require you to think of your own answer. These questions do not give answer choices.

When **writing longer answers**, you must explain your responses. Make sure your explanation is clear and well organized.

When **writing an essay**, be sure to follow the prompt. The prompt will tell you what to include in your essay.

Rubrics are score charts that graders use to grade your tests.

When you **quote** from the text, you use the authors' exact words to support your ideas. Place the author's words inside quotation marks.

Writing clearly involves answering the question that you are asked. It also means writing correctly and using **neat handwriting**.

Keyboarding skills allow you to type your answers and assignments quickly and easily.

For additional practice, please see Chapter 1 Test located in the Teacher Guide.

Chapter 2
Reading Strategies

This chapter covers DOK levels 1–3 and the following fifth grade strands and standards (for full standards, please see page x):

> **Reading Literature 1, 2**
>
> **Reading Informational Texts 1, 2, 3**
>
> **Reading Foundational Skills 4**

In this chapter...

- You will be able to make connections to a text through active reading strategies, including asking questions, making inferences, and evaluating information in a text.

2.1 PURPOSE FOR READING

Just like authors have different reasons for writing, readers have different **purposes for reading**. Think about what you're hoping to get out of a text before you read.

Reading **to be informed** means reading to learn more about a topic. You can always read **to find out** information. Looking up articles about the history of space travel would be a good example. Reading **to be entertained** is also known as reading for fun. Some people like mysteries, and others like books about hobbies. Some people even like reading articles about history or science. Reading **to solve problems** means trying to find out how to do something. This could mean finding medical advice or directions for putting something together.

Readers can read for more than one reason at the same time. Sometimes you'll even find yourself reading for different reasons than expected. You can read a funny story and end up learning something. You can read to find the solution to a problem and enjoy what you're reading. It helps to read with an open mind.

2.2 ACTIVE READING

What is active reading? You know what the word *active* means, right? It means full of motion and energy. It involves participation. When you are an **active reader**, you participate in the text. You engage with it. Active reading is not hard, and it can even be fun. And when you finish actively reading a text, you'll have a much fuller understanding of it!

Think of the acronym SAME to help you with active reading.

- **Survey**
- **Ask questions**
- **Make connections**
- **Evaluate what you have read**

Let's look at each of these in detail.

SURVEY

Surveying (or **previewing**) is a pre-reading strategy you can use. Surveying a text means taking a glance at the whole thing before reading it. Look at the title, headings, subheadings, and first sentence of each paragraph. There might even be graphics for you to scan before you start reading. It's helpful to have an idea of where the article is headed.

Surveying can also help you determine the **purpose** of the text. If the text has headings listing steps, you can tell that the purpose is to give instructions. If the text has illustrations of the story, you can tell the purpose is to entertain the reader.

ASK QUESTIONS

To **ask questions** means to seek answers while reading. What do you already know about this subject? What do you want to find out? You can ask yourself questions, and find the answers as you read. The text may or may not answer all your questions. However, the process of asking questions about the text keeps your mind engaged in what you're reading.

MAKE CONNECTIONS

During reading, you can make connections by making predictions, making inferences, and accessing prior knowledge. When you **make predictions**, you think ahead, guessing what you'll read next. For instance, if you read about a man lost in a cave, you can predict that he might run into a bear or another animal. Or he may even find some hidden treasure!

You might also **make inferences** about what you're reading. When you make an inference, you are making a connection between what is said and not said in a story. For example, imagine you're reading a story about a student studying for a big test. The student studies every evening for a week before the test. She understands the material very well, but on the morning of the test, she wakes up with a stomachache. What inference could you make? The story doesn't say it directly, but you might infer that the student is anxious about the test, which is making her stomach hurt.

You can also infer relationships between characters. Say you're reading about a boy whose parents bring home a new baby sister. The boy has always been well behaved, but he starts misbehaving at home, causing his parents to scold him. You can infer that the boy is probably acting out to get his parents' attention because they're now busy with a baby.

As you read, it is always a good idea to **access prior knowledge**, or think about what you already know. Think about your own experiences and prior knowledge about the subject. By doing this, you will be able to make personal connections with the text. For example, if you are reading a story about a fifth grader who has a fear of moving to a new place, draw upon your own experience. Perhaps you once had to move to a new place. You can then better understand what the character probably feels. Making connections based upon your prior knowledge and experience will help you to connect with the text on a deeper level.

EVALUATE WHAT YOU HAVE READ

So you've finished reading a text, and now you're done, right? Well, not quite. There are still active reading strategies you can use *after* you finish reading. They will help you recall and discuss what you read.

One strategy is to **summarize** the text. To summarize means to give a short version of what you read. For example, think of the last movie you went to see. How long was it? If you wanted to explain to a friend what the movie was about, would your explanation be as long as the movie? Probably not! You would pick out the main events that were important to the overall story and share those details with your friend. The same is true for your reading. When you are asked to summarize, you should think of the most important events and details to share.

Another strategy is to draw conclusions. When you **draw a conclusion**, you use the information in a text to make a statement about a character or event. You also use prior knowledge. Like an inference, a conclusion may not be directly stated. You make a connection between what's said and not said in a text. You can draw conclusions based on how characters act and what they say, how characters interact, and where a text is set. To draw conclusions, look at the details in the text to form a statement about a character or an event in the text.

Practice 1: Summarizing

RL 2, RI 2 (DOK 2)

Read the texts, and answer the questions that follow.

Stevie Wonder

Stevie Wonder is well known for his career as a musician. He was born Stevland Hardaway Judkins in a place called Saginaw, Michigan, in 1950. Some of his famous songs include "Superstition" and "You Are the Sunshine of My Life." Music has been a big part of his life since childhood. As a kid, he played several instruments, including the piano, harmonica, and drums, and sang in the church choir. Although it is a well-known fact that Stevie Wonder is blind, he was not born that way. Stevie's blindness was a side effect of complications related to his being born prematurely. Fans of Stevie Wonder span the world. He is a legendary American.

---

1   Write a summary of the text.

_____

_____

_____

Carrying Capacity

An ecosystem can support only a certain number of organisms in a population. We call this **carrying capacity**. It may go up or down depending on the season. A wet spring may support more plants. However, a dry summer will support fewer plants.

Pollution, weather, and natural disasters all have an impact on the carrying capacity of an area. If humans begin polluting an area, what do you predict will happen to the carrying capacity? It will go down. Anything that harms an environment will reduce the carrying capacity. Improvements to the environment increase the carrying capacity of the area.

2   Write a summary of the text.

_____

_____

_____

The Stone

There was once a poor farming family who lived in a small cabin in rural Oklahoma. One day, just as the father and his son had returned from the field, they noticed the mother and daughter sitting out on the porch. The daughter was weeping.

"What's wrong?" asked the father, concerned as he and the son approached. "Why is our daughter crying?" he wanted to know.

"She is sad that the county dance is approaching, and she has nothing to wear. It would be a shame for her to wear something made from old scraps and worn-out fabrics that we have around here." The mother's brow was heavy with worry. The daughter cried with her face in her hands.

Scratching his head, the son spoke up. "Well, maybe I have something that could help," he said. "I was saving this for another time, but I guess today's as good as any." With that, he reached in his pocket and pulled out a shiny black stone. Looking for a long time at the stone before handing it to his sister, he began to explain. "I won it in a frog-jumping contest. It has magic."

"Magic?" his mother and sister exclaimed at once.

"Well, it is supposed to be worth one wish—anything you want. I suppose you could use it to wish for a new dress."

"Wait a minute," said the father gently. "Now, family, let's think about this. If this stone has powers as my son says, our one wish doesn't have to be for the new dress." Just as his daughter began to protest, the father put up his hand to signal for her to wait. "Think about it," he continued. This could be our chance—our way out. We could wish for a new house or a good crop season—something that could last us."

They all seemed to be thinking about what the father had said. Perhaps he was right. Perhaps they should go for something that would be more long-lasting. The wheels of their minds began to turn, and new ideas came spouting out. A pony, more money, and new floors were among the wishes.

"I think our request should be much broader," said the father. "We should wish to have everything we ever really need!"

After thinking about it for a few moments, the family was on board. Floors would become worn with time. Money could also come and go again, but if they could be assured of having everything they ever needed, they knew that was the best that they could ask for.

Having made the decision, the son handed the stone to the father so that he could make the official wish. With all of the seriousness he could muster, the father held the stone just below his chin and made the wish. "Our wish is that we always have everything we need." He spoke each word slowly and clearly so as not to have any part of the request be overlooked. Not to forget his manners, the father finished up the wish with a firm and solemn, "Thank you."

Just as he spoke the last word, he felt a sensation in his hand. The stone became warmer and warmer until it seemed to bubble inside. Then, it began to dissolve and shrivel until there was nothing left of it. His family watched with bulging eyes as all of this took place.

Waiting for something to happen, the family looked around. Nothing had changed. There was no new dress, no new floors, no bag of money—simply the "same old same old" as it always was. Very disappointed, the family decided they should just go on about their daily business. Perhaps it would just take a little time for their wish to kick in.

As time passed, the family noticed that nothing ever changed. Everything just stayed the same. Eventually, they began to believe that the stone simply had no power. It was a trick. But it never occurred to the family that maybe they just already had everything they needed.

3   Write a summary of the text.

_____

_____

_____

2.3 MODEL OF ACTIVE READING

Here's an example of how you might actively read a text. In the boxes along the sides of the text are questions you might ask yourself as you read the story. See how the graphic follows the pre-reading and during-reading strategies? It's as if you, the reader, are having a conversation with the text you're reading!

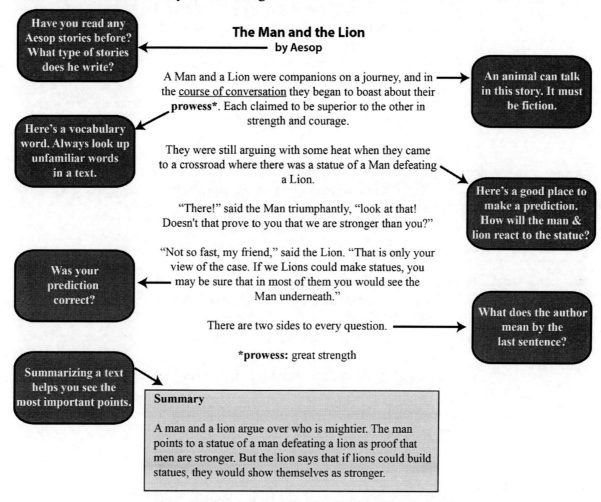

Have you read any Aesop stories before? What type of stories does he write?

The Man and the Lion
by Aesop

A Man and a Lion were companions on a journey, and in the course of conversation they began to boast about their **prowess***. Each claimed to be superior to the other in strength and courage.

An animal can talk in this story. It must be fiction.

Here's a vocabulary word. Always look up unfamiliar words in a text.

They were still arguing with some heat when they came to a crossroad where there was a statue of a Man defeating a Lion.

"There!" said the Man triumphantly, "look at that! Doesn't that prove to you that we are stronger than you?"

Here's a good place to make a prediction. How will the man & lion react to the statue?

Was your prediction correct?

"Not so fast, my friend," said the Lion. "That is only your view of the case. If we Lions could make statues, you may be sure that in most of them you would see the Man underneath."

There are two sides to every question.

What does the author mean by the last sentence?

*prowess: great strength

Summarizing a text helps you see the most important points.

Summary

A man and a lion argue over who is mightier. The man points to a statue of a man defeating a lion as proof that men are stronger. But the lion says that if lions could build statues, they would show themselves as stronger.

Practice 1: Practice 2: Active Reading

RL 1, **RF** 4 (DOK 1, 2)

As you read the following text, respond to the prompts in the spaces to the side.

What's a dilemma? What do you think the text will be about?

Shawn's Dilemma

Shawn would be in hot water. Sitting on the curb, he waited for his mom to pick him up. All through basketball practice he had been no good, because he couldn't concentrate. The only thing on his mind was what would happen when his mom and dad saw how poorly he had done on his history quiz. Coach Harris had yelled at him to "hustle up" and "get the lead out" more than once. Yet, with the big fat red "F" looming over him, there was nothing anyone could say to make him concentrate on shooting hoops today.

Can you make a personal connection to Shawn's problem?

Taking the dreaded quiz paper from his pocket, he unfolded it cautiously. As he opened up the paper, it was as if the large "F" Mrs. Jones penned at the top of the paper lunged out at him, laughing menacingly at his failure. Feeling defeated, Shawn let out a huge sigh. Actually, thinking about it, Shawn had never really been that good in history. Although he could do well enough to keep afloat, understanding history had never come easily. In second grade, it had been the names and dates that threw him. There were so many to remember, and he always got them confused. In third grade, it had been maps and timelines that didn't make sense, and in fourth grade, old historical documents might as well have been written in Greek, because Shawn never had a clue about even where to begin.

What conclusions can you draw about Shawn?

As the minutes slipped away, Shawn began to panic. What would it be? Would he be grounded and miss out on his weekend trek to the skate park? Would he lose his TV and computer privileges? No Xbox? As all of the possibilities swirled around in his mind, a strange thought struck him. For once, he wasn't as concerned about what the punishment would be as he was about what his mom and dad would think of his failing the history quiz. The thought of their disappointment at his quiz grade dwarfed the idea that he would be punished. How could this be?

What do you predict will happen when his mom shows up?

CHAPTER 2 SUMMARY

Just like authors have different reasons for writing, readers have different **purposes for reading**.

- to be informed
- to be entertained
- to solve problems

When you are an **active reader**, you participate in the text.

Think of the acronym SAME to help you with active reading.

- **S**urvey
- **A**sk questions
- **M**ake connections
- **E**valuate what you have read

Surveying (or **previewing**) a text means taking a glance at the whole thing before reading it.

To **ask questions** means to seek answers while reading. What do you already know about this subject? What do you want to find out?

To **make predictions**, you should think ahead, guessing what you'll read next.

When you **make an inference**, you are making a connection between what's said and not said in a story.

As you read, it is always a good idea to **access prior knowledge**, or think about what you already know.

To **summarize** means to give a short version of what you read.

When you **draw a conclusion**, you use the information in a text to make a statement about a character or event.

For additional practice, please see Chapter 2 Test located in the Teacher Guide.

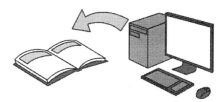

Research Connection

Think about the needs people around the world have. Some possible needs might include food, shelter, warm clothing, and fresh water. Now, think about some ways that you could serve others by meeting those needs. Possibilities include volunteering at a soup kitchen, walking an elderly neighbor's dog, buying a toy for a homeless child, writing a letter to a soldier overseas, collecting clothing for a homeless shelter, or raising money to send to a charity.

First, do some research. Identify a human need that interests you. Next, learn how you can help. Choose a charity, organization, or person to help. Find out exactly what that person or group needs. Third, make a plan for meeting the need. For example, if you are buying a toy for a homeless child, how will you raise the money? What help might you need from an adult? How will you decide what to buy? How will you deliver it to the shelter? Last, do the project.

Now, write a report about what you did. Be sure to include how you chose the project, what you did, and what happened when you finished the project.

Chapter 3
Exploring the Text

This chapter covers DOK levels 1–3 and the following fifth grade strands and standards (for full standards, please see page x):

> **Reading Literature: 1**, 5, **6**, 10
> **Reading Information Texts: 1, 2, 3, 5, 6, 8, 9**
> **Language:** 6

In this chapter...

- You will read and evaluate grade-level text and develop meaning through an analysis of text organization, structure, point of view, and relevance to other texts on the same topic.

- You will compare and contrast texts in order to better understand a topic.

3.1 MAIN IDEA AND SUPPORTING DETAILS

The **main idea** is what the text is all about. It is the point of the text. Sometimes you can find the main idea in the title. For example, take the title "Why I Like Disney Movies." You can tell right away that this text will tell the reasons why the writer likes Disney movies. It is the "big idea" of that text. But in another text, the main idea might be a sentence at its beginning or end. Sometimes you will have to look for supporting details or evidence that supports a main idea.

You should look for the facts, reasons, arguments, and examples that help you understand the key point of the text. These are the **supporting details**. This kind of evidence usually comes after the topic sentence and makes up the rest of the paragraph. Look directly to the text to find these details.

For example, take a look at this short text. Can you figure out what the main idea is?

> I had a great summer. First, I slept late every day. I went swimming with friends. I stayed up half the night watching TV. I even went to camp! I wish summer would never end!

If you guessed that the main idea is why the writer likes summer, then you are right! The supporting details (sleeping late, swimming, watching TV, and going to camp) all show why the writer likes summer so much.

These kinds of details are important in writing. They can help you understand what an author is trying to say or why he thinks as he does. A writer often will use supporting details to provide **evidence** that his opinion is right.

Imagine you are reading your school paper. On the opinions page, different students are giving their ideas about the best ways to communicate. Here is what one student has to say:

E-mail is a better way to communicate than regular mail. E-mail is free, but stamps for regular mail are getting more and more expensive. E-mail is also quicker. An e-mail takes minutes to arrive, but regular mail takes days to get to your house. In all, e-mail is the quicker, cheaper way to write to people.

After you read the first sentence, you know exactly how the author feels about the issue. The author then goes on to give several reasons to support his point. Each of these supporting details is evidence he uses to help prove his point of view.

Perhaps you are reading a longer text, one with multiple paragraphs. Each paragraph should have a main point and evidence to support it. But the paragraphs should also work together as a whole to support the overall main idea of the text.

Practice 1: Main Idea and Supporting Details

RI 2, 8 (DOK 2)

Read the text, and answer the questions that follow.

An Odd Bird with a Cow's Stomach

The hoatzin is an odd bird. Not only does it eat leaves, far more than any other bird, but it digests them like a cow or a sheep, grinding the leaves up in a specialized muscular crop. Up close, the hoatzin smells bad and flies poorly.

Hoatzin by Linda De Volder

Scientists have known about the hoatzin for years. A zoologist first wrote about the bird in 1776! Researchers have been curious about the strange hoatzin ever since. Recently, Wildlife Conservation International conducted a long study of this Venezuelan bird, supplying many more details.

About 85 percent of the hoatzin's diet is made up of green leaves. It prefers young, fresh leaves, which are richer in protein and easier to digest. Since the hoatzin, unlike a cow, has no teeth, it "chews" the leaves up by rubbing them against sandpapery ridges in its crop. It keeps food in its gut twenty hours or more; a chicken digests its food in a few hours. Like a cow, the hoatzin produces fatty acids that aid fermentation, giving the hoatzin the nickname *stinkbird*.

The hoatzin's digestive system has a price: The large crop results in a small breastbone and undersize muscles that limit its ability to fly. On landing it may crash into branches. The bird can fly, however, enough to avoid predators or researchers.

1   What evidence does the author present to support the claim that the hoatzin's digestive system has negative effects? Select **all** that apply.

A) The bird smells bad due to digestive acids. *(circled)*

B) The bird flies poorly because of its crop. *(circled)*

C) The bird is dying out in Venezuela.

D) The bird has no way to escape predators.

E) The bird has no teeth.

2   What detail does the author include to support the idea that scientists have known about the hoatzin for a long time?

"A zoologist first wrote about the bird in 1776!"

3   Fill in the following chart.

	Main Idea
Paragraph 1	The hoatzin is an odd bird.
Paragraph 2	Scientists have know about the hoatzin for years.
Paragraph 3	How the hoatzin was given the nickname stinkbird.
Paragraph 4	It can fly to avoid predators or reseachers.
Entire Text	

3.2 STRUCTURE OF A TEXT

As you read, you will notice that some types of text have certain organizational **structures**. These patterns are the way writers arrange ideas to present to readers. They are important because they show the relationships of ideas. You can become a better reader by knowing some of the common patterns. This section talks about four of them: chronology, problem/solution, cause/effect, and comparison. Let's take a look at each pattern and how it is best used.

CHRONOLOGICAL ORDER

Another way to understand a text is to look to see when each major event happens. When authors write a story, they often use **chronological order**, or a sequence of events. Sometimes this is called time order. Both fiction and nonfiction texts use this type of structure. Sequence of events can go from the first to the last event. Other times, it goes from last to first. Sometimes it can jump around! As you read, you will see clues about the order of events. Steps in a process should always be in a specific order to tell the reader when to finish each step.

Authors often use **transitions** to help their writing flow better. These are words or phrases that show connections between ideas, which makes writing easier to understand. Here are some common transitions to show chronological order.

Chronological Transitions				
finally	last	meanwhile	soon	today
first	later	next	then	when

PROBLEM AND SOLUTION

Sometimes it is not enough just to read a text. You have to involve yourself in it. You may have to figure out the clues in the plot the same way the characters in the book do. There might be a problem that needs to be solved. This is called **problem and solution order**. If you are an active reader, you can think of solutions to those problems. Sometimes you can use real-life situations to help you solve a problem. If you are reading about a fifth grader who wins a big contest, you can identify with that person. Why? Because you are in the fifth grade, too! Maybe you have even won a contest at some point in your life, so you can imagine the joy that person feels. Sometimes you can use technical information to help you solve a problem. For example, if you are trying to put together a model airplane, you might have to read the manual to help you. Also, what are you going to do if you are reading a story and a word pops up that you don't know? You can use a dictionary or another resource to help you. When you do that, you are being an active reader!

Problem/Solution Transitions	
as a result	it turns out
in fact	this is why

COMPARISON

A **compare-and-contrast** paragraph looks at how things are alike and different. If you focus on how they are alike (similarities), you are comparing. If you focus on how they are different, you are contrasting.

The following paragraph is organized to compare and contrast.

Apples and bananas are both healthy fruits. However, they have several differences. First, an apple must be washed. Then, you can eat its skin. A banana does not have to be washed, but it must be peeled. The banana peel is not edible. Apples come in many shapes, colors, and even flavors. The bananas we see at the market are mostly one kind—yellow! Finally, an apple is messier to eat than a banana, since apples are juicy. A banana is not really messy to eat, but you do need to find a place to throw away the peel.

See how this paragraph focuses on comparing apples and bananas? The writer makes a point about one fruit and then describes how the other fruit is similar or different to the first one.

| Compare and Contrast Transitions ||
Compare	Contrast
also	although
as	but
both	however
in addition	instead
like	otherwise
same	unlike
similarly	while

CAUSE AND EFFECT

Another way to understand what is in a text is to look at why events happen. Many events have a **cause and effect relationship**. A cause is the reason why something happens. An effect is the result. Look at the example below:

Cause: Jessica's alarm clock is broken.

Effect: She doesn't get up in time and is late to school.

In this example, a broken alarm clock causes Jessica to be late. A broken clock is the cause. Being late is the effect. When you know how events relate to each other, you can understand a text better.

Cause and Effect Transitions		
as a result	consequently	so
because of	due to	so that

3.3 POINT OF VIEW

All writing has a **point of view**, which tells you who is narrating the text: a character in the story or an outsider. As you know, authors use first-person, third-person, and occasionally second-person point of view. These show who is relating the events or information in the text. But point of view has another meaning. It also refers to the author's perspective or viewpoint—how he or she views a topic.

Two different people can experience the same event in different ways. Each will see it from a different point of view. Each will give a different **account** of what happened.

Read the following texts written in first-person point of view.

Jackson's Account	Reba's Account
"When I first arrived at Blair Elementary two weeks ago, I wasn't sure what to expect. It was scary leaving my friends in Oregon and moving to a small town in North Carolina. My parents recently divorced, and I'm not really sure of anything anymore. I just hope I can make some friends here. I really need some right now."	*"There's a new kid in my class at Blair Elementary. His name is Jackson, and he's pretty quiet. He also acts sad. I don't think he wants to be here. He doesn't seem very friendly."*

Jackson and Reba are experiencing the same event but in different ways. This gives them each a different point of view about what is happening.

When you read, consider who is telling the story. The narrator of the text can affect how the story is told. As you saw above, you can get a different impression of events based on who is telling the story. With Jackson as the narrator, you sympathize with him trying to fit in at a new school. With Reba as the narrator, you wonder why Jackson seems sad and unfriendly.

3.4 COMPARE AND CONTRAST TEXTS

You can also use structure to **compare and contrast texts**. There are a number of things you can compare in texts: characters, settings, plots, concepts, points of view, and writing purposes. You may even compare and contrast the structures of two or more texts.

For example, two texts might tell about similar events, but each might contain different information about those events. Think back to when you learned about the US government moving Native Americans west. If it was a Native American telling the reader about the Trail of Tears, that story would probably sound very different from the story told by the US government at the time.

The Native Americans might start telling the story in a different place than the government did, perhaps beginning many, many years back when white settlers first arrived in America. They may use chronological order to convey the events that occurred. The Native Americans would probably have very different ideas than the government about the events that took place.

In turn, the US government's version of the story would probably contain different details, such as the reasons why they thought that moving the Native Americans was justified. Perhaps the government would use a cause and effect pattern, describing the reasons why they forced the Native Americans to move and the effects it had on the country.

In this example, the characters and concepts in both stories are the same. But the structure and opinions are different because the stories have different narrators, points of view, and writing purposes.

Either way, you must be able to look at each text and see what information it has to offer. When you **integrate information** (include facts) from several texts, you show your readers that you are knowledgeable about your subject.

Practice 2: Structure and Point of View

RL 5, 6, RI 6 (DOK 1–3)

Read the text, and answer the questions that follow.

Friends

Characters: *STELLA, 11 years old, lifelong friend of Peter; PETER, 11 years old, lifelong friend of Stella; JAYNE, 11 years old, friend of both Peter and Stella*

Setting: *The public park in front of the running track*

Act 1

Scene 1

[PETER walks onto the stage and addresses the audience. He places one hand next to his mouth, looks back and forth several times, leans forward and speaks.]

PETER: First of all, I want you to know I'm no coward. I realize I might appear to be one since my solution to my current problem is to hide out until it passes. My problem, you see, involves the upcoming partner triathlon. I have no desire to participate in it, but I am by no means intimidated by it. I have never, however, had the ability to say no to Stella. Stella lives for competitions, in particular, these kinds of tests of strength. She always wants me to be her partner, teammate, or training partner and always feels certain she can't win without me. Since I simply cannot look her in the eye and refuse her request, I will avoid her until the event registration passes. Oh no, here she comes. Gotta run!

[PETER runs away, zigzagging behind trees.]

Act 1

Scene 2

[STELLA and JAYNE enter the stage. JAYNE sits on the bench in front of the track. STELLA puts one foot on the side of the bench and starts stretching.]

JAYNE: I saw the multitude of advertisements for the registration for the triathlon. With the huge number of ads they've put out, the competition is sure to be stiff. I assume you and Peter will partner up for the event.

[STELLA groans.]

JAYNE: Are my ears playing tricks on me, or did you just groan?

STELLA: There's nothing wrong with your hearing.

JAYNE: Do you mean to tell me you don't want to participate in the race?

[STELLA sits next to JAYNE on the bench.]

STELLA: Oh, I want to participate; actually, I want to win. The problem is Peter. Dustin asked me to be his partner, and I think we would definitely make a winning combination. He is a faster swimmer than I am. I am a faster biker than he is, and we both are fast runners. Peter, and I really hate saying this, adds nothing to a partnership in this competition. He is an excellent sport, always gracious and fair minded, but his athletic skills pale in comparison to mine. I would literally die if he ever even came close to tying me in a competition of this type.

JAYNE: Why not just tell him Dustin asked you to be his partner? Honesty is always the best policy.

STELLA: Not when being honest means crushing your best friend's feelings. Peter loves having me as a partner, and I can't disappoint him. He would be destroyed if I told him I wanted to work with a new teammate.

[*STELLA frowns and lets her shoulders droop.*]

JAYNE: I am very diplomatic. I could inform Peter about the situation in a manner that would convince him it was all his idea for you to partner with Dustin.

[*STELLA grins.*]

STELLA: You want to be my personal Atlas and take that huge weight off my shoulders? I should refuse your offer, but I simply can't bear to see the look of disappointment on Peter's face, so you're on!

1   What does the author reveal in Scene 1 that affects your reading of Scene 2? Why **most likely** did the author choose to structure the drama this way?

     _____

     _____

2   Order the sequence of events in this text. Number them from 1 to 4, with 1 being first and 4 being last.
     ___3___ Stella confides in Jayne about her problem with Peter.
     ___1___ Dustin asks Stella if she wants to be partners.
     ___2___ Peter runs away to avoid Stella.
     ___4___ Jayne offers to convince Peter not to compete.

3   Compare and contrast Peter's and Stella's points of view toward their partnership in the triathlon.

     _____

     _____

4   This question has two parts. First, answer part A. Then, answer part B.

Part A

   How does Peter act as the narrator in Scene 1?

   A) He explains events to the audience.   C) He is not a character in the drama.

   B) He knows what Stella and Jayne are   D) He uses third-person point of view.
      thinking.

Part B

How would the text be different without this narrator?

A) The audience wouldn't know who the characters were.

B) The audience wouldn't know Peter's secret.

C) The audience wouldn't understand Stella's ambitions.

D) There would be no difference in the text.

Triathlon Champs Discuss Training Process
by Richie Wyrock

Stella Kowalski and Dustin Jones, the winners of the Fairview Elementary School Triathlon, discussed their training regimen that led to their success. "We began each workout with about ten minutes of deep stretching," said Kowalski. "We wanted to get our muscles warmed up and limber before we started running, swimming, or biking."

Jones added, "Yeah, we also varied the intensity of our workouts, building up our stamina gradually. We didn't want to risk an injury."

The students trained for two months before the triathlon. They credit their balanced diet, persistence, and practice for their win. "Without all the training we did," said Kowalski, "we couldn't have won."

---

5   What is the point of view of this text?

A) first person

B) second person

C) third person

D) The point of view is unclear.

6   How does reading this text add to your understanding of "Friends"? Select **all** that apply.

A) It reveals that Stella won the triathlon.

B) It describes the best ways to train for a triathlon.

C) It reveals that Stella partnered with Dustin for the triathlon.

D) It suggests that Dustin had a sports injury from his training.

7   What organizational pattern does this text use? How does it contrast with the structure of "Friends"?

_____

_____

_____

3.5 USE READING STRATEGIES

Sometimes when you read a text, you will need to use reading strategies to explain how individuals, events, or ideas relate to each other. You will have to describe their **interactions**.

This goes along with cause/effect because you are looking at relationships. Take a look at this text. It explains how photosynthesis works. See if you can identify the **relationships** each element shares with the others.

The Process of Photosynthesis

Have you ever wondered what goes on inside a plant? Plants look pretty and colorful, but there is more to them than meets the eye. Plants are always working at a process called photosynthesis. They take in water through their roots and carbon dioxide from the air. Using sunlight, they convert this water and carbon dioxide into oxygen and glucose. Humans and other living beings need this oxygen to breathe. The glucose, a type of sugar, provides energy to refuel for the process.

How do plants use photosynthesis to help humans?

Look at the text. You know that a plant takes carbon dioxide from the air. Then, helped by the sun, it converts carbon dioxide into oxygen. We use this oxygen to breathe. You have tied together the actions of the plants and the actions of people. You just figured out the interactions between these elements!

Reading strategies also include **drawing conclusions**, **making predictions**, and **making inferences**. What conclusion can you make based on the photosynthesis text above? The text says, "Using sunlight, [plants] convert this water and carbon dioxide into oxygen and glucose. Humans and other living beings need this oxygen to breathe." Therefore, you might conclude that photosynthesis supports life for humans and animals, as well as plants.

Sometimes an author does not tell you everything outright. You may have to infer what the author means. When you make an **inference**, you are making a connection between what is said and not said in a story. In doing so, you use your prior knowledge and experience to help you understand what you are reading. This skill will come in handy, because an author may not state everything that happens in a story. He or she leaves it up to you to make the connection. For instance, look at the following text.

He held his breath and jumped in. The water covered his head and went up his nose. He could hear the muffled sound of his friends laughing and splashing around him. He opened his eyes under the water, looking around. He spotted the yellow ring at the bottom through the clear water and swam swiftly toward it.

Did you guess that the boy had jumped into a swimming pool? If you did, you guessed right. The author does not state this. You can infer the boy is in a pool because he's holding his breath, the water is covering his head, and he's swimming toward a yellow diving ring.

What predictions can you make about this text? There are all sorts of possibilities. Perhaps the boy will grab the diving ring from the bottom of the pool, and he or one of his friends will throw it again.

Practice 3: Use Reading Strategies

RL 1, 6, 10, **RI** 9 (DOK 1–3)

In this practice, you will play detective. A crime has occurred at the local convenience store, and it's your job to interview the witnesses. Read the witness statements below, and answer the questions that follow.

Witness Statements

Act 1

Scene 1

[*A DETECTIVE arrives at Doc Magoo's Convenience Store. He shows his badge to the STORE MANAGER, a man in a dress shirt and tie, at the front counter. They go into the manager's office, and the detective takes out his note pad.*]

Detective: Can you tell me what happened, sir?

Store Owner: Every dime was stolen from the cash register! I know exactly who the culprit is! The red-haired guy with sunglasses stole the money, I know it!

Detective: Okay, walk me through what happened.

Store Owner: Well, he was in here loitering for an hour. I was keeping my eye on him because he seemed like a suspicious character. I went in the back to get some supplies, and when I came back, both he and the money were gone.

Detective: What time was this?

Store Owner: Oh, let me think. [*looking frazzled and perplexed*] It was probably around 4:30. We were about to have our rush period, so I needed to restock the shelves before that happened. [*getting impatient*] Look, I'm sure about this. Arrest him immediately! I've had it with these kids coming in every day and ruining my business! Just last week, another young man rollerbladed through my store and knocked over my display of Salty Snax! He wheeled right out of here before I could catch him! They're all troublemakers!

Scene 2

[*The detective follows the store owner back out to the front counter. A CUSTOMER, a woman with gray hair and glasses, is standing there waiting to be interviewed.*]

Detective: Ma'am, you were here when the theft occurred?

Customer: That's correct, officer. I noticed a few other people in the store with me. One was a red-haired young man, looking in the magazine section. I remember him because he reminded me of my own grandson, Alan. Such a sweet boy my Alan is.

Detective: Mm-hmm, and did you notice anything else?

Customer: As a matter of fact, I also noticed a woman by herself. She didn't seem to be looking for anything in particular, but she sure seemed interested in the store owner. And I did see her near the register when the store owner went into the back.

Detective: Can you describe this woman?

Customer: [*tapping her chin thoughtfully*] Oh, middle aged … about my height. I don't remember much else about her. I was busy filling my cart with cat food for my adorable cat, Muffins.

Detective: Do you know what time it was that the owner went to the back of the store?

Customer: I'd say it was 4:50. I know I had to rush out of here to make the 5:00 bus home, so I was keeping an eye on my watch.

Scene 3

[*Next, the detective meets with the STORE ASSISTANT, a young woman with a ponytail, in the employee break room. She's pulling her lunch out of the fridge as the detective pulls out his note pad.*]

Detective: Miss, you were straightening the shelves near the front of the store when the theft occurred, is that right?

Store Assistant: Yup! My manager asked me to do it, like, as soon as my shift started.

Detective: Did you see the red-haired young man that your manager was keeping an eye on?

Store Assistant: [*laughing*] Of course! The carrot-top's name is Freddy.

Detective: You know him?

Store Assistant: Yeah! He's in my class at school and *OMG*, isn't he cute? I tried to get his attention while he was here, but he was too engrossed in the new sports magazine that came out yesterday. He barely looked up from the magazine rack. I was totally bummed, ya know?

Detective: I see. And when did he leave?

Store Assistant: [*popping her gum*] Hmm, I checked him out at the cash register around 4:15. I know because I was about to go on a five-minute break. When I came back at 4:20, he was gone. So I went back to organizing the shelf.

1   If you were the detective, which account would you consider the **most** reliable? Why?

_____

2   How does the store owner's point of view influence his account of events? Use a quote to support your answer.

_____

_____

3   Based on the evidence, is Freddy the thief? How do you know?

_____

_____

4 Place the letter of each event in the correct spot on the timeline according to the eyewitness accounts.

A) The store owner goes into the back to get supplies.

C) The money from the cash register goes missing.

B) The red-haired man buys a magazine.

D) The store assistant goes on a five-minute break.

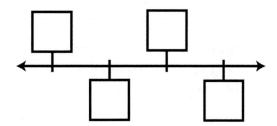

CHAPTER 3 SUMMARY

The **main idea** is what the text is all about. It is the point of the text.

The facts, reasons, arguments, and examples that help you understand the key point of the text are the **supporting details**.

As you read, you will notice that some types of text have certain organizational **structures**. These patterns are the way writers arrange ideas to present to readers.

Chronological order shows the sequence of events.

Problem and solution order describes a problem that needs to be solved.

A **compare-and-contrast** paragraph looks at how things are alike and different.

Many events have a **cause and effect relationship**. A cause is the reason why something happens. An effect is the result.

Authors often use **transitions** to help their writing flow better. These are words or phrases that show connections between ideas, which makes writing easier to understand.

All writing has a **point of view**, which tells you who is narrating the text: a character in the story or an outsider. Point of view can include first person or third person.

The narrator of the text can affect how the story is told.

You can also use structure to **compare and contrast texts**. You can compare characters, settings, plots, concepts, points of view, and writing purposes. You may even compare and contrast the structures of two or more texts.

Reading strategies include drawing conclusions, making predictions, and making inferences.

When you make an **inference**, you are making a connection between what is said and not said in a story.

For additional practice, please see Chapter 3 Test located in the Teacher Guide.

Chapter 4
Vocabulary

This chapter covers DOK levels 1–3 and the following fifth grade strands and standards (for full standards, please see page x):

Reading Literature: 4
Reading Informational Texts: 4
Reading Foundational Skills: 3, 4
Language: 4, 5, 6

In this chapter...

- You will understand how words are built and how each word part adds meaning to a word.

- You will use knowledge of context clues to determine the meaning of unknown words. These include domain-specific words such as those found in scientific, technical, or historical documents.

- You will use reference materials, including dictionaries, thesauruses, and encyclopedias, to learn the meanings of unfamiliar words.

4.1 WORD PARTS

Many English words come from other languages, such as **Greek and Latin**. Learning about **roots**, **prefixes**, and **suffixes** is another way to understand new words. A word can be broken down into parts. The part at the beginning of a word is the **prefix**. The main part of a word is the **root**. The last part of a word is the **suffix**. For example, look at the word *dishonestly*: *dis* is the prefix, *honest* is the root, and *ly* is the suffix. Put together, the word means "not acting in an honest way." Learning the meanings of certain roots, prefixes, and suffixes will help you understand new words.

> **Did You Know?**
>
> Many English words have Greek or Latin roots. This is because our language has always borrowed from other languages. English began as a form of ancient German. However, Rome controlled England from AD 43–436, bringing a heavy influence of Latin and Greek on the developing English language.

Common Root Words		
Root	**Definition**	**Example**
bio	life	biodome
cede, ceed, cess	go, yield	recede, process
chron	time	synchronize
cred	believe	incredible
dem, demo	people	democratic
dict	speak	dictate
equ	equal	equate
geo, terr, terra	earth	geography, terrestrial
graph	writing	telegraph
ject	throw	project
jud, jur, jus	law, justice	jury
metri, meter	measure	perimeter
naut, naus, nav	sea, ships, or travelers	navigate
ped, pod	foot	pedestrian
phon, phono, phone	sound	microphone
rupt	break	interrupt
scrib, script	write	scribble
temp	time, season	tempest
vers, vert	turn	convert

Common Prefixes	
bi	two or twice **Examples:** biannual (every two years), bilingual (someone who speaks two languages), and bicycle (a bike with two wheels)
dis	to take away, the absence of **Examples:** When you take away respect, it's *disrespect*. When you leave school for home, you are *dismissed*.
il, in, in, and un	not **Examples:** When you're not able, you're *unable*. Something not possible is *impossible*. Something not legal is *illegal*. Something not formal is *informal*.
mis	wrong or badly **Examples:** misbehave, misinform, mistake
pre	something that comes before **Examples:** prefix, prepare, preview
re	to do again **Examples:** review, reread, replay
tri	three **Examples:** tricycle (bike with three wheels) and triplets (three babies)

Common Suffixes	
able	capable of being **Examples:** a person who is easy to get along with is *agreeable* or *likable*. Someone we care about is *adorable* or *lovable*.
er	someone who does something or whose job it is **Examples:** A person who runs is a *runner*. Someone who bakes is a *baker*. Someone who gardens is a *gardener*.
ful	full of **Examples:** cheerful, plentiful, frightful, helpful, careful
less	without **Examples:** Someone without fear is *fearless*.
ly	like, in the manner of **Examples:** quietly, easily, hopelessly
ment	an act or instance of doing something or a state of being **Examples:** entertainment, amazement, contentment
ness	state of or quality **Examples:** restlessness, kindness
ous	full of or having **Examples:** A house that has a lot of room is *spacious*. Someone who is full of kindness is *gracious*.

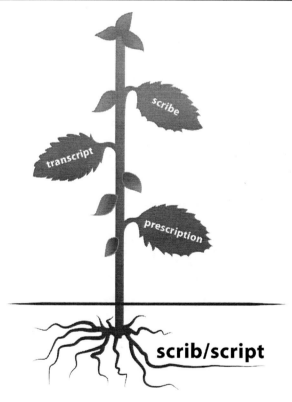

The root word *scrib/script*, which means "write," is the basis for several other words. A *prescription* is a written note from a doctor for a patient's medication. A *scribe* is a writer or clerk. A *transcript* is a written or printed copy of something.

Practice 1: Word Parts

RL 4, L 4.b, RF 3.a (DOK 2)

A. For each of the following words, write the meaning based on your knowledge of roots and affixes.

Word	Meaning
1. dishonor	
2. incredulous	
3. nautical	
4. trilingual	
5. bountiful	

B. Read the text, and answer the questions that follow.

Math on the Mind

Chelsea listened as Ms. McKinney repeated the spelling words for the week. Her mind wandered to what would happen later in the day in math class. Up until this year, math had been her favorite subject. She loved the fun, delightful activities that they did in the early grades, like coloring different shapes in preschool. There was always a game, always a cute math toy; it gave her such enjoyment! Now, somehow, not only had math become boring, but Chelsea felt like she was one of the worst math students in the class. She had come to dislike numbers altogether. Was she misguided in thinking that if she just paid attention in class, she should do well on the tests and quizzes? Would she have to study more? Where would she begin? At home, the Cs and occasional D that she was bringing home from math class were simply not acceptable. She knew she was capable of doing better. She was unafraid to face this challenge. She would have to dig in her heels and get better grades in math.

1   What does the *re* in <u>repeat</u> mean?

A) full of   C) to do again

B) not   D) before

2   Which of the following words has a suffix that means "filled with"?

A) delightful   C) enjoyment

B) capable   D) teacher

3   This question has two parts. First, answer part A. Then, answer part B.

Part A

Which of the following words contains a prefix that means "wrongly or badly"?

A) misguided   C) dislike

B) unafraid   D) preschool

Part B

What does the word you chose in part A mean?

_____

_____

_____

4   What prefix would you add to the word <u>acceptable</u> to make it mean "not acceptable"?

A) dis   C) mis

B) pre   D) un

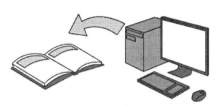

Research Connection

Just as America is comprised of people from many different cultures, the English language has developed over time from many different cultures. Many people's names also come from other places. For example, the common name Nick is actually derived from the Greek name "Nikolaos." This name combines the Greek god of victory, Nike, with the root *laos*, which means "people," to form a meaning of "victor of the people." Research your name to learn where it originated from and what it means.

SYLLABLES

Syllables are chunks of sound. Each syllable has one vowel sound. When you add a prefix or a suffix to a root, you add a syllable. You can see syllables when you speak. Look in a mirror as you say words. See how many times your mouth opens? Each time you open your mouth, you are saying one syllable.

All words have at least one syllable. Some have many. If you read one syllable at a time, you can read long words easier. Here are some examples:

   One syllable: dog, rate, danced

   Two syllables: hammer, swimming, repeat

   Three syllables: delightful, underground, evergreen

When you encounter an unfamiliar word, try breaking it into syllables to see if you can find a word you recognize.

   Example: deafening

You may not recognize this word, but when you break it into syllables, you get deaf – en – ing. You probably recognize the word *deaf*, so you can figure out that this word has something to do with not being able to hear. By learning to recognize common suffixes, you could figure out the rest of the meaning.

SOUNDS AND BLENDS

Some letters work together to make new **sounds**. Vowels (*a*, *e*, *i*, *o*, and *u*) combine in some words. Consonants (all the other letters) also work together in **blends**. Learning the way some words sound can help you figure out what they mean.

SOUNDS

Sometimes the way you read a word can help you know what it means. You just read how vowels can combine with other letters to make new sounds. Say the word *clown* out loud. Now say the word *out*. Did you hear the same **sound** in both words? That sound is spelled *ow* in *clown* and *ou* in *out*.

Here are some other groups of letters that sound the same but have different spellings:

thaw	soil	boat
author	boy	crow

CONSONANT BLENDS

Some words have a **consonant blend**. A blend has two or more consonants that work together. They make the same sound each time. Knowing them can make it easier to read new words that have these blends.

Here are some common blends. Read them aloud so you can hear how they sound.

bl	gl	sp
cr	gr	st
dr	sm	th

Here are some words that use these blends.

Blend	Word	Blend	Word	Blend	Word
bl	bland	gl	glass	sp	spine
	table		angle		gasp
cr	crew	gr	grow	st	step
	acre		angry		last
dr	drink	sm	smile	th	thing
	address		prism		both

4.2 CONTEXT CLUES

Good readers use special skills to understand what they read. Knowing how to use context clues is a good skill to have. **Context clues** are found around a word. They are other words and phrases that help you figure out the meaning of a new word. First, look for the clues that are in the sentence with the unknown word in it. Then, look at the other sentences around it for help. Sometimes, nearby words have a similar meaning to the unknown word or give a definition of it.

For example, if you read an essay about the world's fastest cars, you might see the word *capability* in a paragraph.

> The SSC Ultimate Aero has a speed <u>capability</u> of over 250 mph. The car is built to reach this speed. Of course, few people will ever try to drive this fast.

What can you guess *capability* means from its context? This paragraph says that this car can reach very high speeds. It sounds like *capability* means something like "ability to do something."

Types of Context Clues		
Type	**Definition**	**Example**
Cause/effect	The unknown word depends on the cause/effect relationship it shares with other words. Some words that signal cause/effect relationships are *because, since, consequently, therefore,* and *as a result.*	*Because* the bus was <u>tardy</u>, we were <u>late</u> to the first period at school. tardy: late
Comparison	The unknown word has the same meaning as a familiar word or words in a text. Key words and phrases to look for include *like, in the same way, both, similar,* and *also.*	The <u>tome</u>, *like* most heavy <u>books</u>, was difficult to carry home. tome: book
Contrast	The unknown word has the opposite meaning of a familiar word or words in a text. Key words and phrases to look for include *but, however, not, while, yet, except, on the other hand, instead of, unlike, although,* and *the opposite of.*	My older brother told me my fifth grade teacher, Ms. Stone, was a <u>tyrant</u>. *However,* I think she's <u>nice</u>. tyrant: mean ruler (opposite of *nice*)
Definition or Restatement	The meaning of the unknown word is defined or restated in the sentence or text. Look for key words and phrases such as *is, that is, or, means, who is, that is, in other words,* or *which.*	An <u>entomologist</u>, *or* a <u>bug expert</u>, studies many kinds of insects. entomologist: bug expert
Example	The meaning of an unknown word is explained in an example in the sentence or text. Key phrases are *for example, for instance,* and *such as.*	People use all kinds of <u>vehicles</u> *such as* <u>cars</u>, <u>bicycles</u>, <u>scooters</u>, and <u>motorcycles</u>. vehicles: cars, bicycle, scooters, motorcycles

WORDS WITH MULTIPLE MEANINGS

Sometimes when you are reading, you will come across **words with multiple meanings**. For instance, take the word *address*. If we just look at the word, without a context, it could mean several different things: It could mean your home address, to speak or discuss a problem, or a speech by an important person. It is only when we look at context clues that the meaning becomes clear.

Example: The teacher <u>addressed</u> me in a quiet voice.

The meaning of *address* in this sentence is how someone speaks or talks. Context clues help you figure out the correct meaning of a word. Now that we know how to use context clues to figure out the meanings of new words, let's practice looking at words that have more than one meaning.

Practice 2: Context Clues

RL 4, RI 4, L 4.a, RF 4.c (DOK 2)

Read the text below, and answer the questions that follow.

A New Experience

Shauna hesitated before knocking on the apartment door. Behind her, she could feel the frigid November air, but she stood still, nervous about facing what was in front of her. Suddenly, Shauna experienced a wave of guilt over what was really on her mind. Shauna knew that what she was thinking would be appalling to most. She and her friend Katrina had signed up to be a part of their church's neighborhood outreach program. Shauna just didn't know that she would be the one visiting the homes of the less fortunate to deliver holiday gift baskets.

Rather, Shauna had pictured the project something more like sitting in the comfortable church classroom with her Sunday school friends and thinking of ways to help those in need. Getting out and being the actual hands of help had never crossed Shauna's mind. Although she had learned in a citizenship lesson that being gregarious was a virtue, Shauna was afraid. What would she see in there? How would they treat her? How would the people she encountered be different from the people she knew? Right now, all she wanted to do was to run off back to the comfort of her own cozy suburb, sit down, and have dinner with her own family.

A woman opened the door and invited Shauna in. The room into which she looked was filled with meager provisions, but it was absolutely immaculate. There was not so much as a single item out of place. It was clear that the family who lived here might be poor, but they were certainly careful about keeping their living area tidy. Seeing no one around, Shauna quietly made her way over to a table in the corner. There, she set down her basket of colorful confections and lifted the cover. Cupcakes, cookies, and other decorative pastries sent a sweet aroma into the air. Shauna felt good about what she was doing. This would be the apex of her holiday experience.

Creeping back towards the door, Shauna thought she heard something. Turning around, she saw a little curly-haired girl dressed in a too-small pink ruffled dress. "Thank you," the little girl said shyly. Smiling back, Shauna nodded and waved as she hurried out the door. She felt warm inside.

1   Read this sentence from the text and the question that follows.

    Shauna <u>hesitated</u> before knocking on the apartment door.

What does the word <u>hesitated</u> mean in the sentence?

A) paused   C) ran

B) looked   D) jumped

2   Read this sentence from the text and the question that follows.

    Behind her, she could feel the <u>frigid</u> November air, but she stood still, nervous about facing what was in front of her.

In this sentence, the word <u>frigid</u> means _____.

3   Read these sentences from the text and the question that follows.

    Suddenly, Shauna experienced a wave of guilt over what was really on her mind. Shauna knew that what she was thinking would be <u>appalling</u> to most.

What does <u>appalling</u> mean?

A) enjoyable   C) awful

B) difficult   D) different

4   Read this sentence from the text and the question that follows.

    Although she had learned in a citizenship lesson that being <u>gregarious</u> was a virtue, Shauna was afraid.

What does the word <u>gregarious</u> **most likely** mean?

A) outgoing   C) scared

B) sad   D) stuck-up

5   This question has two parts. First, answer part A. Then, answer part B.

Part A

Read these sentences and the question that follows.

    The room into which she looked was filled with <u>meager</u> provisions, but it was absolutely <u>immaculate</u>. There was not so much as a single item out of place.

What does the word <u>meager</u> **most likely** mean?

A) eager   C) inadequate

B) plentiful   D) delicious

Part B

Underline the word or phrase above that helps you understand what <u>immaculate</u> means.

6 Read this sentence from the text and the question that follows.

There, she set down her basket of colorful <u>confections</u> and lifted the cover.

Based on its context in the text, what does the word <u>confections</u> mean?

A) sandwiches

B) raw vegetables

C) fruit and cheese

D) sweet desserts

7 Read this sentence from the text and the question that follows.

This would be the <u>apex</u> of her holiday experience.

What does the word <u>apex</u> mean?

A) a deep valley

B) a small hill

C) to climb

D) the highest point

In a discovery activity, Mitchell and his science classmates looked at various minerals. They were looking for specific qualities in each mineral. Making observations about color was easy—all they had to do was look. To see the minerals' streaks, they rubbed them against streak plates. To decide about luster, they held them up in the science-lab lights. They were even allowed to break the mineral into pieces. That way, they could see if the pieces would cleave in a sheer, straight way or splinter unevenly.

8 Read this sentence.

To see the minerals' <u>streaks</u>, they rubbed them against streak plates.

Based upon how it is used in the sentence, what does the word <u>streaks</u> mean?

A) to move quickly

B) long, narrow smears

C) flashes of light

D) a disease that spreads quickly

9 Read this sentence.

To decide about <u>luster</u>, they held them up in the science-lab lights.

Based upon how it is used in the sentence, <u>luster</u> means

A) the way light is reflected from a mineral's surface.

B) the inability of a mineral to reflect any light.

C) a mineral's ability to reflect light in a rainbow of colors.

D) a mineral's ability to take in, but not reflect, any light.

10 Read this sentence.

That way, they could see if the pieces would <u>cleave</u> in a sheer, straight way or splinter unevenly.

Based upon how it is used in the sentence, what does <u>cleave</u> mean?

A) to cut into equal pieces

B) to shatter into rough bits

C) to fracture in a definite line

D) to smash into an ornate pattern

The Tongue

The human tongue is a fascinating muscle. It is the only muscle in the human body that is not attached to something on both ends. You can stick it out of your mouth and move it around. This is a handy thing when you get something stuck on your teeth, and there is no toothbrush in sight.

The tongue also houses your taste buds. If you stick out your tongue and look in a mirror, you will see that your tongue is covered with minuscule bumps. Those tiny bumps are your taste buds. The taste buds help a person distinguish between salty, sweet, sour, and bitter tastes. Your tongue holds about 10,000 taste buds. However, these are not permanent residents on your tongue. Your body actually replaces your taste buds about every two weeks.

Another interesting fact is that your tongue, like your fingers, has its own unique print. Someday people may have the technology to identify you with nothing but your tongue print!

11 Read this sentence.

If you stick out your tongue and look in a mirror, you will see that your tongue is covered with <u>minuscule</u> bumps.

What is the meaning of the word <u>minuscule</u>?

A) very large   C) very bright

B) very small   D) very loud

12 Read this sentence.

However, these are not <u>permanent</u> residents on your tongue.

What does the word <u>permanent</u> mean?

A) lasting   C) curled

B) dying   D) sharp

13 Based on the text, what does the word <u>identify</u> mean? Explain your answer.

_____

_____

4.3 WORKING WITH WORDS

Another helpful skill to have when learning new vocabulary is to know how some words are related to other words. This relation can be through their spellings or meanings.

Synonyms are words that have the same or almost the same meaning.

Examples: *Large* is a synonym for *big. Giggle* is a synonym for *laugh. Jump* is a synonym for *leap.*

Antonyms are words that have the opposite meaning.

> **Examples:** *Hot* is an antonym for *cold*. *Tall* is an antonym for *short*. *Day* is an antonym for *night*.

Homophones are words that sound the same but have different meanings and usually different spellings.

> **Examples:** *Meet* and *meat*; *heard* and *herd*; *there* and *their*

Homographs are words that look the same but have different meanings. Sometimes they sound the same, but sometimes they don't.

> **Example:** *does* (to do) – Why *does* Jake always wear a baseball cap?
> *does* (more than one female deer) – We saw three *does* and a buck in the woods.

As you can see, these words are spelled the same way. Yet they are sometimes pronounced differently, and when they are used in a sentence, you can tell they have different meanings.

Here are some more examples of homographs.

bass	My uncle sings **bass** in the choir. Neil caught a huge **bass** on his fishing trip.
bow	Melissa has a big pink **bow** in her hair. It is proper to **bow** before the queen.
wave	Mrs. Reilly greets us with a **wave** every morning at the bus stop. The **wave** crashed on the shore with a noise like a big drum.
wound	My grandma **wound** the old-fashioned clock and made it tick. Jessica cut her finger, and Danny had to bandage the **wound**.

moped

Justin **moped** when he couldn't play outside.

My uncle rides a **moped**.

wind

A tropical **wind** blew through the city.

If I don't **wind** my watch, I won't be on time.

Practice 3: Working with Words

RL 4, L 5.c (DOK 2–3)

Read the text. Then, answer the questions.

The Hottest Ticket in Town!

This Friday is the opening night of the drama club's latest production. This reviewer had an opportunity to see a sneak preview of this unforgettable show. The play, *Positively Me*, was written by our own resident playwright, Mrs. Franklin. It promises to make the audience think, laugh their heads off, and cry buckets of tears. It offers many ideas to discuss with our fellow students long after the play ends.

The play is about two ten-year-old girls who travel back in time. Their goal is to right a wrong that occurred one hundred years in the past. While visiting the past, they learn about many things that influenced the people they know in their own time. When they return, they see the wide-reaching effects of their actions. As one character says, "Changing the past is like tossing a pebble in a pond. It not only creates a splash, but it also creates ripples that change the surface of the water in every direction."

Ably filling the roles of the time travelers are Becky Simpson and Irene Boriss. When I saw the play, I noticed how both girls looked right at home on the stage; you would never suspect the girls had never been in a play before. They performed like professionals. Neither girl dropped a line or stumbled through a scene. The supporting cast was equally impressive.

The play is being staged in our new theater. Spending an evening in this arena is a treat by itself. The chairs are comfortable and are staggered to improve everyone's view of the stage. The climate controls are adjustable, so the theater is neither too warm nor too cold. The lighting and sound systems work perfectly and add to the seamless production.

The production is sure to sell out, so buy your tickets in advance. The play will definitely be the buzz around school next week, so don't be left out. In fact, if I had to see it again and again, I would not object! Tickets purchased ahead of time will be sold at a discount price. Head over to the theater office after school today, and secure your tickets for the play.

---

1 Read this sentence.

It promises to make the audience think, laugh their heads off, and cry buckets of <u>tears</u>.

Which of the following sentences correctly uses the homograph for the underlined word above?

A) My mother cried tears of joy when my sister got married.

B) I tried not to cry when I saw the tears in my brand new shirt.

C) Ava does not like to cry because she hates the way tears taste.

D) Grandma Jane always tears up when she watches *Gone with the Wind*.

2 Read this sentence.

The supporting cast was equally <u>impressive</u>.

The word <u>impressive</u> is a synonym for

A) amazing.

C) troubled.

B) boring.

D) expensive.

3 Read this sentence.

Head over to the theater office after school today, and <u>secure</u> your tickets for the play.

What word is a synonym for <u>secure</u>?

A) forget

C) give

B) lose

D) obtain

4 Read this sentence.

The chairs are <u>comfortable</u> and are staggered to improve everyone's view of the stage.

What word is an antonym for <u>comfortable</u>?

A) cozy

C) cramped

B) roomy

D) spacious

5 Read this sentence.

In fact, if I had to see it again and again, I would not <u>object</u>!

Look at the underlined word above. Name **two** synonyms and **two** antonyms each for the word <u>object</u>. Also, can you think of a word that looks like <u>object</u> but means something else? Give the homograph and its definition for the word <u>object</u>.

_____

_____

_____

4.4 LEARNING NEW WORDS

There are many resources you can use to learn new words. Some of these are in printed form, but you can also find many digital resources online.

Reference materials are books and online tools that help you find out more about words. Here are the most common ones.

A **dictionary** is a book that lists words in alphabetical (ABC) order. On the top corner of each page, you'll see two words called guide words. These words tell you the first word and the last word on that page. This helps you find the word you are looking for. Each word has an entry (section) that tells what the word means. It can tell you other things about the word, too. The entry will show you how to say the word. It will also include the word's part of speech. Of course, the dictionary provides the word's definitions.

Here is a sample word entry:

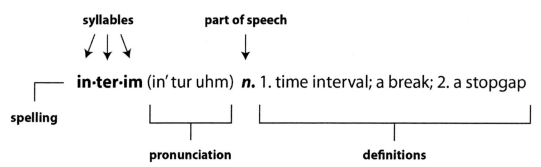

A **thesaurus** is similar to a dictionary, but rather than containing definitions, a thesaurus contains word synonyms (words that mean close to the same thing as the word you look up). When you are writing, a thesaurus comes in handy. It is a great resource to help you generate creative and colorful words to express yourself.

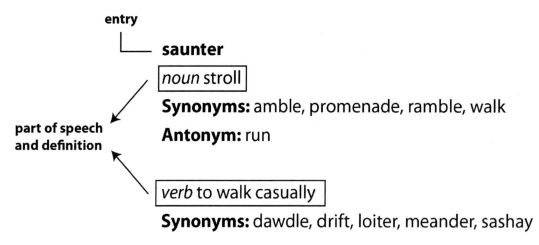

A **glossary** is like a specialized dictionary that is created for a certain text. The text might have special or difficult words that the author needs the reader to understand. A glossary may be at the back of a book, or there may be a short glossary in each chapter. It provides definitions for key terms in the book or in the chapter.

Glossary Page	
Wave: a disturbance that travels through space or time, carrying energy from one location to another	**Weather balloon:** a balloon released into the atmosphere that records data about temperature, air pressure, and humidity
Wavelength: the distance between the crests and troughs in a series of waves	**Weather map:** a map that shows data about weather conditions across an area

All of these resources are also available as online reference tools. You can access them on your computer with an Internet connection. Some online sources even have an audio feature. If your computer has speakers, you can hear how a word is pronounced.

Reference materials are useful when you come across **domain-specific words**. These are words that have a special meaning in a particular subject. For example, the word *compound* has several different meanings. In science, a *compound* means a mixture of two or more elements or ingredients. In English class, *compound* may refer to a compound sentence (a sentence with two or more clauses). Use context clues or a dictionary to help you know what domain-specific words mean.

Practice 4: Learning New Words

RI 4, L 4.c, 6 (DOK 2)

Read the following reference entries, and answer the questions that follow.

> shriek (shreek) *n.* 1 a sharp, loud cry
>
> *v.* 2 to cry out sharply

1 Which sentence uses <u>shriek</u> correctly?

A) The baby shrieked sleepily after drinking a bottle.

B) The ducks shrieked happily while munching their corn.

C) The child shrieked frightfully in the haunted house.

D) The girl shrieked sadly as she watched her ice cream melt.

> word: **depressed**
>
> part of speech: *adjective*
>
> meaning: sad, low in spirits
>
> synonyms: saddened, dismayed, let down
>
> antonyms: cheerful, encouraged, joyous

2 Which word would **best** replace <u>depressed</u> in this sentence?

Dante was depressed about losing the tennis match.

A) cheerful   C) encouraged

B) saddened   D) joyous

anonymous	with no name known
apparition	a ghost
assortment	a group or collection of different items
avarice	greed for riches
belligerent	aggressive and eager to fight
bustle	to move quickly and busily
cantankerous	ill-tempered or bad tempered
consolation	something that makes someone feel better

3 Someone who is <u>cantankerous</u> is which of the following? Select **all** that apply.

A) nice   C) polite   E) eager   G) spry

B) mean   D) lazy   F) cranky   H) mild

4 If you were writing a letter to someone, and you did not want them to know whom it was from, how would you sign it?

_____

_____

Read the text, and follow the directions that follow.

The Printing Press

Before William Caxton set up the first printing press in England in 1476, the only writing available to literate people was handwritten. Books, mostly religious in nature, were labor-intensive and time-consuming products. These coveted manuscripts were relatively few in number. They were accessible to only the educated classes, which made up a small segment of society. Only the nobility and the clergy were literate. All other members of society belonged to the class of laborers, who were generally uneducated and known as "commoners." However, a new merchant class was beginning to emerge in Europe—men who had a basic degree of education as well as some expendable cash.

---

5 Some of the words in the text may be unfamiliar to you. Use the reference source Dictionary.com to look up the following words, and complete this table.
www.dictionary.com

Word	Definition	Part of Speech	Use in an Original Sentence
literate			
labor-intensive			
coveted			
accessible			
segment			
nobility			
emerge			
expendable			

CHAPTER 4 SUMMARY

Words can be broken down into **word parts**.

The part at the beginning of a word is the **prefix**. The main part of a word is the **root**. The last part of a word is the **suffix**.

Syllables are chunks of sound. Each syllable has one vowel sound.

Some letters work together to make new **sounds**. Vowels (*a, e, i, o,* and *u*) combine in some words. Consonants (all the other letters) also work together in **blends**.

Context clues are found around a word. They are other words and phrases that help you figure out the meaning of a new word.

Context clues can help you when you find a word that has **multiple meanings**.

Synonyms are words that have the same or almost the same meaning.

Antonyms are words that have an opposite meaning.

Homophones are words that sound the same but have different meanings and usually different spellings.

Homographs are words that look the same but have different meanings. Sometimes they sound the same, but sometimes they don't.

Reference materials are books and online tools that help you find out more about words.

A **dictionary** is a book that lists words in alphabetical (ABC) order. Each word has an entry (section) that tells what the word means.

A **thesaurus** is similar to a dictionary, but rather than containing definitions, a thesaurus contains word synonyms (words that mean close to the same thing as the word you look up).

A **glossary** is like a specialized dictionary that is created for a certain text. The text might have special or difficult words that the author needs the reader to understand.

For additional practice, please see Chapter 4 Test located in the Teacher Guide.

Chapter 5
Literary Genres

This chapter covers DOK levels 1–3 and the following fifth grade strands and standards (for full standards, please see page x):

Reading Literature: 1, 4, 5, 7, 9, **10**
Reading Foundational Skills: 4
Language: 5

In this chapter…

- You will read grade-level appropriate fiction, nonfiction, drama, and poetry and tell those genres of literature apart.

- You will understand the unique elements of each genre and how to recognize these elements.

- You will understand connections between language and works of literature in the form of figurative language such as metaphors and similes.

You may not realize it, but you have read quite a bit of **literature** in your life. In school and maybe on your own too, you have read stories, whole books, poems, and perhaps even plays. These are all different types or **genres** (ZHON-rahz) of literature. It's time to learn a little more about the genres of literature you are reading.

5.1 FICTION

Fiction is the term used for made-up stories. They are imaginative and are not true. Sometimes an author might take real historical events and people and make up fictional stories around them. But because the author makes up the story, it is fiction. There are many different kinds of fiction.

Novel	A **novel** is a long fiction book. It may have many chapters. It can be any kind of literature, like a fantasy, a legend, a mystery, or a western.
	Example: *Bread and Roses, Too* by Katherine Paterson
Folktale	**Folktales** are simple stories set in the past which have animal, human, or supernatural characters. Supernatural characters use their special powers to solve problems. Often, events in folktales happen in threes.
	Example: "The Tale of the Bamboo Cutter," a Japanese folktale
Fairy tale	**Fairy tales** are also types of folklore that are passed down over many years. They usually begin with "Once upon a time …"
	Example: "Hansel and Gretel"

Fable	A **fable** is a short story that teaches a lesson. Fables often use animals in place of humans. **Example:** "The Fox and the Grapes" by Aesop
Legend	A **legend** is a story that has some true and some untrue parts. Legends are usually about people who really lived, but their legendary deeds are bigger than real life. **Example:** Johnny Appleseed
Myth	A **myth** is a story that explains the world by using made-up events and characters. Most myths are very old. Today, we use science to understand nature. In myths, magic or spirits usually explain natural events. Many cultures have myths about how the world began, why the sun moves in the sky, and where the first people came from. **Example:** "Crow Brings the Daylight," an Inuit myth

There are **subgenres** of novels.

Science fiction	**Science fiction** stories typically are set in the future, or they may be set in outer space. Many science fiction stories include science and inventions that are not yet possible. **Example:** *Jacob Wonderbar and the Cosmic Space Kapow* by Nathan Bransford
Fantasy fiction	**Fantasy fiction** contains elements that aren't realistic, such as talking animals or magical powers. **Example:** *Peter and the Starcatchers* by Dave Barry
Historical fiction	**Historical fiction** consists of written works about plot elements that did not really happen but could have happened in the distant past. **Example:** *Lyddie* by Katherine Paterson
Graphic novel	A **graphic novel** is a book presented in a comic-book format. It blends pictures and words to tell a story. **Example:** *Bone* by Jeff Smith
Realistic fiction	**Realistic fiction** takes place in a world much like the real world. The characters are involved in events that could really happen. This might include a story about a terrible day at school or one about an actress winning an award for her acting. Just like real life, realistic fiction may be about many things. **Example:** *Ramona Quimby, Age 8* by Beverly Cleary

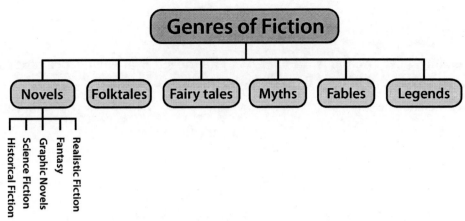

Practice 1: Graphic Novels

RL 7, 10 (DOK 3)

Visit this website, and create your own short graphic novel. Write a story with at least two characters, including dialogue and actions. Share your comics with your class when you are finished.

http://www.makebeliefscomix.com/

Here is an example of how a comic strip panel from a graphic novel might look.

This comic strip was created at MakeBeliefsComix.com; go there to create your own.

Practice 2: Fiction

RL 10 (DOK 2)

These questions have two parts. In part A, write the letter of each genre next to the correct book cover, and in part B, answer the questions.

A. Science fiction   C. Myth   E. Fairy tale

B. Legend   D. Fantasy fiction

1

Part A _____

Part B

How can you tell the genre of this book?

_____

_____

_____

_____

2

Part A _____

Part B

How can you tell the genre of this book?

_____

_____

_____

_____

3

Part A _____

Part B

How can you tell the genre of this book?

_____

_____

_____

_____

4

Part A _____

Part B

How can you tell the genre of this book?

_____

_____

_____

_____

5

Part A _____

Part B

How can you tell the genre of this book?

_____

_____

_____

_____

5.2 NONFICTION

Nonfiction writing is not made up; it is based on true facts. Nonfiction contains information about real-life people, events, or subjects. Like fiction, there are different kinds of nonfiction texts. These **informational texts** give us knowledge about the world around us. Nonfiction texts are often used in research. You will learn more about how they are used in the informational texts chapter.

Autobiography	An **autobiography** is a story about a person's life written by that person. Some autobiographies deal with a person's whole life, while others only cover a few special months or years in that person's lifetime. Many famous people have written autobiographies. **Example:** *It Came from Ohio! My Life as a Writer* by R. L. Stine
Biography	A **biography** is the story of another person's real life. Writing a biography is a little like researching a report. Biographers have to know many facts about their subjects. At the same time, they have to show what their subjects are (or were) like in real life. **Example:** *Eleanor Roosevelt: A Life of Discovery* by Russell Freedman
Journals	**Journals** often include a reflection of the events happening in the writer's life. They may span a certain time that the author lived through. **Example:** *The Journals of Lewis and Clark* by Meriwether Lewis and William Clark
Informational Books	**Informational books** are exactly what they sound like. They are books you read to gain information. They could be your school textbooks or just books that teach you something about a particular subject. **Example:** *Children of the Dust Bowl* by Jerry Stanley
Reference Books	**Reference books** include general information or quick facts about a subject. They include dictionaries, encyclopedias, thesauruses, and glossaries. **Example:** *The Merriam-Webster Dictionary*

5.3 POETRY

Poetry expresses ideas, feelings, or situations in a creative way. Poetry is about words and associations; it uses words that create mind pictures. Poetry does not have regular rules like other writing. Sometimes it doesn't have punctuation. It does not have paragraphs and may not have complete sentences. Instead, it is typically written in lines and stanzas. **Stanzas** are groups of lines within a poem. Usually, stanzas are separated from each other by a blank line.

Some poems contain **rhyme**. This means the poem has words that make the same sounds at the ends of some lines.

Excerpt from "A Dream" by Edgar Allan Poe

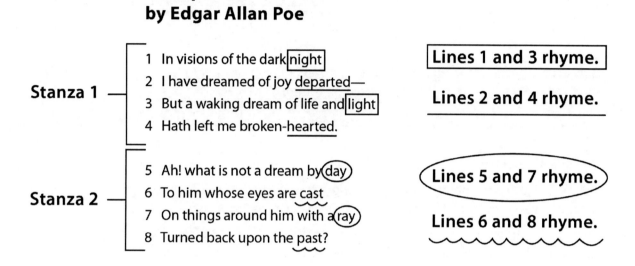

Other poems do not rhyme. Those poems are written in **free verse**, which means the lines do not rhyme or have a set pattern.

> **Example:** Stranger, if you passing meet me and desire to speak to me, why
> should you not speak to me?
> And why should I not speak to you?
> – "To You" by Walt Whitman

There are many different types of poetry. Some are short (just a few lines) and others are as long as books!

Lyric poems	Lyric poems focus on thought and emotion. They sometimes describe images like nature scenes using vivid language. **Example:** "Nothing Gold Can Stay" by Robert Frost
Narrative poems	Narrative poems tell stories. They often include characters, setting, and plots, just like regular stories. They range from a few words about an event to book-size epics about long adventures. **Example:** *Horton Hears a Who* by Dr. Seuss
Nursery rhymes	Nursery rhymes are short poems often taught to young children. **Example:** the poems of Mother Goose
Epic poems	An **epic** is a long, narrative (story) poem that tells about the extraordinary feats of a great legendary or national hero. **Example:** The *Iliad* by Homer
Ballads	A **ballad** is a narrative poem written to be sung to a melody. It is usually based on folklore or legend. **Example:** "The Ballad of the Foxhunter" by William Butler Yeats

STRUCTURED POETRY

There are also several poetry types that follow specific patterns. These patterns might call for a certain number of lines, rhyme scheme, or number of syllables per line.

The **rhyme scheme** refers to which lines rhyme. Read these lines from Robert Frost's "The Road Not Taken." Notice that the rhyme scheme is abaab. The *a* indicates the three lines that rhyme, which are lines 1, 3, and 4. The *b* indicates that lines 2 and 5 rhyme.

1	Two roads diverged in a yellow *wood,*	a
2	And sorry I could not travel <u>both</u>	b
3	And be one traveler, long I *stood*	a
4	And looked down one as far as I *could*	a
5	To where it bent in the <u>undergrowth</u>	b

A new letter of the alphabet is used for each line that introduces a new rhyme. For example, here is the next stanza from the same poem.

6	Then took the other, as just as *fair,*	c
7	And having perhaps the better <u>claim</u>,	d
8	Because it was grassy and wanted *wear*;	c
9	Though as for that the passing *there*	c
10	Had worn them really about the <u>same</u>,	d

Let's look at a couple examples of structured poetry.

Haiku is a form of poetry that came from Japan. A haiku follows a specific format. It has three lines. Lines 1 and 3 have five syllables each. Line 2 has seven syllables.

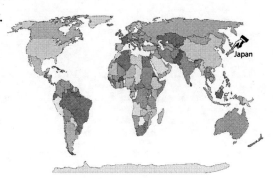

> **Example 1:** Leaves gently falling
> Dancing in the autumn wind
> Crisp flags gold and red

> **Example 2:** Clouds drift through the sky
> Cottony balls of pure white
> Passing by the sun

Limericks are another kind of structured poetry. A limerick is a funny poem of five lines. Its rhyme scheme is aabba. Lines 1, 2, and 5 rhyme with each other. Also, lines 3 and 4 rhyme with each other. People don't know for certain where this type of poem came from, but many attribute it to a region of Ireland called Limerick.

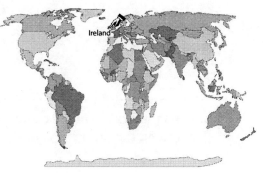

> There was an Old Man with a beard,
>
> Who said, "It is just as I feared!
>
> Two Owls and a Hen,
>
> Four Larks and a Wren,
>
> Have all built their nests in my beard!"
>
> – Edward Lear

When you read a limerick aloud, pay attention to the bouncy rhythm it uses. People usually stress the words in a particular pattern. Look at this example. The capitalized words or syllables are stressed.

> There ONCE was a PIrate named LU.
>
> She SHARED all her GOLD with her CREW.
>
> It WASn't that MUCH—
>
> Just a FEW coins and SUCH,
>
> For her SHIP was JUST a caNOE!
>
> – Anonymous

The rhythm can vary slightly with each limerick. But as you read them, you'll begin to hear how they sound. You'll see how humorous limericks are when the emphasis is in the right place!

Practice 3: Structured Poetry

RL 10, **RF** 4.b (DOK 3)

A. Write your own haiku about one of the following topics.

- the ocean
- winter
- vacations
- a sport
- a puppy or kitten

B. With a partner, take turns reading the following limericks out loud. Grade your partner based on the following questions.

- Did your partner read clearly?
- Did your partner read at a speed that made sense for the poem?
- Did your partner pause at the right moments?
- Did your partner emphasize the right words and syllables?
- Overall, did your partner read the poems well? Why or why not?
- How could your partner improve his or her oral reading ability?

Dear little Jim had a plan.
He'd sneak downstairs to visit Aunt Ann.
For Aunt Ann was a baker,
And a sweet custard-maker,
And bright little Jim wanted flan.

Don was a fast-running horse
Who when racing would never change course.
He ran the whole way
And the whole time would neigh,
And always ended races quite hoarse.

A young girl was quite good in math,
But one problem stood in her path.
She was no fool,
Nay, the brightest in school,
So she showed that math problem her wrath!

There was a young girl from Atlanta
Whose favorite drink was orange Fanta.
She drank it all day,
And always would pray
That a whole case would be brought by Santa.

ELEMENTS OF POETRY

Besides rhyme, there are other **elements of poetry** you should be familiar with. For instance, who is the speaker of the poem? The **speaker** is the "voice" or narrator of the poem. It is not necessarily the author of the poem.

Poems also have a tone. **Tone** is feeling you get when reading a poem. It can be based both on the imagery and the rhythm of the poem. For example, a poem with cheerful images like sunshine and children playing would create a happy tone. A poem with a fast, lively rhythm could create an excited tone.

Meter and rhythm are closely related. Meter measures the pattern of syllables and accents in each line. Just like in music, rhythm refers to the beat and pace of written words. Rhythm creates a sense of movement in poetry. This is achieved by stressing certain syllables. Rhythm becomes important in the overall structure of the poem. Depending on how sounds are arranged, rhythm can be fast or slow, choppy or smooth, pleasant or harsh.

Notice the rhythm of the excerpt from The Song of Hiawatha by Henry Wadsworth Longfellow.

> By the shore of Gitchie Gumee,
>
> By the shining Big-Sea-Water,
>
> At the doorway of his wigwam,
>
> In the pleasant Summer morning,
>
> Hiawatha stood and waited.

The rhythm is repetitive, with the stress on the same syllables in each line. So, it sounds almost like a Native American chant. Meter and rhythm work together within the poem's design.

Many poems also have repetition, a repeating of sounds. Two kinds of repetition are alliteration and assonance.

Alliteration is the repetition of the same or very similar consonant sounds at the beginning of words. Alliteration helps emphasize words.

> **Example:** The whisper of the wind-blown willows (This line repeats the w sound.)

Assonance is the repetition of similar vowel sounds.

> **Example:** "Do you like the color blue?" (These letter combinations have an *oo* sound.)

FIGURATIVE LANGUAGE

Authors of fiction (and especially poets) use **figurative language** to bring their words to life. Figurative language is a colorful way of using words to create a feeling or image in the reader's mind.

Figurative Language	Examples
A **simile** is a comparison using the words *like* or *as*.	Charlie is as sly as a fox. (Since foxes are known for being crafty, it helps you determine the meaning of the word *sly*. "The sound resounded through the house like thunder." – Charles Dickens (If you've ever heard thunder, you know it booms and even creates vibrations if lightning strikes close enough. This helps you understand what *resounded* means. It means "to boom or echo.")
A **metaphor** is a comparison that doesn't use the words *like* or *as*.	James is a beast on the soccer field. (You know that a beast is ferocious. This helps you to understand how James plays.) "All the world's a stage, / And all the men and women merely players." – William Shakespeare (Thinking about how actors are acting, reacting to others, and pretending on stage tells you how Shakespeare sees people in real life.)
Imagery is language that appeals to the senses. Most images are visual; they appeal to the sense of sight, creating pictures that readers can see in their minds. Other images appeal to the senses of touch, taste, hearing, or smell.	Awaking to the aroma of blueberry pancakes And the sizzle pop of bacon frying in Grandma's skillet. Open your eyes to the sunlight beaming through the window with gentle warmth.
Personification is a figure of speech in which a nonhuman thing or quality is given human characteristics. Often, the use of personified objects in literature conjures up vivid mental images that readers can picture.	The numbers danced off the page of my math test.
Onomatopoeia refers to words that sound like what they are describing. Onomatopoeia helps to create the sound imagery of poetry.	*meow, buzz, tick-tock, boom*

Practice 4: Poetry

RL 4, 7, 10, L 5.a (DOK 1, 2)

Read the text, and answer the questions that follow.

Adapted from "A Song of Love"
by Lewis Carroll

Say, what is the spell, when her fledglings are cheeping,

That lures the bird home to her nest?

Or wakes the tired mother, whose infant is weeping,

To cuddle and croon it to rest?

What the magic that charms the glad babe in her arms,

Till it coos with the voice of the dove?

'Tis a secret, and so let us whisper it low—

And the name of the secret is Love!

For I think it is Love,

For I feel it is Love,

For I'm sure it is nothing but Love!

Say, whose is the skill that paints valley and hill,

Like a picture so fair to the sight?

That flecks the green meadow with sunshine and shadow,

Till the little lambs leap with delight?

'Tis a secret untold to hearts cruel and cold,

Though 'tis sung by the angels above,

In notes that ring clear for the ears that can hear—

And the name of the secret is Love!

For I think it is Love,

For I feel it is Love,

For I'm sure it is nothing but Love!

---

1   This text has _____ stanzas.

2   What is the rhyme scheme of the first stanza?

_____

3   This question has two parts. First, answer part A. Then, answer part B.

Part A

   This text is what type of poem?

   A) nursery rhyme   C) lyric

   B) epic   D) ballad

Part B

   How can you tell what type of poem it is?

   _____

   _____

   _____

4   Which of the following lines contain alliteration? Select **all** that apply.

   A) To cuddle and croon it to rest?
      What the magic that charms the glad babe in her arms

   B) Like a picture so fair to the sight?

   C) Till the little lambs leap with delight?

   D) 'Tis a secret untold to hearts cruel and cold

   E) And the name of the secret is Love!

5   Read this line from the poem.

      In notes that ring clear for the ears that can hear—

   This line contains what sound device?

   A) alliteration   C) onomatopoeia

   B) assonance   D) tone

6   Name **two** instances of imagery, and tell what senses they appeal to.

   _____

   _____

7   Name **at least three** ways that the poem personifies love.

   _____

   _____

   _____

8   Who is the speaker of the poem?

   A) Lewis Carroll   C) a tired mother wanting to sleep

   B) love   D) a person happy about love

9   Listen to the multimedia presentation of the poem. What tone does it **most** create?

http://americanbookcompany.com/media/a-song-of-love

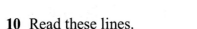

A) joy

B) sadness

C) surprise

D) irritation

10   Read these lines.

> Say, whose is the skill that paints valley and hill,
>
> Like a picture so fair to the sight?

What figurative language do these lines use?

A) onomatopoeia

B) metaphor

C) simile

D) personification

11   Which of the following is an example of metaphor?

A) Or wakes the tired mother, whose infant is weeping, / To cuddle and croon it to rest?

B) What the magic that charms the glad babe in her arms, / Till it coos with the voice of the dove?

C) 'Tis a secret untold to hearts cruel and cold

C) And the name of the secret is Love!

5.4 DRAMA

Drama includes short and long plays. They are pieces of literature that actors perform. Plays can be read aloud or acted out onstage. They include lines of dialogue and stage directions.

> **Example:** *The Best Christmas Pageant Ever* by Barbara Robinson

TYPES OF DRAMA

There are different types of dramas. The most common are comedies and tragedies. A **comedy** is a drama that shows the humor of the world. It is usually funny and has a happy ending. A **tragedy** is usually sad or serious. It shows the problems in the world, and it often has a sad ending.

There are also subgenres in drama. For example, a **melodrama** is a subgenre of drama that deals with serious issues but stops short of being tragic in the end. It usually includes exaggerated acting and appeals to the emotions. A **musical** is a type of drama that includes singing and dancing.

A printed version of a drama is also called a **script**. Not only do stage actors use scripts, but so do actors in a movie or TV show.

ELEMENTS OF DRAMA

A drama is not like a regular story. It tells a story by showing the action rather than telling what happens. There are many parts that make a drama what it is. The following chart will show different **elements of drama**. The examples are from a made-up play called "Research Time."

Elements of Drama		
Type	**Description**	**Example**
cast of characters	the actors in a play	Phil and Lucy, two fifth graders
setting	where the play takes place	the school media center
plot	what happens in the play	Phil and Lucy are partners working on a science project.
dialogue	the words spoken by the characters Dialogue is broken into **lines** (the words of each actor's part in the drama).	Lucy: Why don't we split up the research? I'll look up Jupiter's composition and atmosphere, and you research its moons and orbit. Phil: Sounds like a good plan to me!
stage directions	descriptions of how the actors move (usually in italics and set off with parentheses)	*(Lucy heads to the science section. Phil logs onto a computer.)*
act	a major division in the action of a play The different acts signal major shifts in action. Most full-length plays have three acts, but some have up to five.	Act I
scene	a smaller division in the action of a play Acts are often broken into scenes. Scenes signal a simple change of location, time, or dialogue.	Scene 2: *Phil and Lucy begin their research on Jupiter in the media center.*

Let's look at an example of a play and how it is laid out with the different elements of drama.

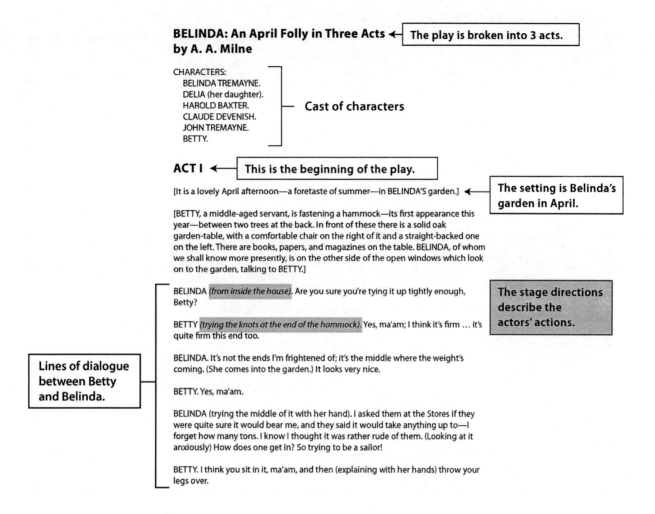

BELINDA: An April Folly in Three Acts ← The play is broken into 3 acts.
by A. A. Milne

CHARACTERS:
  BELINDA TREMAYNE.
  DELIA (her daughter).
  HAROLD BAXTER. — **Cast of characters**
  CLAUDE DEVENISH.
  JOHN TREMAYNE.
  BETTY.

ACT I ← This is the beginning of the play.

[It is a lovely April afternoon—a foretaste of summer—in BELINDA'S garden.] ← The setting is Belinda's garden in April.

[BETTY, a middle-aged servant, is fastening a hammock—its first appearance this year—between two trees at the back. In front of these there is a solid oak garden-table, with a comfortable chair on the right of it and a straight-backed one on the left. There are books, papers, and magazines on the table. BELINDA, of whom we shall know more presently, is on the other side of the open windows which look on to the garden, talking to BETTY.]

BELINDA *(from inside the house)*. Are you sure you're tying it up tightly enough, Betty?

BETTY *(trying the knots at the end of the hammock)*. Yes, ma'am; I think it's firm … it's quite firm this end too.

The stage directions describe the actors' actions.

BELINDA. It's not the ends I'm frightened of; it's the middle where the weight's coming. (She comes into the garden.) It looks very nice.

BETTY. Yes, ma'am.

Lines of dialogue between Betty and Belinda.

BELINDA (trying the middle of it with her hand). I asked them at the Stores if they were quite sure it would bear me, and they said it would take anything up to—I forget how many tons. I know I thought it was rather rude of them. (Looking at it anxiously) How does one get in? So trying to be a sailor!

BETTY. I think you sit in it, ma'am, and then (explaining with her hands) throw your legs over.

Practice 5: Drama

RL 10 (DOK 1–3)

Read the text, and answer the questions that follow.

Erin and Marcy

Characters:

Erin, a ten-year-old girl

Marcy, her best friend

[*Erin and Marcy are sitting together in the library. They start whispering to each other.*]

Erin: Marcy, have you seen my favorite mechanical pencil?

Marcy: You mean the one that plays "Take Me Out to the Ball Game" when you click for lead?

Erin: [*nodding eagerly*] Yep, that's the one.

Marcy: Is it the one that's pink with purple polka dots?

Erin: Uh-huh!

Marcy: [*tapping her chin*] And it has bite marks on it from when your puppy chewed on it?

Erin: Yeah! Have you seen it?

Marcy: [*in a teasing tone*] No, I can't say that I have.

[*The girls burst into giggles.*]

Erin: You're being silly, aren't you?

---

1   Which of the following elements indicate to the reader that this is a drama? Select **all** that apply.

   A) Characters' names precede dialogue.

   B) It takes place in the present day.

   C) It includes stage directions.

   D) It has conflict.

   E) It is set at a school library.

2   What is the purpose of the italicized phases in the text? Select **all** that apply.

   A) They explain where the actors live.

   B) They explain how a line is said.

   C) They explain unknown vocabulary.

   D) They explain what the actors do.

   E) They explain how the set is arranged.

3   This text is an example of a

   A) comedy.

   B) tragedy.

   C) melodrama.

   D) musical.

CHAPTER 5 SUMMARY

Genres, or types, of literature include fiction, nonfiction, poetry, and drama.

Fiction includes the following subgenres: **novels**, **realistic fiction**, **science fiction**, **fantasy fiction**, **historical fiction**, **graphic novels**, **folktales**, **fairy tales**, **fables**, **legends**, and **myths**.

Nonfiction includes autobiographies, biographies, journals, informational books, and reference books.

Poetry expresses ideas, feelings, or situations in a creative way. Types of poetry include lyric, narrative, nursery rhyme, epic, ballad, haiku, and limerick.

Elements of poetry include **rhyme**, **rhyme scheme**, **rhythm**, **meter**, **speaker**, **tone**, and **repetition**.

Writers use **figurative language** to bring their words to life. Examples include **similes**, **metaphors**, **imagery**, **personification**, and **onomatopoeia**.

Drama includes short and long plays. They are pieces of literature that actors perform. Types of drama include **comedies**, **tragedies**, **melodramas**, and **musicals**.

Elements of drama include the **cast of characters**, **setting**, **plot**, **dialogue**, **stage directions**, **acts**, and **scenes**.

For additional practice, please see Chapter 5 Test located in the Teacher Guide.

Chapter 6
Elements of Literature

 This chapter covers DOK levels 1–3 and the following fifth grade strands and standards, please see page x):

Reading Literature: 1, 2, 6, 7, 10
Reading Informational Texts: 2
Reading Foundational Skills: 4

In this chapter...

- You will identify and understand various elements in literature and explain how those elements enhance the work of literature.

- You will understand how characters are developed through speech, action, and dialogue as well as through direct description within a work.

- You will recognize common themes of literature and how theme is developed through a well-structured plot.

- You will make connections between works of literature and multimedia in order to create and interpret works of literature in visual or audio format.

6.1 INTRODUCTION

When you read literature, you can look for certain elements that help enrich your understanding of what you read. All literature includes **story elements**, such as setting, characters, plot, conflict, and theme. Understanding these smaller parts gives you, the reader, a better view of the big picture the author is trying to create.

6.2 SETTING

Setting is where and when a story takes place. A story may take place in any era—past, present, or future. Also, a story may take place in any part of the world, real or imagined. Smaller aspects of setting might be specific places, such as a school, the mall, or a baseball field.

Setting is very important because when and where the action of a story occurs directly affects other elements in the story. For example, the setting can affect the mood and tone of the story. When we discuss **mood** in a text, we mean the feeling a reader experiences while reading the text. The **tone** is the attitude the author has toward the story.

Imagine a story set in an old, run-down, abandoned house. That story would likely have a creepy mood, wouldn't it? Now picture a story set at a carnival on a pleasant summer's evening. The setting would help the author create a happy, excited tone.

6.3 CHARACTERS

Characters are the participants in a story. They can include people, animals, and even objects. Think of some stories you've read or seen on TV. Think about the emotions shown by characters. Just like real people, they get angry about being wronged, become giddy about falling in love, and are torn by difficult decisions. Often characters' emotions can give us clues to their natures. For example, Mary Lennox from *The Secret Garden* may seem like a spoiled, unpleasant girl at first. Soon, we learn more about why she makes certain choices—she was ignored by her parents, orphaned, and sent to live with a gloomy uncle. Though Mary can be rude and bossy sometimes, she gradually becomes a happier and kinder person by tending a forgotten garden on her uncle's property. By sharing the motivations of characters, authors give us more to think about.

CHARACTER DEVELOPMENT

Just as we get to know people in real life, in reading literature, we get to know characters. As readers, we are able to observe the characters' actions, motives, and physical appearances in relation to plot and theme. Let's take a look at how to recognize these qualities.

ACTIONS

One way to learn about a character is through his or her **actions**. What does the character do? How does he or she respond to challenges? How the character acts and reacts to challenges reveals what kind of person he or she is. Just like when you meet new friends, you know what they are like according to their actions or behavior. Nice new friends share and encourage. Not-so-nice new "friends" break the rules and are dishonest. Think about the fairy tale "Little Red Riding Hood." The Big Bad Wolf is a villain because of his actions. He dresses up like Little Red's grandmother and tries to trick the unsuspecting girl into becoming his next meal. It is through his actions that readers know and understand his character in the story.

MOTIVES

Another way that readers can know and understand characters is by understanding the characters' **motives**. A motive is a reason for action. Going back to the "Little Red Riding Hood" example, the Big Bad Wolf is motivated into deception by his desire to eat the little girl. As readers, we recognize the wolf to be dangerous and evil based upon this motive.

CHARACTERS AFFECT PLOT AND THEME

A character can affect a story's plot and theme. Sometimes, the character drives the story's plot or demonstrates theme through his or her experience. In Jerry Spinelli's *Maniac Magee*, Jeffrey Lionel Magee leaves his home in Bridgeport, Pennsylvania, and moves around to different places in a town called Two Mills for a year. In this novel, not only is Maniac Magee the protagonist, but his role in the story is what drives the plot. As he moves around Two Mills, running like a "maniac," it is what he does, where he goes, and whom he meets that create the plot of the novel. Maniac Magee is an example of how a character can be an important part of a novel's plot and overall action.

In some cases, a character in a novel is an important part of the theme, or main idea. Given the example of Spinelli's *Maniac Magee* again, Jeffrey is also an important part of the novel's theme. One key idea in the novel is racism and its danger. One of Jeffrey's character traits is his blindness to skin color. By being blind to skin color, Jeffrey meets people of all skin colors and unites them. In this way, Jeffrey is a huge part of the novel's theme.

INFERENCES AND CONCLUSIONS ABOUT CHARACTERS

In addition to understanding the way characters are developed and how they relate to the plot, a good reader must also be able to **make inferences** and **draw conclusions** about characters. By paying attention to how a character fits in with the story's plot, setting, and other characters, readers will be able to make sound conclusions. Other considerations about a character should include the character's motives and physical appearance.

MAIN AND MINOR CHARACTERS

Sometimes as you read literature, you will notice that some characters in a literary work have greater roles than others. **Main characters** are those with larger roles in a story's plot. **Minor characters** are characters who play smaller roles in the story line. For example, in the fairy tale *Snow White and the Seven Dwarfs*, Snow White would be a main character, while the seven dwarfs would be considered minor characters.

STEREOTYPICAL CHARACTERS

Sometimes, writers use characters in a story to represent an idea that readers will quickly recognize. These **stereotypical characters** are used to represent basic characteristics in human nature—goodness, evil, greed, generosity, and so on. Examples of these stereotypical characters would be the evil stepmother in the fairy tale *Cinderella* or the wicked queen in *Snow White and the Seven Dwarfs*. A reader recognizes these characters as representations of evil. Everything about these characters—their mean actions, unsightly appearances, harsh-sounding voices—help to build their roles as representations of evil. Stereotypical characters can also be used to represent good qualities that readers will also recognize.

FULLY DEVELOPED CHARACTERS

In contrast to stereotypical characters, literary works also contain **fully developed characters** (also called **round characters**). Unlike stereotypical characters, these characters are used not only to represent a character type, but these characters are fully developed. They have many characteristics and are developed from different angles. For example, in Ellen Raskin's novel *The Westing Game*, Turtle Wexler, the novel's protagonist, is a fully developed character. The reader knows her from different angles: as a bratty young girl who runs around swinging her single braid and kicking others and as a smart girl who wins the Westing game. When a character is fully developed, the reader has an opportunity to observe several aspects of this character's personality.

CHANGES CHARACTERS UNDERGO

Within a story, characters often **undergo changes**. These characters are called **dynamic characters** (as opposed to **static characters**, who don't change). They may grow, reach realizations, and develop in ways that readers should recognize. For example, in Louis Sachar's *There's a Boy in the Girl's Bathroom*, Bradley Chalkers is the protagonist. He's the oldest kid in the fifth grade because he's been held back, and the other kids don't like him because they think he's mean and tells lies. Bradley can be unkind sometimes, but he's actually lonely and wishes he could make friends. He starts seeing the school counselor, Carla, a funny, caring young woman. To Bradley's surprise, Carla likes him. She helps him see that he can change. Bradley becomes a more confident, happier kid at the end of the book. He learns what he has to do to gain his classmates' acceptance and friendship. These are changes that an active reader recognizes and understands.

The following chart gives examples of different character types in Louis Sachar's novel *Holes*.

Character Types in *Holes*	
Main character	**Minor characters**
Stanley Yelnats is the unlikely hero and main character of *Holes*.	Squid, X-Ray, and Armpit are other boys at Camp Green Lake. They are minor characters.
Fully-developed character	**Stereotypical character**
Zero seems like a "nobody" who never talks, but he turns out to be a brave, smart kid who helps Stanley.	The Warden is a stereotypical villain: selfish, mean, and scary. She makes the boys dig holes to find long-lost treasure for her.
Dynamic character	**Static character**
Kissin' Kate Barlow starts out as a proper schoolteacher and turns into an infamous outlaw.	Mr. Sir is a counselor at the camp. He remains a rude, obnoxious character throughout the novel.

Practice 1: Characters

RL 1, 2 (DOK 1, 2)

Read the text, and answer the questions that follow.

> # The Bike Trip
>
> Avid athletes, Tom and Terry had been mountain biking for years. Every other Saturday, they'd pack their gear and head out to remote mountain trails for a day trip. One weekend, they invited their friends Martin and Kasey to go with them. Tom and Terry decided they would ride a tough trail up the mountain, and Martin and Kasey agreed.
>
> Because Martin and Kasey had never been mountain biking, they were apprehensive about the trip; they worried they would not be up to the strenuous task. Halfway through the ride, Martin grew tired and started to wobble. Suddenly, he hit a rock in the path and flipped over the handlebars. Everyone else skidded to a stop and ran over to check on him. Fortunately, he was not too badly injured except for a twisted ankle. Tom and Terry knew they could make it over the mountain to get help, but they were unsure if they'd be able to find their way back. Because it was growing dark, they had to make a decision quickly.
>
> Tom and Terry rode hard and fast over the mountain. The sun was sinking, and they were afraid they'd never find help. Exhausted and frightened, they were just about to give up hope when they saw a ranger. Never had they felt so relieved. They all made their way back to Martin and Kasey. Martin was carried down to safety on a stretcher. As soon as they could, they called their families to let them know everyone was safe.

1. Which of the following **most likely** motivated Tom and Terry to ride a tough trail up the mountain?

   A) They wanted to impress Martin and Kasey.

   B) They wanted a challenge since they are good riders.

   C) They thought they could become heroes by doing this.

   D) They would earn rewards for riding tough trails.

2. What roles do Tom and Terry play in the story?

   A) villains   C) heroes

   B) victims   D) students

3. Which of the following actions of Tom and Terry would be considered noble?

   A) inviting friends to bike   C) deciding to take a tougher trail

   B) running away from Martin and Kasey   D) finding help for Martin

4 What words **best** describe the actions of Tom and Terry? Select **all** that apply.

A) brave	C) tired	E) helpful	G) scared
B) angry	D) mean	F) boring	H) rude

5 Based upon the setting and plot, what conclusions can you make about Tom and Terry? What about Martin and Kasey? Support your answer with **at least two** details from the text.

_____

_____

_____

POINT OF VIEW

Another important part of understanding literature is recognizing **point of view**. An author's point of view is the way in which a reader experiences a story. It includes the **perspective**— or mental view—that the author attempts to communicate to the reader. The narrator's or speaker's point of view influences how events in a story are described.

For example, you know the story of "The Three Little Pigs." The pigs are the heroes of the story, and the Big Bad Wolf is the villain. But imagine if it were the other way around. In *The True Story of the Three Little Pigs* by Jon Scieszka, the Big Bad Wolf tells the story, and in his version, he's the victim! He claims that he was only trying to borrow a cup of sugar from each of the three pigs. Because he has a bad cold, he sneezes and accidentally blows down the pigs' houses. As you can see, a change in the perspective can change the story dramatically!

Sometimes, when readers think of point of view, they consider who is telling the story—the narrator. A **first-person point of view** features a story in which the narrator is a part of the story. He or she is a character in the story. You will know that a story is written using a first-person point of view because the narrator will use first-person pronouns, such as *I, me, we, my, us,* and *our.* First-person point of view is important because it gives an insider's view of story events. The reader is able to become a part of the story in a huge way. At the same time, first-person point of view limits a reader to the perspective of the character speaking. For example, the following text is written using first-person point of view.

> I wasn't sure what to expect when I first arrived at Blair Elementary. I had just left my friends in Oregon and moved to a small town in California. My parents had just divorced, and I wasn't really sure of anything at the time.

Another point of view that readers should recognize is third person. **Third-person point of view** tells the story from the perspective of an outside source. A reader can easily recognize the use of third-person point of view, as there will be third-person pronouns, such as *he, she, it, theirs,* and *they.* Third-person point of view often reveals not only what characters do and say but also what they think. At the same time, third-person point of view reveals the narrator's attitude toward the characters. For instance, a narrator may describe a character as selfish while the character wouldn't think or say that about himself. The following would be an example of writing that uses third-person point of view.

Page 105

> She counted the voting slips again and again. Each time, they totaled the same. There were 102 votes for her friend Theresa, two more votes than Cheree had for herself. Her best friend, Theresa, had fairly and squarely beaten her in the contest.

6.4 PLOT

The chain of events that happen in a story is called the **plot**. The plot usually has several parts. There is an exposition, conflict, rising action, climax, falling action, and resolution.

Exposition	The exposition is the beginning of the story (it's sometimes called the introduction). The author introduces the setting and characters. The introduction also reveals the conflict (the main problem) of the story.
Rising Action	The action in a story begins to build. For instance, a character who has been bullied may feel he doesn't have to put up with it anymore. He may start to prepare to face the conflict—the bully—in the story.
Climax	The climax is the turning point in a story. The action of the story is usually at its highest. For example, the character that has been bullied finally stands up to the bully.
Falling Action	The action in the story slows down. The character's life may begin to return to normal. It may even be better. For instance, the character who stands up to the bully is not bullied anymore.
Resolution	The resolution is the ending of a story. All conflict is settled.

Sometimes it helps to understand the plot of a story with a diagram. For example, here is a plot diagram for the novel *Tales of a Fourth Grade Nothing* by Judy Blume.

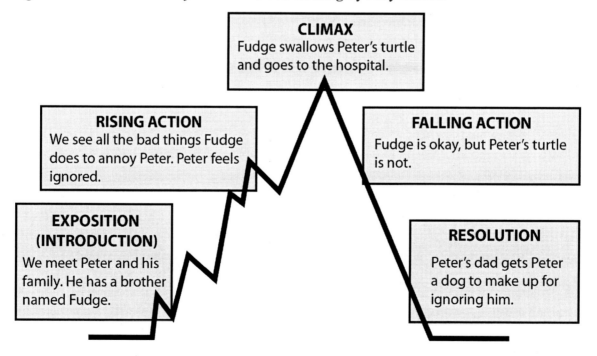

CLIMAX
Fudge swallows Peter's turtle and goes to the hospital.

RISING ACTION
We see all the bad things Fudge does to annoy Peter. Peter feels ignored.

FALLING ACTION
Fudge is okay, but Peter's turtle is not.

EXPOSITION (INTRODUCTION)
We meet Peter and his family. He has a brother named Fudge.

RESOLUTION
Peter's dad gets Peter a dog to make up for ignoring him.

Practice 2: Setting, Characters, and Plot

RL 1, 10 (DOK 1–3)

Read the text, and answer the questions that follow.

Excerpt from "The Treasure Hunters"
by Kim Hill

It began with a simple dare. George, as usual, had started it. He'd yelled with his meaty face flushed, his small eyes narrowed, "I bet you're such a chicken you wouldn't go into the Manchester house alone fer ten minutes!" He had been bugging me for weeks, taunting me after school, on the bus, in the hall, and I'd had enough! It was time to take a stand. No one would call me chicken anymore. I took the dare.

"I ain't no chicken!" I'd said. "Shoot, I'd stay fifteen minutes in that stupid house. Ten minutes is nothin'."

So, here I am, in front of the spookiest house in our town. The fact that no other kid had gone into the Manchester house before interested everyone, and all the neighborhood kids came to watch. I couldn't back down now—too many witnesses.

The Manchester house was legend in our neighborhood. Everyone knew about it, and everyone had a spooky tale to tell in hushed tones on camping trips and in the schoolyard. It's said that old Mister Manchester, a scientist, used to perform strange experiments there. That people would go in and never come out. Then, one day, old Mister Manchester just disappeared, never to be heard from again. Whether or not any of it was true was beside the point. In matters of legend, you only had to make sure the reciting was entertaining.

The house was at the end of our five-mile town. It had once been a beautiful mansion back during the Civil War or something. But now it stood in ruins: large, dark, abandoned, decrepit, and covered in cobwebs … haunted looking.

Looking at the creepy house, I wished I hadn't let George get to me. I wished I didn't have to go in. Taking a deep breath, I started walking. Behind me, I heard someone yell, "Dead man walking!" I stopped before I took my first step up the stairs, thinking about turning around and leaving.

"Come on, Toby! Ya scared or somethin'?" George taunted from the safety of the street, far from the house.

"Yeah, Toby, ya really are chicken, ain't ya?" joined Scooter, George's puny sidekick. "Chicken! Chicken! Chicken!" they chanted together.

"I'm goin' already! I ain't no chicken neither!" I hollered back.

I walked up the steps, each one creaking loudly. I made it to the sagging front porch and put my hand on the doorknob.

"Just get it over with," I said out loud. I could still hear George and Scooter yelling "Chicken!" from the street. As soon as I turned the knob, they stopped.

Silence descended like a suffocating blanket on a hot summer night, thick and sticky. They all watched, holding their breath as I opened the heavy, squeaking door. Gulping, I stepped into the darkened entryway, the pungent smell of dust, mildew, and age hitting me in the face. I looked around.

Everything was still. Not even the dust swirled from the breeze I let in. It just lay like a heavy weight on everything. The windows were covered in grime so thick it blocked out most of the midday sun. It was so dark I could barely make out the crumbling curve of the staircase to my right or the cobweb-draped chandelier above my head. I closed the door behind me. The sound of the latch clicking into place and the thud of wood against wood echoed through the mansion like a pin dropping in a tomb—sealing me in.

1   What motivates Toby to go into the Manchester house?

A) to prove that he's not afraid   C) to see if anyone lives there

B) to impress all of his friends   D) to confirm it is not haunted

2   Why **most likely** is George making Toby go into the house?

A) He wants to help Toby overcome his fear.   C) He wants to be the hero and rescue Toby.

B) He knows there is nothing bad in the house.   D) He is secretly afraid to go in himself.

3   Describe the setting of the story, using details from the text.

_____

_____

_____

4   What will Toby **most likely** do next? Use details from the text to support your answer.

_____

_____

_____

5   This question has two parts. First, answer part A. Then, answer part B.

Part A

This story uses _____ point of view.

Part B

The story is told from whose perspective?

A) George's   C) Mr. Manchester's

B) Toby's   D) an unknown narrator's

6   Fill in the plot diagram with details from the story.

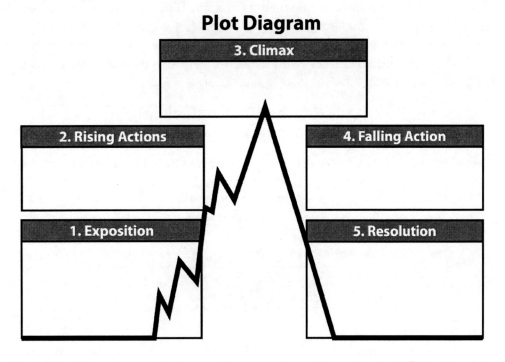

6.5 CONFLICT

Any good plot has a conflict. A **conflict** is a challenge that a character must face and overcome. Many stories have multiple conflicts. Here are some of the most basic kinds.

Kinds of Conflict	
Type	**Description**
character vs. character	This occurs when two characters have a problem with one another. Comic books often show heroes facing villains. Another example is a romantic comedy about a person in love with someone who doesn't realize it.
character vs. self	In this type of conflict, a character's own mind or body is the obstacle. For instance, a character could practice to get better at playing chess. Another might try to overcome a fear. This is also called internal conflict.
character vs. nature	These conflicts are usually about characters trying to survive outdoors or overcome an animal or natural force. In the book *Island of the Blue Dolphins*, Karana is a young girl trying to survive alone on an island in the Pacific.
character vs. society	This conflict pits characters against groups of people. *Charlotte's Web* uses this type of conflict. The story shows a pig trying to survive in a world where pigs are considered food.
character vs. supernatural	This conflict sets the characters against God or another religious figure, ghosts, or other unearthly figures. In *A Christmas Carol*, Ebenezer Scrooge is visited by three spirits who show him how lonely his life is because of his greed.

Here is an example of multiple conflicts. You just read that the novel *Charlotte's Web* has the conflict of character vs. society. The main character, Wilbur, is afraid the farmer, Mr. Zuckerman, will turn him into bacon. The story revolves around whether Mr. Zuckerman will change his mind when he sees how Wilbur is "some pig." This is an example of character vs. character conflict. (In fiction, animals who speak are considered characters. Other times, a conflict with an animal would be considered character vs. nature.)

Practice 3: Conflict

RL 1 (DOK 2, 3)

Watch this video that shows three different conflicts. Then, fill in the table below.

	Conflict 1	Conflict 2	Conflict 3
What type of conflict is shown?			
How would you solve the problem if you were one of the characters?			

6.6 THEME

Theme is the underlying meaning or point of a story. It is an important idea about life that the story reveals. A story can have more than one theme, but there usually is a main theme within the story. Themes that can be understood by people all over the word are **universal themes**. You'll learn more about universal themes in the next chapter.

> **Examples:** Health is more important than possessions.
> You are beautiful to those who love you.
> It is best to be honest at all times.

Do not confuse the theme with the subject or topic of a text. For example, say you ask someone what the story of "Goldilocks and the Three Bears" is about. Here is how the story's topic and theme might be explained:

Topic: The story is about a girl who goes into the house of some bears while they are not home, eats their food, and uses their furniture. The bears are very sad and upset when they return.

Theme: "Goldilocks and the Three Bears" shows by example how important it is to respect the property of others, have good manners, and take responsibility for your own actions.

Generally, a theme is not stated directly; instead, it is implied, which means you must infer it from what you read. Some themes are stated, though. These include the lessons you can learn from reading fables. At the end of a fable, the lesson is written out for you. Usually, however, you will need to figure it out. When you are looking for a theme, consider how the main character changes or learns a lesson during the story.

Take a look at this short text. See if you can identify the theme.

Adaptation of "The Gift of the Magi"
by O. Henry

A long time ago, there was a young married couple who didn't have much money but loved each other dearly. As Christmas approached, they worried about how to get each other a nice gift with what little money they had. The wife, Della, loved her long, beautiful hair. But she loved her husband, Jim, even more. She decided to cut off and sell her hair so she could buy him a watch chain for his pocket watch.

When Jim came home from work, he was surprised to see Della with her hair cut short, but he said nothing. It was time for them to exchange gifts. Della handed him his present first. She watched eagerly as he opened the box and pulled out the handsome watch chain.

Oddly, Jim didn't seem overjoyed like she'd hoped. "That's very nice, Della," he said. "Thank you."

"What's wrong?" Della asked anxiously. "Don't you like it?"

"I think you'd better open my gift to you," he replied. Della took the box he handed her and pulled off the paper quickly. Inside was the beautiful hair comb that she'd been admiring in the store window for the past month.

"Oh!" Della cried. She reached up to touch her shortly cropped hair. How could she wear the comb now? "I sold my hair to buy you your present," she said.

"I sold my watch to buy you the comb!" Jim said. They looked at each other for a moment and then started laughing. They hugged each other, happy with the gifts they'd given and received.

What is the theme of this text?

A) People can sell their hair for money.

B) Pocket watches without a chain can get lost.

C) Love is the most valuable gift of all.

D) Never sell your most prized possession.

If you said C, then you are right! The text does talk about how a character sells her hair for money, but that is a detail, or fact, of the text. The text doesn't say anything about pocket watches getting lost without a chain. It does not tell people never to sell their most prized possession, either. In fact, the two characters sacrifice their most prized possessions and realize how much they love each other. The real point that the story makes is that love is the most valuable gift of all. Della and Jim are willing to make a sacrifice to show their love for each other. So C is the best answer.

How Characters Can Show Theme

We all have qualities that make us different from everyone else. The same is true for characters in a story. An author has to make characters come alive so they are realistic to readers.

The way characters respond to events and challenges in a story is one way writers can show theme. For example, the famous author William Shakespeare wrote a play called *Macbeth*. A main theme of the play is that too much ambition can be dangerous. In the play, there is a character named Macbeth. He wants power so much that he betrays his king to take over the throne. Macbeth regrets his decision, but he is too crazy for power to stop his bad behavior. Shakespeare uses Macbeth's actions to show that sometimes it is hard to stop acting badly when you are focused on achieving a goal at all costs.

Practice 4: Theme

RL 2 (DOK 2, 3)

Read the texts, and answer the questions that follow.

> ### Time for a Friend
>
> Chelsea boarded the morning school bus and plopped down her backpack in the seat beside her. Saving a seat for Tanya was her usual routine. Rain or shine, every morning bus ride since first grade had been this way. Tanya was only her best friend in the whole wide world. Today, though, Chelsea was a little preoccupied; she had a science test on her mind. Even though she had been studying all week long, Chelsea was worried. It couldn't hurt her to get in a few more minutes of study on the way to school. Unzipping the pocket of her backpack, she pulled out her flash cards and began reviewing vocabulary.
>
> When the bus pulled up to Tanya's stop, it was only a few moments before Tanya was aboard and in the seat next to Chelsea. "Hey, T," Chelsea said, barely looking up. "What's up?" Not hearing a peep out of her usually chatty friend, Chelsea used her finger to save her spot in her stack of note cards and looked at her friend. Right away she knew something was wrong. Tanya looked disheveled and had a puffy redness around her eyes. It was clear she had been upset. Studying for the science test would have to wait. Now it was time to be a friend.

A Time to Talk
by Robert Frost

When a friend calls to me from the road

And slows his horse to a meaning walk,

I don't stand still and look around

On all the hills I haven't hoed,

And shout from where I am, What is it?

No, not as there is a time to talk.

I thrust my hoe in the mellow ground,

Blade-end up and five feet tall,

And plod: I go up to the stone wall

For a friendly visit.

1   Which of the following **best** states a theme found in both texts?

A) Work is not really that important.

B) Stopping to talk is more fun than doing work.

C) It is important to care about our friends.

D) Time for friends should come after work is done.

2   Which lines from the text "Time for a Friend" **most** reflect the theme? Select **all** that apply.

A) It couldn't hurt her to get in a few more minutes of study on the way to school.

B) Today, though, Chelsea was a little preoccupied; she had a science test on her mind.

C) It was clear she had been upset.

D) Studying for the science test would have to wait.

E) Now it was time to be a friend.

3   What makes both Chelsea and the narrator feel like they need to stop what they planned to do?

_____

_____

4   Compare and contrast the two texts. How does each text develop the theme of friendship? Use evidence from both texts to support your answer.

_____

_____

6.7 MULTIMEDIA

Aside from the words an author uses, there are other things that give a text meaning. **Multimedia elements** like pictures, sound, and other elements can **add meaning, tone, or beauty** to a text. This adds to your understanding and enjoyment of what you read.

Have you ever heard someone say, "A picture is worth a thousand words"? It's true: a picture can often show something more easily than words can describe. Pictures are a quick way to add meaning to a text. Think about comic books or graphic novels. You are reading a story, but you are also looking at the action as it happens. This helps you understand the text in a new way.

Say you are reading a poem about a rainbow that appears in the mist of a waterfall. The author may include a photo of a rainbow in a waterfall with the poem. This helps readers who have not seen this type of rainbow before understand how it looks. This visual element adds a certain beauty to the text that the reader did not sense before.

Sound is something a writer can use to show mood and tone. If you've ever seen a TV show where people are running in fear, you've probably heard urgent, frightening music to go along with the scene. Or at the end of a movie, after all the exciting action is over, the music might become soft and tranquil. This device also can work using words. Describing sound is one way a writer can show emotion.

Besides pictures and sound, PowerPoint presentations are another way to add meaning to a text. When your teacher stands in front of the class giving a lecture, does it help you understand better if there are pictures to go with the words she is speaking? PowerPoint is a presentation software program. The speaker can make a slide show and run the show while speaking so the audience can see images at the same time. Charts, music, and videos can all be part of a PowerPoint presentation. Visual displays in presentations are a way to enhance your ideas. Your listeners will have something to follow along with as they listen to your ideas.

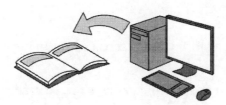

Research Connection

Think of your favorite book, play, or poem that has been adapted into a film. Then, research the film's director and the making of the film. Next, view the film and write a report about how the film differed from the original story and why you believe the director made the choices he did regarding the plot and the casting of the characters. Remember to take notes as you watch the movie in order to keep track of how the film is different from the original. It may also help to reread the book before viewing the movie.

Suggested Books with Film Adaptations

Tuck Everlasting by Natalie Babbitt

Peter Pan by J. M. Barrie

The Wonderful Wizard of Oz by L. Frank Baum

Matilda by Roald Dahl

Little Women by Louisa May Alcott

Holes by Louis Sachar

Charlie and the Chocolate Factory by Roald Dahl

Shiloh by Phyllis Reynolds Naylor

The Indian in the Cupboard by Lynn Reid Banks

The Tale of Despereaux by Kate DiCamillo

Bridge to Terabithia by Katherine Paterson

Coraline by Neil Gaiman

CHAPTER 6 SUMMARY

Setting is where and when a story takes place. The setting can affect the mood and tone of the story.

When we discuss **mood** in a text, we mean the feeling a reader experiences while reading the text. The **tone** is the attitude the author has toward the story.

Characters are the participants in a story. Authors develop characters through their actions, dialogue, and descriptions.

An author's **point of view** is the way in which a reader experiences a story. It includes the **perspective**—or mental view—that the author attempts to communicate to the reader.

A **first-person point of view** features a story in which the narrator is a part of the story. **Third-person point of view** tells the story from the perspective of an outside source.

The chain of events that happen in a story is called the **plot**. There is an exposition, conflict, rising action, climax, falling action, and resolution.

A **conflict** is a challenge that a character must face and overcome. Types of conflict include character vs. character, character vs. self, character vs. nature, character vs. society, and character vs. supernatural.

Theme is the underlying meaning or point of a story. It is an important idea about life that the story reveals.

Multimedia elements like pictures, sound, and other elements can **add meaning, tone, or beauty** to a text.

For additional practice, please see Chapter 6 Test located in the Teacher Guide.

Chapter 7
Understanding Literature

This chapter covers DOK levels 1–3 and the following fifth grade strands and standards (for full standards, please see page x):

Reading Literature: 1, 2, **3**, 4, **5**, 6, 7, **9**, 10
Language: 3, 5

In this chapter…

- You will make connections between characters, themes, settings, and plots—within and across works of literature.

- You will understand how aspects of language, such as dialect, impact a work of literature as well as how common sayings are portrayed in literature.

- You will analyze the structure and organization of a work of literature and how authors use organization as a tool.

7.1 COMPARING AND CONTRASTING LITERATURE

Comparing and contrasting is the process of looking for similarities and differences. On the Common Core test, you may be required to answer questions about similarities and differences between literary elements, such as characters, events, themes, and so on.

Many stories are alike in certain ways. They share similar elements. For example, say you are asked to compare and contrast the **characters**, **plot**, **themes**, **points of view**, or other **literary devices** in two different stories. You can look at characters or setting or even the plot to see what is the same.

For example, one story you might read is *Because of Winn-Dixie* by Kate DiCamillo. The main character is a little girl named Opal. She is very shy and needs a friend. Opal finds a stray dog and names him Winn-Dixie. He becomes one of her closest friends. As a result, she has the courage to meet new people in her town, like the librarian and the pet-store clerk. Winn-Dixie teaches Opal to be brave and helps her build relationships with the people around her.

Another story you can read is *Bridge to Terabithia* by Katherine Paterson. The main character is Jesse, an angry and sad little boy. He makes friends with a neighbor named Leslie. She opens his mind up to a make-believe world called Terabithia, where they can imagine new creatures and play all day. Leslie teaches Jesse to be brave and let go of his sadness.

The characters in these stories are not the same, but they have one thing in common: they are lonely and need friends. Also, the plots are not exactly the same, but some of the events are the same, such as the main character making a new friend and learning to be brave. You just compared these two stories! Now think about a time when you made a new friend. You just connected these stories to your own life!

You can also compare and contrast themes in different works. Many pieces of literature use similar themes. No matter the genre, setting, or culture, some themes occur over and over. Themes that can be understood by people all over the word are **universal themes**. For example, one theme of *Adventures of Huckleberry Finn* is the negative effect of racism on victims and racists alike.

Racism is something anyone in any culture can experience. So the peril of racism is a universal theme. Works from many cultures deal with this theme, including *The House on Mango Street* by Sandra Cisneros or *Darby* by Jonathan Scott Fuqua.

Practice 1: Comparing and Contrasting Literature

RL 1, 2, 9 (DOK 2, 3)

Read the texts, and answer the questions that follow.

The Town Mouse and the Country Mouse
by Aesop

Once upon a time, a Town Mouse went on a visit to his cousin in the country. This Country Mouse was rough and ready, but he loved his town friend and made him heartily welcome. Beans and bacon, cheese and bread were all he had to offer, but he offered them freely.

The Town Mouse rather turned up his long nose at this country fare and said: "I cannot understand, Cousin, how you can put up with such poor food as this. But, of course, you cannot expect anything better in the country. Come with me, and I will show you how to live. When you have been in town a week, you will wonder how you could ever have stood a country life.

No sooner said than done, the two mice set off for the town and arrived at the Town Mouse's residence late at night. "You will want some refreshment after our long journey," said the polite Town Mouse, and took his friend into the grand dining room. There they found the remains of a fine feast, and soon the two mice were eating up roasts and ham, cakes and jellies, and all that was nice. Suddenly, they heard growling and barking. "What is that?" said the Country Mouse. "It is only the dogs of the house," answered the other. "Only!" said the Country Mouse. "I do not like that music at my dinner." Just at that moment the door flew open, in ran two terriers, and the two mice had to scamper down and run off.

"Good-bye, Cousin," said the Country Mouse, "What! Going so soon?" said the other.

"Yes," he replied … "Better beans and bacon in peace than roasts and cakes in fear."

Switching Places

"That's it!" Mom said with a loud sigh. "I'm tired of picking up after you kids!"

My brother Toby and I barely glanced up from the TV to see what she was angry about. Our favorite show was on, and we didn't want to miss anything. Suddenly, the screen flicked off. "Hey!" we shouted. "We were watching that!"

Mom stood behind us holding the TV remote. She scowled. "You kids aren't listening to me! Look at the mess all over this den. I've asked you three times to pick up your toys and clothes."

"It's not fair!" Toby whined. "Why do we have to do everything? Clean up, do chores, do homework … The work never ends!"

To our surprise, Mom's face cracked into a smile. "You think you have it bad?" she said. "What do you think I do all day?"

"I dunno," I mumbled. "You get to stay home while we're at school. You can do whatever you want because you're a grown-up."

"Is that so?" Mom said. "I have an idea. Tomorrow is Saturday. Why don't we switch places for a day? I'll do everything you kids do, and you can fill my role."

Toby and I looked at each other, interested. A whole day as Mom? Was she serious?

Mom *was* serious. The next day when we woke up, Mom was sitting on the couch watching cartoons. She looked at us. "I'm hungry. What's for breakfast?" We went into the kitchen and poured her a bowl of cereal. She asked to eat it on the couch while she watched TV.

We wanted to join her. "Don't you have something to do?" she reminded us. "The laundry needs to be washed and folded." Toby and I trudged to the laundry room and started working.

The work went on and on. Mom trailed behind us as we swept and mopped the floor, made sandwiches for lunch, fed the dog, and vacuumed the living room. Just as we finished, Mom walked into the room, kicked off her dirty shoes, and stretched out on the couch with a big bowl of popcorn. She dropped a bunch of pieces on the floor as she ate and read a magazine.

"Hey! We just finished cleaning in here!" Toby protested.

"Oh, sorry," Mom said. "I didn't notice." Seeing our pouting faces, she broke into a wide grin. "Are you ready to switch back now?"

"Yes!" we said in unison.

1   Based on "The Town Mouse and the Country Mouse," how do you predict the story concludes?

   A) The country mouse leaves and is happy at home.

   B) The town mouse convinces the country mouse to stay.

   C) The town mouse follows the country mouse home.

   D) The country mouse never lets the town mouse visit him again.

2   In "Switching Places," why does the mom suggest she and the children switch places?

   A) She wants to feel young again.

   B) She wants her kids to appreciate what she does.

   C) She thinks it would be funny to see her kids dress as adults.

   D) She doesn't want to hire a housekeeper.

3   What plot element is the same in both texts?

   A) enjoying good food and drink   C) cleaning the house for company

   B) saying goodbye to a friend   D) seeing how someone else lives

4   Contrast the elements in the texts.

	The Town Mouse and the Country Mouse	Switching Places
Setting		
Plot		
Characters		
Genre		

5   This question has two parts. First, answer part A. Then, answer part B.

Part A

What theme appears in both texts?

A) The grass is not always greener on the other side of the fence.

B) If you are unhappy with your life, take a vacation.

C) Sometimes, the early bird does not get the worm.

D) Don't count your chickens before they hatch.

Part B

How does each story reveal this theme?

_____

_____

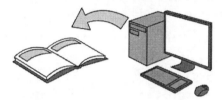

Research Connection

Choose two pieces of literature, one from each list.

Novels

Hatchet by Gary Paulsen

The Light Princess by George McDonald

The Phantom Tollbooth by Norton Juster

From the Mixed-Up Files of Mrs. Basil E. Frankweiler by E. L. Konigsburg

Tuck Everlasting by Natalie Babbitt

Bud, Not Buddy by Christopher Paul Curtis

Poetry

Any poem from *Now We Are Six* by A. A. Milne

Any poem from *Where the Sidewalk Ends* by Shel Silverstein

"A Bird Came Down the Walk" by Emily Dickinson

Read your two choices. After you have studied both sources, think about the characters, setting, plot, conflict, and theme of each one. Choose one of these elements to focus on. Then, write a short essay on your own paper. Compare and contrast this element as it is used in the two sources of literature you choose. Tell how the elements are alike and different. Give examples from the literature. Write three to four paragraphs as a response.

7.2 LANGUAGE

Another element that can be different among literature is language. Sometimes the way authors use words depends on where the author is from. Or it could depend on where the piece of literature is set. There are many **varieties of English** an author can use.

A **dialect** is a form of spoken language for a particular region, community, or social group. Have you ever heard the expressions *Down yonder* or *y'all*? These phrases are part of Southern US dialect. In the North, you'd be more likely to hear *pop* or *soda* whereas in the South you'd be offered a *coke* or a *soft drink*. All of these expressions are examples of dialects spoken informally in the United States.

Many dialects are informal ways of speaking and writing. There are other times when you need to write and speak more formally. A **register** is a level of formality used for certain settings or occasions. Have you ever been to a wedding? There are certain words and phrases you might hear during the ceremony. These include *dearly beloved* and *holy matrimony*. You don't normally hear those words in an everyday conversation. However, in this setting of a wedding ceremony, a very formal register is common. When you talk with adults, such as your parents or a teacher, your register should be formal. But when you talk to friends and classmates, your register is usually casual. Your speech might be filled with slang words and fillers like "ya know."

For example, think of Mark Twain's novel *Adventures of Tom Sawyer*. In this story, young Tom is the main character. He uses words and phrases like *ain't*, *I reckon*, and *give a dern*. The dialect he uses reflects that he is from the Deep South.

Practice 2: Dialect

L 3.b (DOK 3)

Read the text, and follow the directions that follow.

Excerpt from *Adventures of Huckleberry Finn*
by Mark Twain

Jim sings out:

"We's safe, Huck, we's safe! Jump up and crack yo' heels! …"

I says:

"I'll take the canoe and go and see, Jim. It mightn't be, you know."

He jumped and got the canoe ready, and put his old coat in the bottom for me to set on, and give me the paddle; and as I shoved off, he says:

"Pooty soon I'll be a-shout'n' for joy, en I'll say, it's all on accounts o' Huck; I's a free man, en I couldn't ever ben free ef it hadn' ben for Huck; Huck done it. Jim won't ever forgit you, Huck; you's de bes' fren' Jim's ever had; en you's de ONLY fren' ole Jim's got now."

I was paddling off, all in a sweat to tell on him; but when he says this, it seemed to kind of take the tuck all out of me. I went along slow then, and I warn't right down certain whether I was glad I started or whether I warn't.

---

1 Rewrite this passage using your own dialect.

FIGURATIVE LANGUAGE

Using colorful words is one way writers add meaning to text. Paying attention to how a writer uses words is one way to get more out of what you read.

Writers of prose and poetry try to communicate an experience or emotion to readers. They want to create a feeling or an image or make ordinary experiences seem exciting and new. Authors often use figurative language to help them do this. **Figurative language** is a colorful way to use words. Thinking about these words can help you to determine meaning (You learned about some of these types of figurative language in the chapter covering genres of literature.).

A **simile** is a comparison using the words *like* or *as*.

> **Examples:** My fingers look like raisins when I stay in the water too long.
> Her icy stare was like a dagger into his heart.

A **metaphor** is a comparison that doesn't use the words *like* or *as*.

> **Examples:** Your smile is a beam of light brightening up the room.
> The classroom was a beehive of activity as the students prepared their science projects.

A **hyperbole** adds emphasis in writing through exaggerating. It says things that clearly aren't true but add color to the writing.

> **Examples:** Tim threw the ball so fast and hard it landed in Texas.
> I'd rather take a bath with a man-eating shark than give a speech in front of the whole school!

Imagery is language that appeals to the senses (sight, smell, taste, touch, and hearing).

> **Examples:** The children raced down the pebbly beach, shrieking with joy, to wade through the warm, gently lapping waves.
> The cold clay oozed between her fingers, sending a shiver up her spine.

Practice 3: Imagery

RL 7, L 5 (DOK 2, 3)

Read the text, and answer the questions that follow.

Background

Alfred, Lord Tennyson's poem "The Lady of Shalott" is based on a legend about a beautiful woman locked in a tower. The legend is set in the time and place of **Camelot**, the kingdom where King Arthur and his knights lived and had adventures.

The Lady of Shalott is under a curse that keeps her from leaving the tower. She is not even allowed to look out the window at beautiful lords and ladies of Camelot that cross in front of her tower every day! Instead, the only way she can view the outside world is through a mirror propped up opposite the window. She looks in the mirror all day and weaves beautiful tapestries of the reflections she sees passing by.

One day, Sir Lancelot, a handsome knight, trots past her tower on his great steed. The Lady of Shalott is so struck by his beauty that she breaks the rules of the curse and stares out the window at Lancelot. Instantly, her tower room erupts in chaos with yarn flying and the mirror shattering. She runs out of the tower to escape and floats away on a boat she finds at the river's edge. Read the following excerpt from the poem and explain how the artwork shown beneath it captures and enhances the imagery of the poem.

The Lady of Shalott Painting by
John William Waterhouse

Excerpt from "The Lady of Shalott"
by Alfred, Lord Tennyson

She left the web, she left the loom,

She made three paces thro' the room,

She saw the water lily bloom,

She saw the helmet and the plume,

She look'd down to Camelot.

Out flew the web and floated wide;

The mirror crack'd from side to side;

"The curse is come upon me," cried

The Lady of Shalott.

In the stormy east-wind straining,

The pale yellow woods were waning,

The broad stream in his banks complaining,

Heavily the low sky raining

Over tower'd Camelot;

Down she came and found a boat

Beneath a willow left afloat,

And round about the prow[1] she wrote   [1] prow: the front part of a boat

The Lady of Shalott.

And down the river's dim expanse

Like some bold seer[2] in a trance,   [2] seer: a person who can foretell the future

Seeing all his own mischance—

With a glassy countenance[3]   [3] countenance: facial expression

Did she look to Camelot.

And at the closing of the day

She loosed the chain, and down she lay;

The broad stream bore her far away,

The Lady of Shalott.

Lying robed in snowy white
That loosely flew to left and right—
The leaves upon her falling light—
Thro' the noises of the night
She floated down to Camelot:
And as the boat-head wound along
The willowy hills and fields among,
They heard her singing her last song,
The Lady of Shalott.

1   The poem uses strong imagery to paint a picture of the events in the reader's mind. Name **at least three** examples of imagery in the poem, and tell what sense(s) they appeal to.

_____

_____

_____

2   What imagery from the poem does the painting capture? How does seeing the imagery with your eyes differ from "seeing" it by reading?

_____

_____

3   Listen to an adaptation of the poem sung by Loreena McKennitt.

http://americanbookcompany.com/media/lady-of-shalott

*Special thanks to Loreena McKennitt for the permission to use her song in this practice. Visit her website www.quinlanroad.com/ for more information.

The song skips the stanza that begins with "Lying robed in snowy white." Why most likely did McKennitt choose to omit this stanza and continue to the next stanza of the poem? Describe other ways McKennitt's song contributes to the meaning, tone, and beauty of the poem. Write an essay on your own paper.

FIGURATIVE SAYINGS

Sometimes authors like to use sayings that have deeper meanings than the simple words they use. These sayings add color to the writing and allow the readers to use their imagination.

Here are some examples.

An **adage** is a short saying that has been popularly accepted over a long period of time. Writers use adages to share ideas about how to live life.

Example: The grass is always greener on the other side. (It means that we tend to think other people are better off than we are.)

More Adage Examples	
Better late than never.	Curiosity killed the cat.
Better safe than sorry.	A team is as strong as its weakest player.
A leopard can't change its spots.	A person is known by the company he keeps.
A picture is worth a thousand words.	A penny saved is a penny earned.
A secret's only worth keeping if it's worth telling.	All good things must come to an end.

An **idiom** is a common phrase that is not taken literally. Authors use idioms to spice up their writing.

Example: You think you're getting into the show for free? Don't hold your breath. (It means don't bother waiting for something to happen as it probably won't.)

More Idiom Examples	
Break a leg!	Bite off more than you can chew
Let the cat out of the bag	When pigs fly
Costs an arm and a leg	Hit the books
Piece of cake!	Heard it on the grapevine
Caught between a rock and a hard place	On the ball

A **proverb** is a saying much like an adage. It is simple but can have a deeper meaning and is often used to give advice.

Example: To fail to prepare is to prepare to fail. (It means that you should be prepared before starting something. It gives you an advantage.)

More Proverb Examples	
Give a man a fish and you feed him for a day; teach a man to fish and you feed him for a lifetime.	Absence makes the heart grow fonder.
All that glitters is not gold.	Even a small star shines in the darkness.
It's better to have loved and lost, than never to have loved at all.	After the game, the king and pawn go into the same box.
The squeaky wheel gets the grease.	When the going gets tough, the tough get going.

Look up these examples of adages, idioms, and proverbs if you are unsure of their meanings. Can you and your classmates think of more examples that you commonly use in conversation?

Practice 4: Figurative Language

RL 4, L 5 (DOK 2, 3)

A. Fill in the chart with the definition of each term. Then, provide an example for each one that is not seen in the book.

Term	Definition	Example
Metaphor		
Simile		
Hyperbole		
Imagery		
Adage		
Idiom		
Proverb		

B. Read the texts, and then answer the questions.

The Eagle
by Alfred, Lord Tennyson

He clasps the crag with crooked hands;

Close to the sun in lonely lands,

Ringed with the azure world, he stands.

The wrinkled sea beneath him crawls;

He watches from his mountain walls,

And like a thunderbolt he falls.

1   Based on the poem, what color is <u>azure</u>?

   A) red   C) purple

   B) yellow   D) blue

2   Read this line from the poem and the question that follows.

     And like a thunderbolt he falls.

This simile tells you that he falls

   A) quickly.   C) fearfully.

   B) slowly.   D) gracefully.

3   Read this line from the poem.

     He clasps the crag with crooked hands

Why do you think the author words the description in this way?

_____

_____

Murphy's Law

Taylor dashed down the stairs with her duffel bag over her shoulder. She had slept late and had rushed to pack the last of her things for the family's camping trip. Now they would be late leaving and might even miss the waterfall hike they had planned. Taylor jumped down the last step and skidded to a stop in front of her mother, panting hard.

"OK," she gasped. "I had a million and one things to do, but now I'm ready!"

"Hmm," said her mother. "We seem to have hit a snag. While you were packing, I got a call from the kennel. The lady said that Rover is not current on his shots, and they can't board him after all."

Taylor groaned. "It's Murphy's law," she said. "'If something can go wrong, it will.' So are we going camping at all now?"

---

4   4 The phrase "I had a million and one things to do" is an example of

   A) hyperbole.   C) metaphor.

   B) adage.   D) simile.

5   What type of saying is "hit a snag"? What does it mean?

_____

_____

6   What type of saying is "Murphy's law"? What does it mean?

_____

_____

7 Have you ever had a moment when Murphy's Law interrupted your plans? Using your own paper, write a brief narrative about what happened and explain how Murphy's Law applied.

7.3 STRUCTURE

All writing, whether it's a story, drama, or poem, follows a logical **structure**. When you read books, you'll notice that they're usually broken into chapters. Each chapter tells a part of the story. If the author shuffled the chapters around or left some out, the story would be very different! In a similar way, authors often break poems into **stanzas** (groups of lines) and dramas into **scenes**. The chapters, scenes, or stanzas of a literary work all fit together to provide structure to the story. Each chapter, scene, or stanza holds some importance to the story as a whole.

Take a look at the following text.

Makayla's Big Save

The chapters of this book are summarized as follows:

Chapter 1

Makayla, a fifth-grade student, struggles in gym class. She's not out of shape but very clumsy and uncoordinated. She tends to drop the ball and can't throw it very far. She is always picked last for team sports.

Chapter 2

The whole school is excited about the upcoming field hockey game. The Comets will be playing against their biggest rivals, the Grizzly Bears. Makayla is worried about the game. She knows she probably won't be picked to play, but she still wants her team to win.

Chapter 3

It's the day of the big game. Makayla sits on the bench and cheers on her team, the Comets. During the opening minute, the Comets' star goalie sprains her ankle. Somehow, the Comets gain a one-goal advantage in the final minutes. But during the play, their backup goalie also sprains her ankle.

Chapter 4

The Comets' coach is desperate. She turns to Makayla. "You're up! Try to stay in front of the ball. Just don't sprain your ankle!" Makayla is shocked. She can't be the goalie! Her teammates are also upset. "Makayla can't do it!" one of them protests. Nervously, Makayla takes the field.

Chapter 5

In the last seconds of the game, the Grizzly Bears take the offense and head toward Makayla's goal. A player takes a shot. Panicked, Makayla ducks and covers her head. To her amazement, the ball hits her in the chest and bounces away. She's blocked the goal! The buzzer rings. The Comets have won! Makayla's teammates rush to give her a humongous group hug. "You did it!" they cry.

Do you see how the author breaks the story up into chapters? The chapters follow a logical structure, telling the events in chronological order. What would happen if chapter 1 was missing? The reader wouldn't know that Makayla was bad at sports. When Makayla makes the big save at the end of the game, the reader wouldn't understand why her teammates are so amazed and surprised. As you can see, if one chapter of a book or stanza or line in a poem is missing, the overall meaning can be missed. Each part of a text is important to the understanding of its message.

Practice 5: Structure

RL 5, 10 (DOK 1–3)

Read the texts, and then answer the questions.

> 1   Colin had been nervous all day. He had been practicing his history oral report for three weeks, yet he felt unprepared. He shuddered to think how he would feel standing in front of his classmates trying to remember details about it.
>
> 2   At lunch, all he could think about was that his speech would be next period during social studies. Colin felt just like a newly hatched chick––he wanted to crawl right back into his shell. He ate his lunch slowly, lost in thought, going over the speech in his head.
>
> 3   Due to his anxiety, Colin forgot to grab a napkin and wipe his mouth after lunch. He quickly dropped off his tray, ducked his head, and avoided everyone as he left the cafeteria.
>
> 4   Finally, it was Colin's turn to speak. He got up and walked slowly to the front of the classroom, turning to face the other students. A soft giggle skipped around the room. When Mrs. Boles looked up from her notes to see what the children found so amusing, she had to hold back her own giggle. "Colin, dear," she said in her gentle way, "you are wearing a milk mustache."

1   How would the story be different if the author didn't include paragraph 3?

A) The reader would be surprised at the end by Colin's milk mustache.

B) The reader would think that Colin didn't eat his lunch.

C) The reader would think that Colin was eager to give his oral report.

D) There would be no difference in the story.

2   How do the first three paragraphs build up to the concluding paragraph?

_____

_____

3 Read the concluding line of the text.

"Colin, dear," she said in her gentle way, "you are wearing a milk mustache."

What role does this line play in the story?

A) It reveals why the students are laughing at Colin.

B) It shows that Colin's teacher is mean.

C) It suggests that Colin's favorite drink is milk.

D) It provides no conclusion to the story.

The Echoing Green
from *Songs of Innocence and Experience* by William Blake

The sun does arise,
And make happy the skies;
The merry bells ring
To welcome the Spring;
The skylark and thrush,
The birds of the bush,
Sing louder around
To the bells' cheerful sound;
While our sports shall be seen
On the echoing green.

Old John, with white hair,
Does laugh away care,
Sitting under the oak,
Among the old folk.
They laugh at our play,
And soon they all say,
"Such, such were the joys
When we all—girls and boys—
In our youth-time were seen
On the echoing green."

William Blake illustrated many of his own poems.

Till the little ones, weary,

No more can be merry:

The sun does descend,

And our sports have an end.

Round the laps of their mothers

Many sisters and brothers,

Like birds in their nest,

Are ready for rest,

And sport no more seen

On the darkening green.

4   What **best** describes the role of the first stanza of this poem?

A) It wraps up the story by telling the ending.

B) It tells how to solve a problem.

C) It sets the scene for the activities to come.

D) It tells why the old people are sad.

5   The poem begins with the "rising sun." It ends with a "darkening green." What might these time clues be talking about, and why did the author choose to say them this way?

_____

_____

_____

CHAPTER 7 SUMMARY

Comparing and contrasting is the process of looking for similarities and differences. You can compare and contrast the **characters**, **plot**, **themes**, or other **literary devices** in two different stories.

Themes that can be understood by people all over the word are **universal themes**.

Another element that can be different among literature is language. There are many **varieties of English** an author can use.

A **dialect** is a form of spoken language for a particular region, community, or social group.

A **register** is a level of formality used for certain settings or occasions.

Figurative language is a colorful way to use words. This includes **metaphor**, **simile**, **hyperbole**, and **imagery**.

Figurative sayings include **adages**, **idioms**, and **proverbs**.

All writing, whether it is a story, a poem, a play, or a myth, has logical **structure**. Each part of a text (for example, a chapter or a stanza) is important to the understanding of its message.

For additional practice, please see Chapter 7 Test located in the Teacher Guide.

Chapter 8
Informational Texts

 This chapter covers DOK levels 1–3 and the following fifth grade strand and standards (for full standards, please see page x):

> **Reading Informational Texts** 1, 2, 3, 4, **5, 6, 7, 8, 9, 10**
> **Writing** 2, 8, 9

In this chapter...

- You will use active reading strategies and knowledge of informational text features to interpret informational text.

- You will use multiple sources in order to solve a problem.

8.1 INFORMATIONAL TEXT FEATURES

When you are reading for information, you will find many **text features** that will help you. Text features are helpful aids that make your reading more productive. They can help you identify the main idea and supporting details. For example, the title and headings of a text let you see at a glance the main points of a text. The table of contents can help you see how a text organizes its ideas. Let's take a look at some of these.

Text Features	
Type	**Explanation**
Format	One text feature that jumps out at you as a reader is **format**. How is the text organized? Is the information presented in a logical format? Paying attention to a writer's choice of formatting helps a reader to gain the most from any text.
Glossary	Located at the back of a book, **glossaries** are like specialized dictionaries created specifically for a text. They provide definitions for key terms in a book.
Headings and Subheadings	Many informational texts use **headings and subheadings** to organize ideas. Headings help readers to know the big idea of a text. For example, if you are reading a chapter about research in your language arts textbook, you might see headings such as Choosing a Topic, Finding Sources, or Citing Sources. These would be examples of key ideas that the chapter has to offer. Under the heading Finding Sources, you might find subheadings— titles of smaller chapter sections or ideas, such as Electronic Sources, Primary Sources, or Print Sources. Subheadings tell the reader what ideas he or she can find within a section of a text.

Index	Sometimes you will need to quickly locate information in a text. A great tool to help you do this is the **index**. Located at the back of a book, an index gives you a list of key ideas and where to find them in a text. Indexes are arranged alphabetically to help you quickly find the information you need.
Italics	Another common text feature is the use of **italics**. You can recognize italics by the way that letters have a slight forward slant (*like this*). Writers use italics for emphasis. When you are reading a text, pay special attention to italicized words. They may be key vocabulary terms and/or important to the main idea of what you are reading.
Sequence	One commonly used format that a reader will recognize involves **sequence**. When information is arranged sequentially, it is in time order or chronological order—the order in which events occurred. Having a piece of writing in the correct sequence is important, especially when following multistep directions to accomplish a task. If the directions are not written in the correct order, it will be hard to follow them.
Table of Contents	A **table of contents** is a list of chapters in a book. Many tables of contents also often include headings and subheadings.

For example, look at how a science textbook uses text features to organize its ideas.

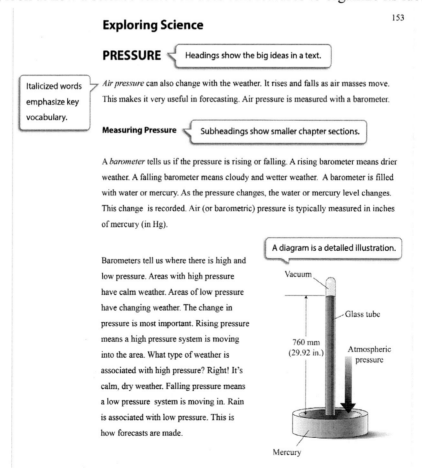

Exploring Science

153

PRESSURE — Headings show the big ideas in a text.

Italicized words emphasize key vocabulary.

Air pressure can also change with the weather. It rises and falls as air masses move. This makes it very useful in forecasting. Air pressure is measured with a barometer.

Measuring Pressure — Subheadings show smaller chapter sections.

A *barometer* tells us if the pressure is rising or falling. A rising barometer means drier weather. A falling barometer means cloudy and wetter weather. A barometer is filled with water or mercury. As the pressure changes, the water or mercury level changes. This change is recorded. Air (or barometric) pressure is typically measured in inches of mercury (in Hg).

Barometers tell us where there is high and low pressure. Areas with high pressure have calm weather. Areas of low pressure have changing weather. The change in pressure is most important. Rising pressure means a high pressure system is moving into the area. What type of weather is associated with high pressure? Right! It's calm, dry weather. Falling pressure means a low pressure system is moving in. Rain is associated with low pressure. This is how forecasts are made.

A diagram is a detailed illustration.

Vacuum

Glass tube

760 mm (29.92 in.)

Atmospheric pressure

Mercury

Page 136

GRAPHICS

Writers of resource materials use **graphics** to help readers. Graphics are pictures that help readers understand the writing. Think of them as visual representations of what you read or learn. Commonly used graphic features are diagrams, illustrations, charts, and maps.

Types of Graphics	
Type	**Explanation**
Charts	**Charts** give a reader information in an organized, easy-to-follow format. A table is a type of chart that uses columns and rows to organize information for the reader. A schedule is a type of table that shows items like times and dates and sometimes places.
Diagrams	A **diagram** is a detailed illustration. It often uses labels to identify specific parts of the pictured item. For example, a science book might use a diagram to show the Earth's layers.
Illustrations	Many texts use **illustrations**—pictures—to help the reader understand the information of the text. Illustrations provide a visual for the reader. They help the reader gain a deeper understanding from what they read.
Maps	A **map** is a flat drawing of all or part of the earth. With every map, there is a map legend. It tells about the items on the map, such as symbols or areas of different patterns or colors. It also tells you the cardinal directions— north, south, east, and west. Usually, north is at the top of a map, south is at the bottom, east is to your right, and west is to your left.

ORGANIZING AND UNDERSTANDING INFORMATION

Organization is key to understanding informational text. Readers and writers alike need to be able to **organize and understand information**. They do this by using common organizational structures. These structures include chronological (time) order, problem and solution order, comparison and contrast order, and cause and effect order (For more information about organizational structures, review chapter 3.).

The text features you read about earlier can help you organize and understand information. Headings, subheadings, format, and sequence may help you figure out the text's organization. If you see headings that say "Before the War," "During the War," and "After the War," you can tell the author uses chronological order. If the sequence of information begins with a cause, you may find the author uses cause/effect order. Italics or bolded words draw your attention to important concepts. The glossary tells you what unfamiliar words mean. The index and table of contents allow you to find the information you need. Knowing and using these text features will make understanding informational texts much easier.

Graphics in informational texts work the same way. If a text includes a graphic, it holds important information. You should pay close attention to the graphic. You should also look for parts of the text that explain why the graphic might be important. A text that includes a diagram might also have a description using words. A text with a map might discuss important landmarks or physical features.

Another type of graphic to look out for is timelines. **Timelines** help organize ideas and events into chronological order. They help you see how one event follows another in a time sequence. Timelines are useful for explaining historical events. They can also help show the events of a person's life.

Example:

Timeline of Author Judy Blume's Life

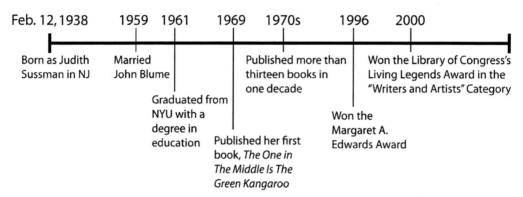

Practice 1: Organizing and Understanding Information

RI 1, 2, 3, 5 (DOK 1–3)

Answer the following questions.

> **Mama's Chicken Soup**
>
> ### Ingredients
>
> | | |
> |---|---|
> | 2 1/2 cups wide egg noodles | 1 cup chopped celery |
> | 1 teaspoon vegetable oil | 1 cup chopped onion |
> | 12 cups chicken broth | 1/3 cup cornstarch |
> | 1 1/2 tablespoons salt | 1/4 cup water |
> | 1 teaspoon poultry seasoning | 3 cups diced, cooked chicken meat |
>
> ### Directions
>
> 1. Bring a large pot of lightly salted water to a boil. Add egg noodles and oil, and boil for 8 minutes, or until tender. Drain, and rinse under cool running water.
>
> 2. In a large saucepan or Dutch oven, combine broth, salt, and poultry seasoning. Bring to a boil. Stir in celery and onion. Reduce heat, cover, and simmer 15 minutes.
>
> 3. In a small bowl, mix cornstarch and water together until cornstarch is completely dissolved. Gradually add to soup, stirring constantly. Stir in noodles and chicken, and heat through.

1   How does the author break up the **two** specific sections of this passage?

A) headings   C) italics

B) table of contents   D) glossary

2   Which step comes first?

A) Drain noodles.   C) Bring water to a boil.

B) Add cornstarch.   D) Stir in celery and onion.

3   If this text came from a book, where would be the **best** place to look up cooking terms you may not understand?

A) table of contents   C) subheadings

B) glossary   D) headings

4   How is this passage organized?

A) compare and contrast   C) order of importance

B) cause and effect   D) sequential order

Read this excerpt from a science textbook. Then, answer the questions that follow.

Classifying Plants

1   How do scientists know which living things are animals and which ones are plants? As it turns out, plants, like animals, are multicellular living things. However, unlike animals, plants can make their own food. Plants use sunlight to make their food. Another unique plant characteristic is that plants cannot move by themselves. Plants can slowly grow larger or bend toward the light source. But this usually takes several days or weeks. Unlike animals, plants cannot walk, run, swim, or fly over a distance in a matter of seconds.

2   When grouping plants, scientists use the plants' physical structure and life cycle, similar to the way animals are grouped. The two main groups of plants are **non-vascular** plants and **vascular** plants.

3   You are probably more familiar with the vascular plants. Vascular plants are the most common type of plant found on land. This group of plants has a special group of cells, or tissues, that move water and food around inside the plant. Tissues are groups of similar cells that work together to complete a particular job. **Xylem** (ZI-luhm) is the name for the tissues that move water inside the plant. And **phloem** (FLOH-em) is the name for the tissues that move food inside the plant. Vascular plants usually have roots, leaves, and stems. However, in some plant groups, the roots, leaves, and stems have special names you will learn at another time. Some examples of vascular plants include flowering plants, (including deciduous trees that lose their leaves in the fall), conifers (like pine trees), ferns, cactus, cycads, and ginkgos.

4   Vascular plants are further divided based on whether or not they make seeds. Plants that make seeds are called **seeded vascular plants**. A seed is a small baby plant made from special plant parts. An entire new plant can grow from one seed. The other main group of vascular plants is called the **seedless vascular plants**. These plants make spores instead of seeds. Plant groups can be seen in the diagram below.

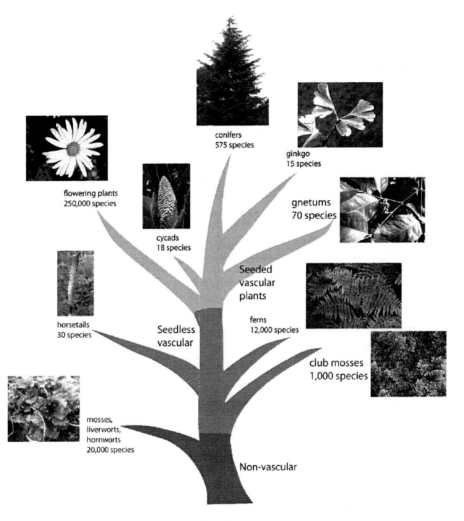

Figure 10.4 Plant Groups

5   In contrast to vascular plants, **non-vascular plants** are without specialized tissues. As a result, non-vascular plants usually have a very simple structure when compared to vascular plants. Because they don't have any transport tissues, non-vascular plants must live in wet or moist environments and are limited to a small size. Some examples of non-vascular plants are mosses, liverworts, and hornworts.

5 Select **two** main ideas of this text.

A) Plants and animals are both multicellular living things.

B) Plants are classified based on their physical structures.

C) Plants are classified into several different groups.

D) Vascular plants are probably most familiar to you.

E) Some plants do not have any seeds.

6 How does the author use information in paragraph 3 to support **one** of the main ideas of the text? Use details and quotations from the text to support your answer.

_____

_____

_____

7 How would the reader's understanding suffer if Figure 10.4 were **not** included?

A) The reader would not know that vascular plants are most common.

B) The reader would not understand vascular plant structure.

C) The reader would not know the difference between the plant groups.

D) The reader would not know what each type of plant looks like.

8 Which of the following would **best** support the main idea of the text?

A) Classifying plants is important because it helps scientists better understand them.

B) Animals are classified based on whether they have a backbone, or vertebrae.

C) The word *xylem* comes from the Greek word for wood.

D) Non-vascular plants were the first plant group to evolve.

9 Summarize the text. Include main ideas and supporting details.

_____

_____

_____

8.2 INFERENCES

In chapter 3, you learned how to make **inferences**. Your inference skills can help you solve problems using informational texts. Sometimes you will need information that is not stated. But you can use clues from the text to help you make logical educated guesses.

For example, read this text. Then, try answering the questions, and read the explanations that follow.

A Sweet Experiment

Have you ever grown candy? This sweet science experiment will show you how.

Safety First!

1. The first rule of all science experiments is safety. You will use boiling water to grow your rock candy. Work carefully under the supervision of an adult.

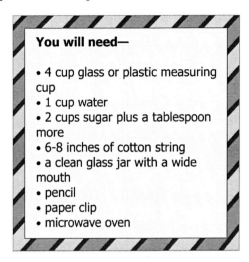

You will need—

- 4 cup glass or plastic measuring cup
- 1 cup water
- 2 cups sugar plus a tablespoon more
- 6-8 inches of cotton string
- a clean glass jar with a wide mouth
- pencil
- paper clip
- microwave oven

Let's get started!

2. After gathering your materials, tie one end of the string to the pencil and the other end to the paper clip. Next, pour one cup of water into the measuring cup. Then, add one cup of sugar to the water and stir. After the sugar dissolves, place the measuring cup in a microwave. Heat the sugar-water solution on high for two minutes. Carefully take the measuring cup out. The liquid will be very hot.

3. Stir the sugar water again. This will keep the sugar dissolved. Add a second cup of sugar to the solution, and stir some more. Be careful not to spill or splash the liquid. Put the cup back in, and heat it for an additional two minutes. Remove the hot liquid from the microwave, and stir until all of the sugar dissolves in the water. Put the liquid back in the microwave one last time. Heat it for one minute, and remove the sugar water.

4. Lay the pencil across the mouth of the jar. Drop the paper clip into the jar. It will work like an anchor holding the string in place. Wind the string around the pencil so the string hangs straight without touching the bottom of the jar. Remove the pencil and string from the jar without unwinding the string. Slowly, pour the hot liquid into the jar.

5. Dampen the string with cool water, and roll it in the extra tablespoon of sugar. Lay the pencil across the mouth of the jar again, and drop the paper clip anchor into the liquid.

Be patient!

6. Wait a couple of hours before making your first observation. Then, look for crystals forming on the string. Let the rock candy crystals grow for about a week before removing them from the jar. The solution cannot be used again. Discard the remaining liquid and wash the jar with soapy water. Break off a piece of your rock candy, and enjoy your sweet science experiment!

Based on the line "The first rule of all science experiments is safety," what can you infer about conducting science experiments?

A) Safety is not an important part of science experiments.

B) People are sometimes harmed when conducting experiments.

C) Your parents will not let you experiment if you are not safe.

D) This will be a very dangerous experiment to conduct.

Did you answer B? You are correct. The text does not say it directly, but it stresses the importance of being careful while conducting experiments. You can, therefore, infer that sometimes people are harmed when they are not careful.

What **most likely** is the author's reason for placing some information in a separate box?

A) to make it easier to know which materials to gather

B) to suggest that other experiments can be done with the same materials

C) to warn that the project requires supplies not found at home

D) to show that it isn't a main part of the article

Did you answer A? That's the correct answer. By placing the items people will need for the experiment in a box, the author makes it easier for readers to find what they need. They don't have to read the entire text word for word to pick out all the items they need for the experiment.

The author uses several text features to help the reader. The headings give clues about what the experiment will involve. The numbered paragraphs help you see that this text involves a process to follow in sequence. As you can see, a text's format allows you to infer what the text covers and in what manner.

Practice 2: Inferences

RI 1 (DOK 3)

Inferences can be very important to solving problems. Working logic puzzles is a great way to practice your critical thinking and inference skills.

Each clue below gives you information about the logic puzzle. Read each clue, make inferences, and mark off the boxes. When you know that two categories cannot go together, mark an X. When you know that two categories must go together, mark an O.

Example: 1. Critter is not a morning animal.

Inference: I should not visit Critter at 8 a.m. (The correct box is marked with an X below.)

Summertime is here and many of your neighbors are going on vacation. Each neighbor has asked you to take care of his or her family's pets while they are out of town. You need to create a daily schedule to make sure you keep track of all the furry friends. Using the information below, complete the chart below. You will need to use your inference skills to figure everything out. Determine which pet each family owns, what type of animal each pet is, and what time of day you need to visit each pet. Good luck!

Clues:

1. Critter is not a morning animal.
2. Kate Fox is allergic to fur.
3. The Bishops' pet is slow.
4. The Field pet likes late walks through the neighborhood.
5. The cat naps from 2 p.m. to 8 p.m.
6. Marbles' favorite toy is a bone.
7. Jax likes to eat seeds.
8. Biscuit spends the morning and evening sleeping under his heat lamp.

	Critter	Jax	Biscuit	Marbles	8:00 am	12:00 pm	3:00 pm	7:00 pm	Dog	Cat	Turtle	Bird
The Fox Family												
The Bishop Family												
The Portnoy Family												
The Field Family												
Dog												
Cat												
Turtle												
Bird												
8:00 am	X											
12:00 pm												
3:00 pm												
7:00 pm												

8.3 INTEGRATING SOURCES

When you read or do research, you will often need to look at several sources to find the information you need. Often, each source will come from a different point of view or have a slightly different focus. The sources might even be different types of texts. Reading these different texts gives you a better understanding of a topic. For example, say you are researching water conservation, and you find these two sources.

Source 1

There are many ways to conserve water at home. The three main places in the house where people use water are the kitchen, the laundry room, and the bathroom. Here are some tips to cut down on water use.

In the kitchen

- Don't leave the tap running as you wash dishes by hand. Instead, fill up one half of the sink with soapy water for soaking, and the other half with fresh water for rinsing.

- Use the garbage disposal as little as possible—or better yet, turn food waste into compost!

- When you wash fruits and vegetables, do it in a bowl filled with water rather than running tap water over them.

In the laundry room

- When you do the laundry, make sure you only run full loads. Gallons of water are wasted on less-than-full loads.

- If your washing machine allows it, choose a lighter cycle if you have just a few items to wash.

In the bathroom

- Turn off the sink faucet while you brush your teeth.

- Make sure your showerhead and toilet are water-efficient models, and fix leaky faucets.

- Reducing your shower time by just a minute or two can save up to 150 gallons of water each month!

Not only does conservation help the environment, it also saves your family money on the water bill.

Source 2

> Protecting our water supply is a very important issue. Conserving water is critical because it is our planet's most valuable resource. Water shortages don't just happen to people in other nations—they can happen here in our hometown. Right now, our town is experiencing a severe drought. You have probably noticed that the levels of our rivers and reservoirs are dangerously low. The city has set up water restrictions to protect our dwindling supply. Households can water their lawns only for short periods and at certain times of the day. It's a brutally hot summer, and many lawns are drying up. Of course we want to turn on the hoses and sprinklers, but we all have to do our part to use water responsibly. Otherwise, we'll all be in serious trouble. So be smart about conserving! Put out a barrel to collect rainwater for your yard. Use water-efficient appliances. You can't say that you don't care about water conservation. Everyone drinks water to survive. Everyone needs to protect it.

Both sources address water conservation, but they do so in different ways. Source 1 gives tips on how to conserve water at home. The text's purpose is to inform readers about ways to save water. The text names some benefits of conserving water, such as helping the environment and saving money on the water bill. But the text keeps a neutral, informative tone.

In contrast, Source 2 states an opinion that it is everyone's duty to conserve water. Since the text's purpose is to persuade, it uses strong, forceful language to urge readers to do their part. The text warns what will happen if people don't conserve water: we will run low on our planet's most valuable resource.

You must be able to look at each text and see what information it has to offer. Both sources describe ways to conserve water, but they take different approaches in conveying information. When you **integrate information** (include facts) from several texts, you become knowledgeable about your subject. You can use the facts from different sources to fill in gaps in your knowledge. For example, by integrating information from the two texts, you learned that water-efficient appliances help save water. Filling in gaps in information helps you solve more complex problems. When you combine information from multiple sources to create something new or to gain a better understanding of the material, you are **synthesizing**.

Practice 3: Integrating Sources

W 8, 9, **RI** 6, 7, 9 (DOK 3)

You are responsible for planning a family dinner. You must prepare a meal that is both within your budget and meets the dietary needs of all family members. Using the sources provided below, design a three-course (appetizer, main course, dessert) meal that is budget-friendly and healthy for all.

Guest List

- Dad: Your father is diabetic. He has to make sure not to eat very much sugar.

- Mom: Your mother has no special dietary needs.

- Jonathan: Your brother, Jonathan, is allergic to shellfish.

- You: You have no special dietary needs.

Budget: $35.00

Appetizers

Shrimp Cocktail

Ingredients

1 lb peeled shrimp
12 oz jar cocktail sauce

Nutrition

Calories 90	Sugar 12g
Fat 1g	Protein 8g
Carbohydrates 14g	

Chips and Salsa

Ingredients

13 oz bag tortilla chips
16 oz jar salsa

Nutrition

Calories 156	Sugar 2g
Fat 7g	Protein 3g
Carbohydrates 23g	

Cocktail Meatballs

Ingredients

1 lb frozen meatballs
Toothpicks

Nutrition

Calories 230	Sugar 2g
Fat 15g	Protein 14g
Carbohydrates 8g	

Main Courses

Honey Glazed Ham and Sweet Potato Casserole

Ingredients

1 lb pre-glazed ham	1 cup sugar
4 c sweet potatoes	4 tbs butter
spices	

Nutrition

Calories 350	Sugar 29g
Fat 10g	Protein 17g
Carbohydrates 41g	

Seafood Soup and Salad

Ingredients

1 c chicken broth	2 c milk
1 small onion	1 lb cooked lobster
2 tbs butter	1 bag salad greens

Nutrition

Calories 290	Sugar 9g
Fat 13g	Protein 20 g
Carbohydrates 13g	

Turkey Burgers and Green Beans

Ingredients

1 lb ground turkey	1 small onion	16 oz can
8 whole wheat	1 tomato	green beans
hamburger buns	spices	

Nutrition

Calories 400	Sugar 8g
Fat 14g	Protein 33g
Carbohydrates 36g	

Desserts

Yogurt Parfait

Ingredients

32 oz yogurt
2 c berries
1/2 c granola

Nutrition

Calories 300	Sugar 15g
Fat 8g	Protein 26g
Carbohydrates 35g	

Brownie Sundae

Ingredients

2 c brownie chunks
2 c ice cream

Nutrition

Calories 400	Sugar 40g
Fat 17g	Protein 5g
Carbohydrates 58g	

Milkshake

Ingredients

2 c ice cream
2 c milk

Nutrition

Calories 255	
Fat 12g	Sugar 27g
Carbohydrates 27g	Protein 10g

1   Which appetizer have you chosen? Why?

   _____

   _____

   _____

2   Which main course have you chosen? Why?

   _____

   _____

   _____

3   Which dessert have you chosen? Why?

   _____

   _____

   _____

CHAPTER 8 SUMMARY

Authors use **organization** to make their ideas clear. **Text features** and **graphics** help you understand the text's organization.

When you make an **inference**, you are making a connection between what is said and not said in a story.

Integrating information from multiple sources helps you learn more about a topic. **Synthesizing** is combining information to make something new.

For additional practice, please see Chapter 8 Test located in the Teacher Guide.

Chapter 9
Grammar

This chapter covers DOK levels 1–3 and the following fifth grade strand and standards (for full standards, please see page x):

Language: 1, 2, 3

In this chapter...

- You will tell the difference between parts of speech and comprehend how to use each part of speech in a sentence.

- You will gain understanding of different verb tenses and the functions of conjunctions, prepositions, and interjections in a sentence.

- You will use conventions of the English language appropriately in writing.

- You will use spelling conventions correctly in order to be more precise in your writing.

- You will also understand how commas are used correctly in sentences and learn how to repair sentence errors such as run-on sentences and sentence fragments.

9.1 PARTS OF SPEECH

Words are the building blocks we use to create our messages. Sentences are made up of words. Every word in a sentence has a special role to play.

The way each word works in a sentence explains its part of speech. There are eight **parts of speech**. Learning all the parts of speech and how to use them will improve how you write and speak.

NOUNS

A **noun** is a word that names a person, place, thing, or idea. Look at the following sentence.

Example: <u>Tommy</u> had the <u>courage</u> to rescue the <u>kitten</u> from the <u>tree</u>.

In this sentence, *Tommy, courage, kitten,* and *tree* are nouns. Tommy is a person. A kitten and a tree are things. Courage is a noun, too, even though you can't touch or see it. It's an idea.

Nouns can be common or proper. A **common noun** names a general person, place, or thing. A **proper noun** names a specific person, place, or thing. Proper nouns are always capitalized.

Common Nouns	Proper Nouns
building	White House
boy	Luke
city	Detroit
TV show	*Legend of Korra*

PRONOUNS

A **pronoun** is a word used in the place of one or more nouns. Pronouns help keep you from having to repeat a word over and over.

There are three basic types of pronouns: nominative, objective, and possessive.

Nominative (or subject) pronouns are used whenever a pronoun is used as a subject.

> **Example:** Amy and I are going water skiing.

In this example, *I* is the part of the subject.

Objective pronouns are used when the pronoun answers the questions, "What?" or "Whom?" after the action verb.

> **Example:** I heard him in the courtyard.

In this example, *him* answers the question, "Heard whom?"

Possessive pronouns are used to show ownership or attachment.

> **Example:** His laptop is broken.

In this example, *His* answers the question, "Who owns the laptop?"

Personal Pronoun Forms		
Nominative	**Objective**	**Possessive**
I	me	my, mine
you	you	your, yours
she	her	her, hers
he	him	his
it	it	its
we	us	our, ours
they	them	their, theirs
who	whom	whose
whoever	whomever	whose

ADJECTIVES

An **adjective** is a word that describes or adds details to a noun or pronoun. An adjective answers the following questions:

- What kind?

- Which one?

- How much?

- How many?

The most common adjectives are *a, an*, and *the*. These are called articles. But there are many other adjectives that add vivid description. Let's take a look at some adjectives.

Examples: The <u>stealthy</u>, <u>graceful</u> ninja scaled the building.

Stealthy and *graceful* are adjectives in this sentence. They tell what kind of ninja.

Bob ate <u>sixteen</u> hot dogs for the competition.

Sixteen is an adjective that tells how many hot dogs.

ADVERBS

An **adverb** is a type of word that describes or adds details. It can modify a verb, an adjective, or another adverb. Adverbs add details in many ways. They can tell the following:

- **time** (when?)

- **place** (where?)

- **manner** (how?)

- **degree** (how much? to what extent?)

Now, let's take a look at some adverbs.

Examples: We will arrive at the water park <u>soon</u>.

Soon is an adverb. It tells when we will arrive.

Maggie eyed the apple pie <u>hungrily</u>.

Hungrily is an adverb. It tells how Maggie eyed the apple pie.

Practice 1: Nouns, Pronouns, Adjectives, and Adverbs

L 1 (DOK 1)

Read the following sentences. Then, place the words from the sentences in the appropriate place on the chart.

1   Gabriel cheerfully rode his shiny, new scooter to the playground.

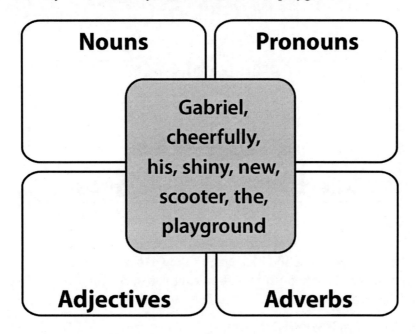

2   Rachel and her twin sister were quite content to give their presentation extra early.

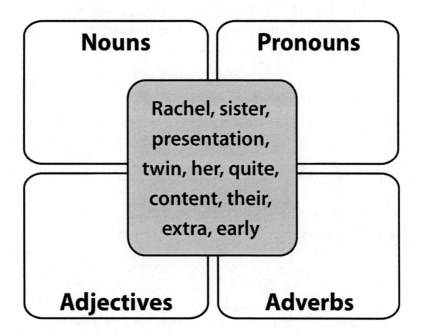

3   My brother, Daniel, is a very accomplished saxophonist.

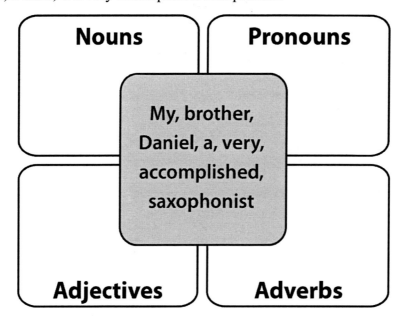

VERBS

Verbs are words that show what action happens, or they can show the state of being of a noun. There are two types of verbs: action verbs and linking verbs. As you can tell from their name, **action verbs** show action. Look at the sentence below.

> **Example:** Six squirrels <u>gobbled</u> the nuts. (the action verb *gobbled* tells what the squirrels are doing)

Some verbs show state of being. They include verbs like *can, could, may, might, must, should, would,* and forms of the verb *to be*. These can be used as **linking verbs** as well, which means they can connect a noun to another verb or an adjective.

> **Example:** Those squirrels <u>are</u> greedy. (the linking verb *are* connects the noun *squirrel* with the adjective *greedy*)

Some verbs have no meaning on their own but help give another verb meaning. Examples of **helping verbs** include *can, could, should, would, must, shall,* and *may*.

> **Examples:** Jacoury <u>can whistle</u> "The Star-Spangled Banner." (*can* helps the verb *whistle* by saying Jacoury has the ability to whistle)
> Melissa <u>may join</u> us at the skating rink tonight. (*may* helps the verb *join* by saying there's a possibility Melissa will join us)

VERB TENSES

There are several verb tenses. **Verb tense** shows when something happens. Look at this table of the three main verb tenses. As you know, helping verbs may be added to action verbs to form the tense (or time) of a particular action.

Verb Tenses		
Tense	**Description**	**Example**
Present	Something is happening now, or it is a recurring action.	David <u>plays</u> electric guitar.
Past	Something happened in the past but is no longer happening.	David <u>played</u> electric guitar at a concert last night.
Future	Something will happen in the future.	David <u>will play</u> electric guitar on tour this summer.

PERFECT TENSE

As you know, there are many different verb tenses, but one in particular is called the perfect tense. The **perfect tense** helps you show when one event occurs before or during another event. The tense is formed by combining a form of *to have* with the past participle of the verb.

Perfect Verb Tenses		
Tense	**Description**	**Example**
Present perfect	Something happened at one point in the past and continued up to the present.	David <u>has played</u> electric guitar for three years.
Past perfect	Something happened before something else in the past.	David <u>had played</u> electric guitar for a year when he started taking lessons.
Future perfect	Something will be completed at some point in the future.	Next year, David <u>will have played</u> the guitar for four years.

Remember, you usually form the past participle of a verb by adding *-ed*, *-en*, or *-t*.

Examples: burn → burnt
eat → eaten
finish → finished

Examples:

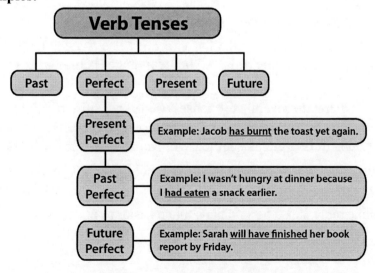

Practice 2: Verbs

L 1.b–c (DOK 2)

Read the paragraph.

> Julie's birthday party was last weekend. On the day of the party, Julie's friend Katie arrived before Tommy. Tommy was already sliding down the Monkey Chute ride when Jack got to the party. Sam arrived last, after Kylie and Mickey arrived. Kylie had already started eating a hot dog when Mickey showed up. Sayuri appeared just before Sam but after Mickey had begun filling water balloons. Dre had been so eager for the party that he arrived twenty minutes before anyone else. His best friend, Oscar, had been the next guest to appear, right before Katie. When Julie's mom saw all the kids assembled, she said, "Time for cake!"

Now, determine the order in which each party guest arrived. Use the timeline below to order the guests.

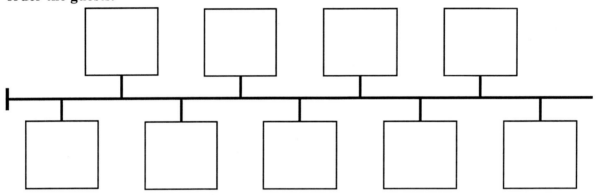

SHIFTS IN VERB TENSE

As you can see with these different tenses, verbs can be used in many different ways. They show sequences of events, and they show the time events happened.

In writing, verb tense should not change without a reason. When it does, that's called a **shift in verb tense**. This can confuse the reader. Read this example.

> **Incorrect Example:** Shawna plays softball after school. She is a good hitter and ran fast. Sometimes she even hits home runs. All her teammates had thought she is a great player.

See how confusing that is? There are several verb tenses used. The entire paragraph should be written in present tense. Sentences 1 and 3 are in present tense. But the tenses are mixed up on sentences 2 and 4. Try substituting the present tense of *ran* and *had thought* instead.

> **Corrected Example:** Shawna plays softball after school. She is a good hitter and runs fast. Sometimes she even hits home runs. All her teammates think she is a great player.

See how the sentences make more sense now? That's much easier to understand!

Practice 3: Shifts in Verb Tense

L 1.d (DOK 2)

The following sentences have verb tense errors. Rewrite the sentences, correcting the verb tense errors.

1   Andy has seen five fireflies before he caught one in a jar.

   _____

2   Shirley signed up to be hall monitor before she knows what the duties are.

   _____

3   After we finished dinner, Dad will say we can go ice skating.

   _____

4   At all her recitals, Martha danced beautifully and sings at least one solo.

   _____

5   By next year, the animal shelter will have rescued dozens of dogs and finding them new homes.

   _____

6   Scott and Jean grow their own tomatoes and had sold them at the farmers' market.

   _____

7   My cousin, Xavier, went to Peru this summer and sends everyone postcards.

   _____

8   Because I freeze the turkey last night, I had to thaw it this morning.

   _____

PREPOSITIONS

A **preposition** is a word used to link a noun, pronoun, or phrase to other words in a sentence. It shows the relationship between ideas. Prepositions tell directions (*on, in, under, around*). Some help show time (*after, until, while*). Others show contrast (*although*). There are many prepositions. Learn to use the right one to say what you mean. Here are some examples.

   Examples: My cousin likes to see the flamingos <u>at</u> the zoo.
   Her father made her study <u>for</u> her math test.

There are dozens of prepositions. Here's a list of the most common ones.

about	behind	except	on	to
above	below	for	onto	toward
across	beneath	from	out	under
after	beside	in	outside	underneath
against	between	inside	over	until
along	beyond	into	past	up
among	by	like	since	upon
around	despite	near	through	with
at	down	of	throughout	within
before	during	off	till	without

Objects of the preposition are the nouns after prepositions. The preposition and its object make up a prepositional phrase.

> **Example:** The driver pulled the car <u>into</u> the **garage**. (*Into* is the preposition. *Garage* is the object.)

Use prepositional phrases to add description and interest to a sentence.

> **Example:** The boy <u>with the brown hair and freckles</u> is <u>in my class</u> this year.

CONJUNCTIONS

A **conjunction** joins together similar words or phrases. **Coordinating conjunctions** connect related words, phrases, or clauses. You use this type of conjunction when linking two complete sentences together. The most common coordinating conjunctions are *for, and, nor, but, or, yet,* and *so*. Some people remember these by thinking of the initials *FANBOYS*.

For
And
Nor
But
Or
Yet
So

> **Examples:** We have grapes, apples, <u>and</u> bananas.
> Jordan runs, <u>but</u> Angelica swims.

Correlative conjunctions are pairs of conjunctions that work together to connect sentence parts. Some of these pairs include *either ... or, if ... then, both...and,* and *neither ... nor*.

> **Examples:** <u>Either</u> you clean your room, <u>or</u> you cannot go to the movies.
> <u>Neither</u> the boys <u>nor</u> the girls wanted to partner up for the dance.

Be careful with agreement when using correlative conjunctions. If you connect two subjects with a correlative conjunction, the second one must agree with the verb that follows.

Example: Every morning <u>either</u> her **cats** <u>or</u> the alarm **clock** *wakes* Julie up. (The word *clock* is singular, so it needs a singular verb.)

If the subjects had been switched, it would have looked like this:

Example: Every morning <u>either</u> the alarm **clock** <u>or</u> her **cats** *wake* Julie up.

INTERJECTIONS

An **interjection** is a word or phrase that expresses strong feeling or surprise. It adds extra emotion to a sentence. Most of the time, interjections have an exclamation point. They also can be set off by commas when the emotion is not as strong.

Examples: <u>Hey</u>! Bring back that bike!
<u>Gee</u>, I guess I won't be playing outside today.

Here is a list of some common interjections.

Ah	Gee	Oh	Well
Aha	Golly	Oops	Whew
Argh	Ha	Ouch	Woo-hoo
Bah	Hey	Psst	Wow
Eek	Hooray	Ugh	Yay
Eh	Huh	Uh-huh	Yikes

Practice 4: Interjections

L 1.a (DOK 2)

A mother and her child are texting each other about their missing cat. Fill in the appropriate interjections, exclamation points, and other words where they are needed.

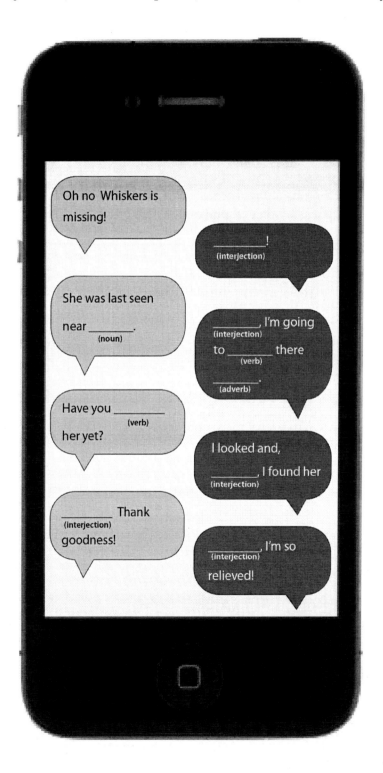

9.2 SENTENCE STRUCTURE

A **sentence** is a group of words. These words work together to tell a complete thought.

Here are things to know about sentences:

- A complete sentence must have a subject and a verb.
- A sentence is also called an independent clause.
- An independent clause can stand alone.
- A dependent clause is a group of words that cannot stand alone as a complete thought.

When you are writing, you will want to vary the lengths of the sentences you use. There are many ways to vary your sentences.

COMBINING SENTENCES

Simple sentences can be joined to make a compound sentence. A compound sentence is made up of two or more independent clauses. **Combining sentences** often aids in the meaning of the sentences as well as adding interest and style to writing.

For example, read these two sentences.

> **Example:** TV commercials are broadcast daily. TV commercials influence watchers to buy new products.

These two sentences are fine written the way they are. However, they share the same subject. Look at the sentences now when they are reduced to one sentence.

> **Example:** TV commercials, which are broadcast daily, can influence watchers to buy new products.

Here are some other ways to combine sentences.

In compound sentences, use a **comma and coordinating conjunction** (*for, and, nor, but, or, yet, so*) between clauses.

> **Example:** Bobby likes to play baseball, <u>and</u> he enjoys being in the school anime club.

Notice that this sentence has two clauses. This is called a **compound sentence**. Each clause could stand alone.

> **Independent clause 1:** Bobby likes to play baseball.
>
> **Independent clause 2:** He enjoys being in the school anime club.

The comma plus the conjunction *and* join the clauses together. Be sure to use the right conjunction that makes sense with the two clauses being joined.

A **semicolon** can be used with two independent clauses that are not joined by a conjunction. Semicolons can replace a period to join a pair of sentences that are closely connected.

> **Example:** Gray bats live in Tennessee; they are currently endangered.

Sometimes, when you have two sentences that you want to join, you can use an **introductory phrase** or **dependent clause**. Look at these two simple sentences.

Example: He read a magazine. He read it at the end of the day.

This is a repetitive way to tell what happened. Look how these ideas can be combined using one sentence as a dependent clause instead. Notice that the introductory phrase or clause must have a comma after it.

A **complex sentence** is a sentence with an independent clause and a dependent clause.

Example: At the end of the day, he read a magazine.

You can also use compound-complex sentences to vary your style. A **compound-complex sentence** has multiple independent clauses and at least one dependent clause.

Example: The messy dog lived in the backyard, but the cat, who didn't make messes, lived inside the house. (*The messy dog lived in the backyard* is an independent clause. So is *The cat lived inside the house*. Combining the two requires a comma and a *but*. Adding the dependent clause *who didn't make messes*, which describes *cat*, requires another pair of commas.)

SENTENCE FRAGMENTS AND RUN-ONS

When you write, you want to be sure to use sentences correctly. Two common sentence errors are **fragments** and **run-ons**. Let's look at fragments first.

A **fragment** is a group of words that is punctuated like a sentence but is really not a sentence. It might lack a subject, predicate, or both. Look at some examples.

Examples: Mailed a package. (Who mailed a package? The subject is missing.)
Debbie's dress. (This could be a subject, but what is the predicate? What about her dress?)
During social studies class. (What is the subject? What is the predicate?)

To fix a fragment, simply add whatever part of the sentence is missing.

Correct Examples: Melanie mailed a package. (added a subject)
Debbie's dress has a leopard print. (added a predicate)
We had a fire drill during social studies class. (added a subject and predicate)

A **run-on** occurs when a writer joins two or more complete sentences using improper punctuation or no conjunction.

Incorrect: Yoko visited her grandmother they worked on their scrapbook.

There are two complete sentences here. There are three ways to correct this error.

1. Turn the run-on into two separate sentences. A period must follow each sentence.

Correct: Yoko visited her grandmother. They worked on their scrapbook.

2. Another solution is to use a semicolon between the two sentences.

Correct: Yoko visited her grandmother; they worked on their scrapbook.

3. Another way to join the sentences is to use a comma and a conjunction.

Correct: Yoko visited her grandmother, and they worked on their scrapbook.

Page 162

Keep in mind that you can use either a semicolon OR a comma and conjunction. Never use a conjunction with a semicolon.

Incorrect: Kim wrote the answer on the board; and the teacher said she did well.

Correct: Kim wrote the answer on the board; the teacher said she did well.

Practice 5: Sentence Fragments and Run-ons

L 1 (DOK 1)

Identify whether each sentence is a complete sentence, a fragment, or a run-on.

	Complete sentence	Fragment	Run-on
1. Practicing for her piano recital.			
2. I'm excited about the field trip next week.			
3. When you finish setting the table.			
4. Jono loves spaghetti he begged his mom to make it.			
5. Wipe your shoes, you're tracking mud through the house.			
6. Carol Anne won a blue ribbon at the swim meet.			
7. Because Stephen was the first to finish the quiz.			

Practice 6: Sentence Structure

L 3.a (DOK 2–3)

Read the text. It contains mistakes. Then, answer the following questions.

The Dust Bowl

Environmental factors tend to affect the economy. Years ago, World War I had created high demand for farm products. Farmers plowed and farmers planted large amounts of crops to meet this demand. They made profits. But the farmers were in a hurry to farm the land. The farmers often damaged the soil.

The fact that farmers had often used poor farming techniques. Which left much of the soil of the Midwest lacking nutrients. By the mid-1920s, demand for farm products dropped. This caused farm prices to drop too. This hurt farmers.

In the early 1930s, dry weather, strong winds, and poor soil combined to create the Dust Bowl. This was a period in which strong storms would blow tons of dirt and dust into the air, they created gigantic dust clouds. Dust covered farms. Dust covered houses. Dust even covered entire towns.

Many farmers lost everything. Falling prices and the Dust Bowl were the cause of this loss. Parts of the Midwest became uninhabitable. People had to leave in search of work.

1 Read this sentence.

Farmers plowed and farmers planted large amounts of crops to meet this demand.

What is the **best** way to rewrite this sentence?

A) Farmers plowed and planted large amounts of crops to meet this demand.

B) Farmers plowed and they planted large amounts of crops to meet this demand.

C) Farmers plowed and planted large amounts of crops to meet the farmers' demand.

D) Farmers plowed and farmers planted large amounts of crops to meet the farmers' demand.

2 Read these sentences.

But the farmers were in a hurry to farm the land. The farmers often damaged the soil.

What is the **best** way to combine these sentences?

A) But the farmers were in hurry to farm the land, so the farmers often damaged the soil.

B) But in the farmers' hurry to farm the land; the farmers often damaged the soil.

C) But in their hurry to farm the land, farmers often damaged the soil.

D) But the farmers hurried to farm the land; farmers often damaged the soil.

3 Read this paragraph and the directions that follow.

The fact that farmers had often used poor farming techniques. Which left much of the soil of the Midwest lacking nutrients. By the mid-1920s, demand for farm products dropped. This caused farm prices to drop, too. This hurt farmers.

The paragraph contains sentence fragments. Rewrite the paragraph, correcting the sentence fragments.

_____

_____

_____

4 Read these sentences.

This caused farm prices to drop too. This hurt farmers.

What is the **best** way to combine these sentences?

A) This caused farm prices to drop, too, so that hurt farmers as well.

B) This caused farm prices to drop, this too hurt farmers.

C) This caused farm prices to drop, too; and this hurt farmers.

D) This caused farm prices to drop, too, which hurt farmers.

5   Read this paragraph.

> In the early 1930s, dry weather, strong winds, and poor soil combined to create the Dust Bowl. This was a period in which strong storms would blow tons of dirt and dust into the air, they created gigantic dust clouds. Dust covered farms. Dust covered houses. Dust even covered entire towns.

One sentence in the paragraph is a run-on. Rewrite the sentence, correcting the run-on.

_____

_____

_____

6   Read these sentences.

> Dust covered farms. Dust covered houses. Dust even covered entire towns.

What is the **best** way to combine these sentences?

_____

_____

_____

7   Read the last paragraph.

> **[1]** Many farmers lost everything. **[2]** Falling prices and the Dust Bowl were the cause of this loss. **[3]** Parts of the Midwest became uninhabitable. **[4]** People had to leave in search of work.

How would the paragraph be improved if the author combined sentences 1 and 2 and sentences 3 and 4?

_____

_____

_____

9.3 CONVENTIONS

There are some important rules about using language. They help readers to understand text. When you write, you need to keep them in mind. When you use them well, people will know exactly what you mean.

Conventions are rules in language. These rules include knowing which words to capitalize. Conventions also include how to use punctuation marks. Let's look at some of these rules.

PUNCTUATION

Punctuation includes periods, commas, and other marks that help you know how to read a sentence.

COMMAS

Commas are punctuation marks used within a sentence. They can separate ideas or parts of a sentence. There are many ways to use commas in your writing. Here are some common ways to use them.

When a month and day are used with a year, a comma separates the day from the year. If the sentence continues after the date, another comma also follows at the end of the date.

> **Examples:** May 17, 2010
> On May 17, 2010, we bought a new house.

Use a comma to separate a city and state. If the sentence continues after the state, use another comma after the state. This is also the way to punctuate a city and country.

> **Examples:** Honolulu, Hawaii
> We flew from Honolulu, Hawaii, to Nuremberg, Germany, in sixteen hours.

Use a comma between three or more items in a series.

> **Example:** Aaron, Julian, and Greg play basketball together.

Use a comma in a direct address.

> **Example:** Lisa, please bring me the dishes from the table.

Use a comma after an introductory phrase or clause.

> **Example:** Knowing it would be dark soon, Corey hurried home from his friend's house.

Use commas before conjunctions (*for, and, nor, but, or, yet, so*) in compound sentences.

> **Example:** Amelia drew a picture, and Randall painted it for her.

Use a comma to set off the words *yes* and *no*.

> **Example:** Yes, I would love some pecan pie.

Use a comma to set off a tag question from the rest of the sentence.

> **Example:** You're not going to eat that, are you?

Use commas to punctuate dialogue. The comma comes before the opening or closing quotation mark.

> **Examples:** Denny asked, "Can someone please give me a ride to practice?"
> "Don't forget to pack your poncho," Mrs. Ferris said.

FORMATTING TITLES

Rule 1. **Titles of books, magazines, plays, movies, music albums, and television programs should be either italicized or underlined. If you are handwriting an essay, it will be easiest to underline titles. If you are typing a report on a computer, you should pick one or the other way to write titles and stick with it throughout the paper.**

Examples: Last Sunday, I read Norton Juster's *The Phantom Tollbooth* for class and then watched ancient reruns of *I Love Lucy*.
We went on a field trip to see the musical *You're a Good Man, Charlie Brown*.

Rule 2. **Use quotation marks to signify a short work of literature, poem, article, song, or a speech. Also, use single quotation marks (' ') when the title of a short work is inside a person's quotation.**

Examples: Elie Wiesel delivered his "The Perils of Indifference" speech in Washington, DC.
Samuel Clemens wrote a story called "The Celebrated Jumping Frog of Calaveras County."
"I just read the story 'To Build a Fire,'" Holly declared.

Practice 7: Formatting Titles

L 2.d (DOK 1–3)

Answer the following questions.

1   Which of the following sentences contains a title that should be italicized?

A) I love the song Little White Church.

B) I enjoy reading Newsweek magazine.

C) Bill is now the fifth grade class president.

D) Did you read that article What's Hurting American Education?

2   Which of the following sentences contains a title that should be in quotation marks?

A) Sports Illustrated has an awesome article this week on college football.

B) Have you finished reading the novel Uncle Tom's Cabin?

C) One of my favorite movies is the classic Blackbeard.

D) Rodeo Bullfrog is my favorite funny short story.

**Look at the following graphics. For each one, write a sentence including the title. Make
sure you format each title correctly.**

3

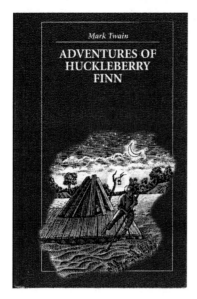

_____

_____

_____

_____

_____

4

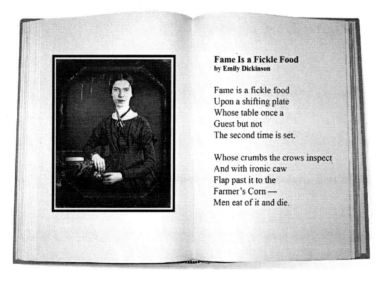

_____

_____

_____

5

I HAVE A DREAM.

_____

_____

_____

9.4 SPELLING

There are many spelling rules to remember. Let's start with some common spelling rules to follow when you add a suffix to a word.

ADDING SUFFIXES

A suffix is something added to the end of a word. When you add a suffix to a word, follow these spelling rules.

Rule 1. **If a suffix begins with a consonant, like _-ment, -ness, -less,_ or _-ful,_ keep the final _e_ of the root word.**

    Examples: agree → agreement

                care → careful

Rule 2. **If the word ends in _s, x, z, ch,_ or _sh,_ add _-es._**

    Examples: bus → buses

                fax → faxes

                mash → mashes

                beach → beaches

Rule 3. **When making nouns that end in _f_ or _fe_ plural, change the _f_ to _v_ and add _-es._**

    Examples: knife → knives

                elf → elves

Rule 4.   **With a word ending in *y*, change *y* to *i*, then add *-ed* or *-es*.**

>   **Examples:** carry → carried
>   tory → stories

Rule 5.   **If the base word has an *ie* ending, change *ie* to *y* before adding *-ing*.**

>   **Examples:** die → dying
>   tie → tying

CONSONANT DOUBLING

Consonant doubling is just what it says. When you add certain suffixes to words, you might have to add another consonant. Here is an easy way to know when to double a consonant. Ask yourself these three questions:

- Does the word have one syllable?
- Does the word have one vowel?
- Does the word have one consonant at the end?

If you answer "yes" to ALL of these questions, then double the consonant. If you answer "no" to any of them, do not double it. Look at these examples.

drop	ring
one syllable? YES	one syllable? YES
one vowel? YES	one vowel? YES
one consonant at end? YES	one consonant at end? NO
Change it!	Don't change it!
drop + ed = dropped	*ring + ing = ringing*

THE I BEFORE E RULE

You might already know the famous *i* before *e* rule. It goes like this: "Put *i* before *e*, except after *c*, or when sounded like *a* as in *neighbor* and *weigh*." It's a good rule most of the time. Take a look at these words.

>   **Examples:** s<u>ie</u>ge, rec<u>ei</u>pt, br<u>ie</u>f, dec<u>ei</u>ve, gr<u>ie</u>ve, bel<u>ie</u>ve, c<u>ei</u>ling

However, there are plenty of words that do not follow this rule, like *protein, scientist, society, heist, glacier,* and *ancient.* You will simply need to learn these words one by one. Some words are just weird. Hey, there's another one: *weird.*

Practice 8: Spelling

L 2.e (DOK 1–2)

Read the text. It contains mistakes. Then answer the questions.

The Legend of Lorelei

Winding its way through Germany, the Rhine River is one of the most important rivers of Europe and the world. No other river in the world has as many old and famous cities along its banks. Several industrial cities lie along the Rhine. It is a major transport route for all of Europe.

The middle section of the Rhine is often considered the most beautyful. Towering rock cliffs look over the river, and many anceint castles and fortresses are scattered along the high banks. Near Sankt Goarshausen (St. Goars) is a nearly vertical rock cliff rising over 430 feet above the water level. This is one of the most difficult points of the Rhine to navigate. The river is at its narrowest and deeppest here.

The rock cliff known as Lorelei overlooks it. The cliff is known as Lorelei because it is connected with one of the most famous legends of Germany. It is a tale of betrayal and revenge.

According to the legend, a beautiful young maiden named Lorelei jumped off the cliff into the river from that rocky point. As with so many legends, her despair was over her unfaithful beloveed, a boatman on the river.

It is said that since her death she sits atop the cliff combing her hair and singing songs to all men who pass by on the river. Just like the Sirens of Greek mithologgy, her singing is so enchantting that the men are cot up in the beauty of the song and in looking up to catch a glimps of Lorelei. Actually, this is Lorelei's revenge. She is blamed for all the boat accidents that happen their.

---

1 Read this sentence.

The middle <u>section</u> of the Rhine is <u>often</u> <u>considered</u> the most <u>beautyful</u>.

Which of the underlined words is **not** spelled correctly?

A) section   C) considered

B) often   D) beautyful

2 Read this sentence.

Towering rock cliffs look over the river, and many anceint castles and fortresses are scattered along the high banks.

This sentence contains a spelling error. Rewrite the sentence, correcting the **one** sentence error.

_____

_____

_____

3 Read this paragraph and the directions that follow.

> Near Sankt Goarshausen (St. Goars) is a nearly vertical rock cliff rising over 430 feet above the water level. This is one of the most difficult points of the Rhine to navigate. The river is at its narrowest and deeppest here.

One sentence contains a spelling error. Rewrite the sentence, correcting the spelling error.

_____

_____

_____

4 Read this sentence and the question that follows.

> As with so many legends, her despair was over her unfaithful beloveed, a boatman on the river.

What correction should be made to this sentence?

A) change *despair* to *despare*

B) change *unfaithful* to *unfaitheful*

C) change *beloveed* to *beloved*

D) correct as is

5 Read this sentence and the directions that follow.

> Just like the Sirens of Greek <u>mithologgy</u>, her singing is so <u>enchantting</u> that the men are <u>cot</u> up in the beauty of the song and in looking up to catch a <u>glimps</u> of Lorelei.

Rewrite this sentence spelling **all** the underlined words correctly. Use a dictionary if you need to.

_____

_____

_____

6 Read this sentence.

> She is blamed for all the boat accidents that happen <u>their</u>.

What is the **best** way to correct the underlined word?

A) there

B) they're

C) thier

D) correct as is

CHAPTER 9 SUMMARY

There are eight **parts of speech**.

A **noun** is a word that names a person, place, thing, or idea.

A **pronoun** is a word used in the place of one or more nouns.

An **adjective** is a word that describes or adds details to a noun or pronoun.

An **adverb** is a type of word that describes or adds details. It can modify a verb, an adjective, or another adverb.

Verbs are words that show what action happens, or they can show the state of being of a noun.

Verb tense shows when something happens.

The **perfect tense** helps you show when one event occurs before or during another event.

A **shift in verb tense** happens when a writer switches tenses abruptly. The shift can confuse readers unless it occurs for a reason.

A **preposition** is a word used to link a noun, pronoun, or phrase to other words in a sentence.

A **conjunction** joins together similar words or phrases.

Coordinating conjunctions connect related words, phrases, or clauses. Some people remember these by thinking of the initials *FANBOYS*.

Correlative conjunctions are pairs of conjunctions that work together to connect sentence parts.

An **interjection** is a word or phrase that expresses strong feeling or surprise.

Combining sentences often aids in the meaning of the sentences as well as adding interest and style to writing.

A **fragment** is a group of words that is punctuated like a sentence but is really not a sentence. It might lack a subject, predicate, or both.

A **run-on** occurs when a writer joins two or more complete sentences using improper punctuation or no conjunction.

Commas are punctuation marks used within a sentence. They can separate ideas or parts of a sentence.

Titles of books, magazines, plays, movies, and television programs should be either italicized or underlined.

Use quotation marks to signify a short work of literature, poem, article, or a speech.

There are spelling rules for **adding suffixes**, **consonant doubling**, and *i before e*.

For additional practice, please see Chapter 9 Test located in the Teacher Guide.

Chapter 10
Writing

This chapter covers DOK levels 1–3 and the following fifth grade strands and standards (for full standards, please see page x):

> **Writing 1, 2, 3, 4, 5, 6,** 7, 8, 9, **10**
>
> **Reading Literature 4**

In this chapter...

- You will produce effective writing for a range of purposes and audiences.

- You will use the writing process to improve your writing.

- You will use narrative strategies, including dialogue, details, and descriptions, to write narrative stories.

- You will use reasons and information to support your opinion in persuasive essays.

- You will examine a topic and convey ideas and information clearly in expository essays.

- You will plan the order of your writing assignments. You will include an introduction, support, and a conclusion in your writing.

- You will link opinion and reasons using words, phrases, and clauses (e.g., consequently, specifically). You will signal changes in time in narrative stories. You will link ideas in expository essays.

- You will include figurative language and avoid clichés in your writing.

You might think to yourself, "I don't like to write." But if you think about it, you write every day. You might fill out a form for a contest, send a thank-you card to your grandma, or make a list of your homework assignments. You might even write a funny story to cheer up a friend. In school, you will need to write in different ways for different purposes. Sometimes your writing will be short and informal, and sometimes you will have to write over several days to create a formal piece of writing. This chapter has some ideas to help you make your writing better.

10.1 The Writing Process

The **writing process** is a list of steps writers use to make their writing easier and better. Dividing the writing into several small steps makes writing less overwhelming. Here are the steps of the writing process.

The Writing Process	
Step	**What You Do**
Brainstorming	Come up with ideas and write them down.
Planning	Select a topic. Organize ideas.
Drafting	Write a first draft.
Revising	Make sure ideas are clear. Add precise words and details.
Editing	Fix any errors.
Publishing	Type your essay or report. Print it, or upload it onto a computer for others to read.

BRAINSTORMING

Brainstorming is like thinking on paper. Think of a topic, and then list everything about that subject that pops into your head. After you do that for a few minutes, look over your list and pick your best ideas. Here is a sample Tim made based on this prompt.

Your class is putting together a book of great foods to try. Your teacher has asked you to write about your favorite food or meal.

Before you write, think about what you love to eat. If you could only have one of these foods or meals, which would it be?

Write a multi-paragraph essay about your favorite thing to eat. Describe it so that others can tell why you like it.

Foods I Like

ice cream
apple pie
spaghetti
hot dogs
enchiladas
french fries
macaroni and cheese

After listing some different foods, Tim decided his absolute favorite is spaghetti. Now, Tim can use other tools to help him brainstorm more about his topic.

FREEWRITING

Freewriting is another way to write down ideas that you can use for an essay. When you freewrite, you simply start writing and see what happens. Don't worry about grammar and spelling. If you get stuck and don't know what to put next, write "I don't know what to write." Just keep writing, and let the ideas flow. Look at how freewriting helped Tim with his essay about spaghetti.

> I really like my mom's spaghetti with meatballs. She makes great sauce, the meatballs are just a little spicey, I put grated cheese on top too. it's best to put the cheese on when it's really hot so it melts a little. Spaghetti is one food you can kindof play with cause you twirl the noodles on your fork. It's fun to eat and dilicious!

USING GRAPHIC ORGANIZERS

It would be hard to write directly from a brainstorming list or freewriting notes. The ideas don't follow any logical order. You need to **focus your ideas** by grouping and organizing them. This is where **graphic organizers** can be helpful. There are many kinds of graphic organizers. Some are specific to certain types of essays.

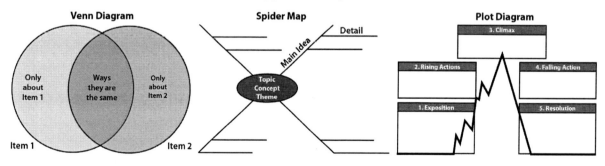

A **Venn diagram** shows similarities and differences of two items. It has two circles that overlap in the center. On the overlapping part of the circles, write the similarities that the two items share. In the other parts, write the differences. Similarly, you can also use the plot diagram you learned about in chapter 6 to help you focus your ideas when you write a story.

Mapping helps you think through main ideas and supporting details. The map in the center is a **spider map**. It shows a main topic or theme, and each of its "legs" is an idea or detail about that topic. Another common type of map is the **fishbone map**. It helps you see cause and effect relationships.

> **Example:** Jiri is writing about why he is a good soccer goalie. This fishbone mapping example is like something that Jiri might come up with.

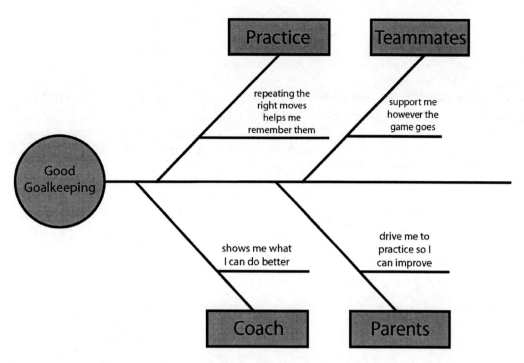

Another type of graphic organizer is a cluster map. In **clustering**, you write the main idea in the middle of a sheet of paper. Supporting ideas branch off the main idea. Finally, specific examples or details branch off the supporting ideas. Clustering shows you how the parts of your essay fit together. You can see if you have enough support for the main idea.

Remember Tim's prompt about what his favorite food is? This clustering example is like something that Tim might come up with:

Tim's Clustering for Essay about Spaghetti

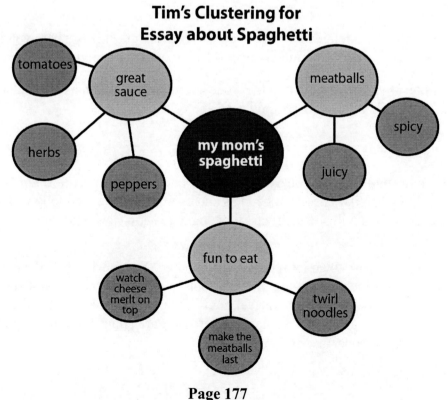

Practice 1: Brainstorming

W 4, 5 (DOK 2)

Make a brainstorming list using the prompt below. Then, use your own paper to make two graphic organizers to help you explore your ideas.

> Every year, *TIME* magazine chooses the most influential people in the world. Your teacher has asked you to write about the most influential person in your life.
>
> Before you write, think about a person who has had a great positive influence on you. How has knowing this person made you a better person?
>
> Write a multi-paragraph essay about the most influential person in your life. Describe him or her so others can tell why you chose this person.

Save your work. You will use it in other practices later in this chapter.

PLANNING

No matter what you write about, you will need to **organize your writing**. A well-organized piece of writing is an effective tool. You can organize your writing better if you know the important parts of a written response. Let's walk through an example here. This will show you the main parts that all your writing for school should have.

INTRODUCTION

In the **introduction**, you tell readers what your essay is about. This is where you introduce characters in a story, give your opinion on an issue, or begin to explain a topic.

> **Example:** If you are ever lost in the woods, knowing how to make a shelter, find water, build a fire, and get food can save your life.

SUPPORT

Now you need to **support** what you said in the introduction. You must **develop your topic**. This means adding details. These can be facts and examples or steps to follow. If you're writing a narrative, you will add conflicts or dialogue to show how your character responds to a situation.

> **Example:** It is wise to go into the woods prepared. You must expect the unexpected. This includes having the right tools and skills to take care of yourself. Always take basic survival items into the woods with you. Also, hikers should always tell someone where they are going and how long they expect to be gone.

CONCLUSION

The **conclusion** is the last thing your reader sees. It is your last chance to make your point. Wrap up your ideas by reminding the reader of your main idea. Or if you are writing to give an opinion, leave your reader with a final thought or question. If you're writing a narrative story, this is where your ending would go.

Example: Being prepared helps you stay safe.

PLANNING AN ORDER

As you know, there are several ways to organize your ideas. These are called **organizational structures**. There are different ways to place your supporting points in order. They include chronological order, comparison and/or contrast, and order of importance. Organizing your ideas is the first step to developing a coherent essay. For his essay about spaghetti, Tim decided to use order of importance. So he will first write about what he likes most about his mom's spaghetti, then what he likes second best, and so on (You can read more about organizational patterns in chapter 3.).

OUTLINING AN ESSAY

Once you have an idea of the order you would like to use, you might use **outlining** to organize your ideas. Outlining is a way to plan your essay by writing the **main ideas** and **supporting details** you plan to discuss. Outlines usually look something like this.

I. Introduction

II. Support

    a. Main idea

        i. Supporting detail

        ii. Supporting detail

        iii. Supporting detail

    b. Main idea

        i. Supporting detail

        ii. Supporting detail

        iii. Supporting detail

    c. Main idea

        i. Supporting detail

        ii. Supporting detail

        iii. Supporting detail

III. Conclusion

After outlining your essay, you have most of the ingredients you need to begin writing a first draft.

STORY ORGANIZATION

A **plot diagram** is good to use when you are organizing a narrative story. A sample of this is shown below. This graphic organizer looks like a mountain. Each part of a story has its own place in the graphic. At the left side of the mountain is the **exposition**, or introduction, of the story. During the exposition, you must introduce the characters and the main conflict in the story. Continuing up the mountain, you build up the conflict through the **rising action**. Next is the **climax**, the highest part of the mountain. This is also the most exciting part of the story. Here, the conflict is addressed head on. Then, the story's **falling action** and **resolution** go on the other side. In the falling action, you write about the consequences of the climax. In the resolution, you tie up loose ends so that your reader's questions are answered. These parts of a narrative provide your story with a clear beginning, middle, and end.

Plot Diagram

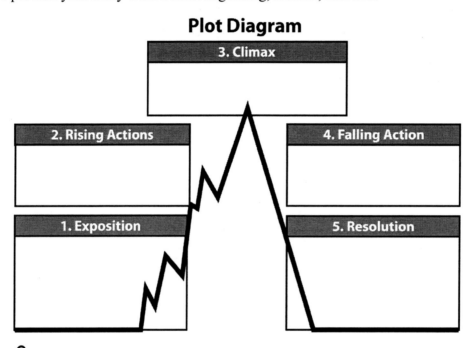

PROVIDING CLOSURE

When you reach the end of your essay or story, you should be sure to provide your reader with **closure**. Closure is the feeling that something is complete, or closed. In writing, this means all the reader's questions are answered and loose ends are tied up. One way to provide closure to your reader is to tie your conclusion back to your introduction in some way. For example, if you introduced your essay with a question, you might end with a possible answer. If you began your story with an image of a garden, you might end your story in the same garden.

Practice 2: Story Organization

W 3, 5, 10 (DOK 2)

Think of the last time you had a disagreement with a parent, sibling, or friend. Complete the plot diagram below as if you were planning to write a narrative about the disagreement.

Exposition Who was involved in the disagreement? What was the disagreement about?

Rising Action What happened leading up to the disagreement?

Climax Describe the actual disagreement.

Falling Action What happened after the disagreement?

Resolution How was the problem solved?

WRITING A DRAFT

Once you have finished brainstorming and planning, it's time to get your ideas on paper. **Write a draft** using the ideas you came up with when you were planning your essay. Refer back to your outline, cluster map, or other planning methods you used. Flesh out your ideas by going into greater depth. In your draft, you should not worry about spelling or punctuation. You will fix these small errors later. For now, you should focus on expanding your ideas. Do write in complete sentences. If some sentences are not correct, that's all right.

Make sure to include a **topic sentence** for each paragraph. Topic sentences are clear statements of the main ideas of your essay. They help your reader follow your ideas. Fill out each paragraph with supporting details. If you made an outline, use it to help you write your supporting details in sentence form.

Practice 3: Writing a Draft

W 4, 5, 10 (DOK 2)

Take the brainstorming list or graphic organizer you created in Practice 1 on page 178. Use the graphic organizer below to help you fill out your ideas into sentence form.

Main Topic: _____

Subtopic 1 topic sentence: _____

Supporting sentence 1: _____

Supporting sentence 2: _____

Supporting sentence 3: _____

Closing sentence: _____

Subtopic 2 topic sentence: _____

Supporting sentence 1: _____

Supporting sentence 2: _____

Supporting sentence 3: _____

Closing sentence: _____

Subtopic 3 topic sentence: _____

Supporting sentence 1: _____

Supporting sentence 2: _____

Supporting sentence 3: _____

Closing sentence: _____

Save your work. You will use it again for other practices in this chapter.

REVISING FOR CLEAR WRITING

Revising means improving your writing. In this step, you read your own work and look for ways to make it better. You can ask yourself these questions as you read your essay:

Writing Checklist Questions

☐ Did I respond to the prompt?

☐ Is my main idea clear?

☐ Do my details all support the main idea?

☐ Did I make the best word choices?

☐ Are my points all in a logical order?

☐ Are all my sentences complete?

☐ Are there any errors in usage, grammar, punctuation, and spelling?

USE PRECISE WORDS

As you write, read it back to yourself. Can your readers tell what you mean? Can they picture what you describe? One way to help people picture what you are saying is to use **precise words**. These are words that describe clearly. Avoid vague words like *good*, *bad*, *great*, *awesome*, *stuff*, and *thing*.

Think back to the topic of your favorite food. Here is the first draft of Tim's paper. Look at the underlined parts. Do you see how they might make his writing seem a bit dull?

Now look at Tim's revised draft. He uses more precise words, which helps make his writing more clear.

> My favorite meal is my mom's spaghetti. <u>I love it</u>. It tastes <u>yummy</u>. It is fun to eat.
>
> The best part is the homemade sauce. Mom uses canned tomatoes and paste, but she also cuts up fresh tomatoes. <u>Fresh herbs too</u>. She adds <u>cut up peppers</u>.
>
> The <u>next best thing</u> is the meatballs. There a little spicy but not too hot. They are always <u>cooked just right</u> and stay juicy. They are never dry or hard.
>
> The <u>last best thing</u> is that spaghetti is fun to eat. I like to put the grated chees on top to melt while its hot and twirl the noodles on my fork. The chalenge is <u>getting the meatballs to last</u>.
>
> <u>This is why</u> my mom's spaghetti is my favorite meal. Whenever she makes it, I give her a big hug. I'm so glad my mom is <u>a great cook</u>.

Tim's Revised Draft

> My favorite meal is my mom's spaghetti. <u>She makes it from scratch,</u> and I love it. It tastes <u>mouth-wateringly dilicious</u> and is fun to eat.
>
> The best part is the homemade sauce. Mom use canned tomatoes and paste, but she also cuts up fresh tomatoes. Fresh herbs too<u>, like oregano and basil</u>. She adds peppers <u>cut into little cubes</u>.
>
> <u>Also scrumptious are</u> the meatballs. There a little spicy but not too hot. They are <u>always cooked to perfection</u> and stay juicy. They are never dry or hard.
>
> The <u>final reason I love spaghetti</u> is that it's fun to eat. I like to put the grated chees on top to melt while its hot and twirl the noodles on my fork. The chalenge is getting the meatballs to last<u>, so I cut them up and have a piece of meatball with each fork of noodles.</u>
>
> <u>The flavor and fun of my mom's spaghetti make it</u> my favorite meal. Whenever she makes it I give her a big hug. I'm so glad my mom is <u>such a wonderful cook</u>.

USING TRANSITIONS

Be sure to add **transitions** as you revise your draft. Transitions are words that show the relationship between your ideas. Transitions may show similarity, difference, cause and effect, time order, or other relationships. These words also help your reader follow your ideas. Read this paragraph from a student's essay about her morning routine.

> I get out of bed. I go to the bathroom to get ready. I comb my hair. I brush my teeth. I change clothes. I go downstairs to breakfast. My dad makes waffles. I eat breakfast with my two brothers. I am always the last one finished eating. My brothers eat too fast. We gather up our homework from the night before. We dash out to the bus stop just in time to catch the bus.

Can you see how the ideas in this paragraph seem disconnected? This is because the student used no transitions. Now read this paragraph with transitions added.

> <u>After</u> I get out of bed, I go to the bathroom to get ready. <u>First,</u> I comb my hair, <u>and then</u> I brush my teeth. I change clothes <u>before</u> I go downstairs to breakfast. My dad makes waffles, <u>so</u> I eat breakfast with my two brothers. I am always the last one finished eating <u>because</u> my brothers eat too fast. We gather up our homework from the night before. <u>Finally,</u> we dash out to the bus stop just in time to catch the bus.

Do you see how the transitions make the student's ideas clearer?

INCLUDE RELEVANT DETAILS

In addition to colorful words, there are other **details** you can include. They can make your writing more interesting. When you **conduct research**, you will get more facts to use to support your points. Supporting sentences tell details about your point. Supporting sentences contain examples, facts, and stories. They give your reader more information.

Concrete details are facts, like "Trees use light to create energy." These facts, along with your **reasons and evidence**, give proof that what you are saying is right. If you are writing a story, use **descriptions** to give depth to your characters and settings. These descriptions help you grab your reader's interest so that he or she will want to read what you wrote. **Sensory details** are descriptions that appeal to your senses, like "The golden light shimmers on the fluttering green leaves." Sensory details are similar to **imagery**, which you read about in chapters 5 and 7. Use imagery and sensory details to paint pictures in your reader's mind.

Make sure the facts and details you include in your writing are **relevant**. *Relevant* means that the information matters to your topic and isn't out of place. Every detail you add should support your topic. If it does not give support, take it out.

CLICHÉS AND FIGURATIVE LANGUAGE

When you revise your draft, be certain to **avoid clichés**. Clichés are expressions that are worn out or dull because they have been used so much.

> **Example:** Davey is sad that his friend moved away, but <u>time heals all wounds</u>.

Do you see how this expression seems overused and boring? You can replace the clichés in your writing by adding your own **figurative language**.

You might recall from chapter 5 that figurative language is a colorful way to use words. You can use **similes**, which are comparisons using *like* or *as*.

> **Example:** Davey is sad that his friend moved away, but <u>a sad heart is like a wound that heals</u>.

A similar type of figurative language is the **metaphor**. These comparisons do not use *like* or *as*.

> **Example:** Davey is sad that his friend moved away, but <u>a sad heart is a wound that heals</u>.

Do you see how the metaphor does not say the sad heart is *like* a wound that heals? Instead, it says the sad heart *is* a wound that heals.

You might even add **personification** to your writing. Personification describes an object or idea as if it were a person.

   Example: Davey is sad that his friend moved away, but in time, his <u>sadness will flee</u>.

Each revision uses new and vivid language instead of old clichés. Using figurative language rather than clichés improves your writing.

Practice 4: Details and Figurative Language

W 2, 3 (DOK 3)

The image below is a picture of the Sistine Chapel ceiling, painted by the Renaissance artist Michelangelo. In order to paint the Sistine Chapel, Michelangelo had to lie on his back and paint upside down.

With your teacher's permission, tape a sheet of paper to the bottom of your desk. Lie under your desk and imagine you are Michelangelo. Write a short descriptive essay about how difficult it was to paint the Sistine Chapel ceiling. Use concrete details, sensory details, and figurative language in your essay.

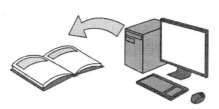

Research Connection

Research a modern-day artist of your choice. Compare his or her work to Michelangelo's work in the Sistine Chapel. Then, write one or more paragraphs about how art today is different from Renaissance art.

ADD DIALOGUE

An important part of revising stories or narrative essays is adding engaging **dialogue**, or conversations between the characters. Dialogue helps move your story along. It can help you break up descriptions of events, too. But your dialogue needs to be exciting. Many parts of the conversations we have every day are too boring to read about. For example, look at this comic strip.

Do you see how this dialogue is not very engaging? As a reader, you probably don't get much out of this dialogue. It doesn't keep your attention. Now, look at this comic strip.

See how the second comic strip uses attention-grabbing dialogue? You can tell the speaker's feelings from the words. The words also show what is happening in the story.

Practice 5: Dialogue

W 3 (DOK 2)

A) **Write a paragraph explaining why the dialogue in the second comic strip is more interesting than the first.**

B) **Read this excerpt from "Goldilocks and the Three Bears." Then, use the story board below to practice writing dialogue. Don't just use the dialogue from the original story—be creative!**

The three bears at last returned from their walk. They found their door open, their porridge tasted, and their chairs disturbed. Poor Baby bear found his chair broken into pieces. Father bear saw his bed had been slept in. Mother bear saw her bed had been slept in. Poor Baby bear saw that his bed had been slept in, and the culprit was still there!

Goldilocks heard the commotion of the returning bears and woke up with a shriek. She bolted out of the bears' house and back through the forest, never to bother the three bears again.

EDITING

When you **edit** your writing, you find and fix small errors. This includes looking for and fixing errors in areas like these:

• spelling	• agreement	forms
• punctuation	• verb tenses	• conjunctions
• capitalization	• noun and pronoun	• prepositions

Because some of these errors are small, you might miss them. But small mistakes matter. Look over your writing closely when you edit. Look back at chapter 9 for more review of these topics. Did you notice the errors in Tim's essay?

Here they are, underlined for you to see.

My favorite meal is my mom's spaghetti. She makes it from scratch, and I love it. It tastes mouth-wateringly <u>dilicious</u> and is fun to eat.

The best part is the homemade sauce. Mom uses canned tomatoes and paste, but she also cuts up fresh tomatoes. <u>Fresh herbs too, like oregano and basil.</u> She adds peppers cut into little cubes.

Also scrumptious are the meatballs. <u>There</u> a <u>litle</u> spicy but not too hot. They are always cooked to perfection and stay juicy. They are never dry or hard.

The final reason I love spaghetti is that it's fun to eat. I like to put the grated <u>chees</u> on top to melt while its hot and twirl the noodles on my fork. The <u>chalenge</u> is getting the meatballs to last, so I cut them up and have a piece of meatball with each fork of noodles.

The flavor and fun of my mom's spaghetti make it my favorite meal. <u>Whenever she makes it</u> I give her a big hug. I'm so glad my mom is such a wonderful cook.

Now, let's look at some errors that Tim found to correct.

Spelling: There are several spelling errors that Tim needs to fix. They include *dilicious* in the first paragraph and *litle* in the third paragraph. The third paragraph uses the wrong homonym (*there*) when Tim really meant the contraction for *they are* (*they're*). In the fourth paragraph, the second sentence has the wrong form of *its/it's*, and *chees* and *chalenge* <u>are both</u> misspelled.

Sentence structure: The second paragraph has a fragment. The fragment needs a subject and verb: "She puts in fresh herbs, too, like oregano and basil."

Punctuation: In the last paragraph, there is a comma missing after the introductory phrase in the second sentence, "Whenever she makes it."

Practice 6: Revising and Editing

W 2, 3, 5, 10 (DOK 3)

Go back to the essays you have worked on throughout this chapter. Revise and edit them to make sure they are clear and free of errors. Use the checklist in this chapter to help you.

PEER EDITING

Because many errors are small, it may be difficult to catch them all by yourself. You should use **peer editing** to help you catch the tricky errors. Peer editing means having a friend or classmate edit your work. It is much easier to find other people's errors than it is to find your own. When you trade papers with a friend and edit each other's work, you both find more errors than you would find alone. Both of you end up with much better writing.

When you use peer editing, it can be helpful to use a checklist like this one. First, edit your own work and mark your progress in the "Writer's Check" column. Then, trade papers with a classmate and fill in the "Peer Editor's Check" column.

Did you make sure...	Writer's Check	Peer Editor's Check
Each sentence forms a complete thought?		
Each sentence contains a noun and a verb?		
There are no sentence fragments?		
There are no run-on sentences?		
Each sentence begins with a capital letter?		
Each sentence uses correct punctuation (commas, periods, question marks, exclamation points, and so on)?		
All dialogue has quotation marks in the right places?		
All words are spelled correctly?		

PUBLISHING

When you are done working on it, you can **publish your writing**. This means you share the final version of your essay with others. Always do a final review of your work when you are ready to publish. Check for neatness if you are writing by hand. You can type your essay on the computer. Then, you can print copies of it to give to your teacher or to other students. You can also put a version of your finished essay online. If your class has a website, there may be a webpage to see student essays.

Publishing your work helps you share it with others. Then, if you like, you can ask for outside help. Or you can work with a group to create new stories and improve each other's writing.

Activity

W 6 (DOK 2)

Have you finished writing your essays? Now it's time to publish them!

A. Take one of your essays, and make a small book out of it. There are different ways you can do this. You can print your essay on paper and then bind it together with staples. You also can punch holes on the left side of the pages and run yarn through the holes. You might make a book out of construction paper and then write your story in it. Or you can glue the printed pages inside. Add some pictures to help tell the story. Show the things you want your readers to picture in their minds as they read your words.

B. Take another essay, and publish it to a webpage. Ask your teacher or tutor for help.

10.2 TYPES OF WRITING

Before you start to write, ask yourself why you are writing. What is your purpose? All writing has a **purpose**, or reason. It might be to convince someone to do something you want or agree with your ideas. It could be to teach someone something new. It could be just to make someone smile.

PERSUASIVE WRITING

You might need to write about what you think. For example, the teacher could ask you to pick which character you relate to the most in a story. This means you have to give your opinion. You need to explain your point of view. When you do this, you are doing **persuasive writing**.

But you can't just give an opinion only. You want people to agree with your argument. So you have to give reasons for your opinion. You must support what you think. This means including facts and details from the story. The details you select for this should show that you are right.

EXPOSITORY WRITING

You might also need to write to inform or to explain. The purpose here is to teach your reader something. An example is a report you might write about the human heart for science class. Writing meant to inform or explain is also called **expository writing.**

When you get ready to write an expository essay, think about what you know. Use sources to learn more facts about your topic. Focus on telling your readers what you want them to know.

NARRATIVE WRITING

There are times when you will write to **tell a story**. When you write about a trip you went on or another experience you have had, you are telling a story. This type of writing is called **narrative writing**. When you write a narrative, your goal is to show your reader what happened. Think of details to include when you begin writing a narrative.

Practice 7: Types of Writing

W 1–3 (DOK 2)

Each of the paragraphs below is a different type of writing. Read each paragraph, and decide whether it is an example of persuasive, expository, or narrative writing. Write your answer in the blank provided.

The first fire departments in London were founded after the Great Fire of London. This fire consumed the city, destroying homes and buildings. The damage even extended to St. Paul's Cathedral, a large historic church. The fire lasted for three days. After the fire, insurance companies thought it would be wise to develop fire brigades. The fire brigades helped to put out fires before they reached the massive size of the Great Fire of London.

1   What type of writing is this text? _____

Today was a big day for Gordon County Fire Department. It's the dry season, so we came in this morning knowing that fires were likely. Our first call came from a homeowner whose brush pile caught fire. Fortunately, the brush pile was far from any buildings. Later, we were called to a restaurant where a grease fire had started in the fryer. The restaurant's fire extinguisher was empty, so the fire went out of control. With a good few squirts of the hose, we were able to put it out.

2   What type of writing is this text? _____

Our town needs a new fire truck. Our current fire truck is over twenty years old, so it is outdated. The current fire truck has a shorter hose, a shorter ladder, and less room for firefighters than current fire trucks on the market. The people of our town deserve a well-prepared fire department to protect them from dangerous fires. We must come together to help raise money for a new fire truck.

3   What type of writing is this text? _____

10.3 WRITING A PERSUASIVE ESSAY

When you write persuasively, you want others to agree with your opinion. You should assert your opinions, but you should not be aggressive. Sounding too aggressive, or mean, may keep your audience from listening to your ideas. You must present your ideas clearly. Order your ideas logically so that your audience can follow your thought process.

You have already read about how **transitional words and phrases** connect ideas. In a persuasive essay, transitions explain the relation between supporting details and your opinion. There are many transitions you can use. Look at the underlined words in the sentences below.

Example: I am most like Laura from *The Little House on the Prairie* because I am always playing outside. My mother calls me a tomboy. For example, I was walking to the bus stop the other day, and my brother wanted to race to the stop sign. I was in the lead, but I tripped on a rock, fell down, and skinned my knee. But I did not cry. Laura is active, <u>too</u>. She always climbs trees, rides horses, and goes sledding. <u>Because</u> we are both active, I am most like Laura from *The Little House on the Prairie.*

You can see how the transitional words can make your ideas more clear. The information flows from one thought to the next in a logical way. This helps convince your reader that you are right. Notice, too, that the paragraph ends with a concluding sentence. The concluding sentence restates the point and wraps up the paragraph.

10.4 WRITING AN EXPOSITORY ESSAY

Expository writing needs to have many facts, not opinions. Always remember to cite the sources of your facts as well (See chapter 11 for more information on citing sources.). Of course, you need to provide solid descriptions and details, too.

When you write expository essays, use transition words like *another*, *both*, and *in contrast* so readers can see how your facts link to each other. You might even use quotations from experts. In chapter 4, you learned about **domain-specific vocabulary** words. These are words that are specific to the subject you are writing about. Using domain-specific vocabulary shows your reader that you are knowledgeable about your topic. Use **precise words** to discuss and help your readers understand the topic.

You might also use **headings** to break up your essay into sections. This can make the essay easier to read. You might also use bullet points, graphics, or other types of formatting to help you organize your ideas.

10.5 WRITING A NARRATIVE

Narrative writing includes many details. It describes how things look, sound, smell, taste, and feel. A narrative story should have good description. When you describe, you use clear adjectives and vivid verbs. **Sensory details** help the reader to see, hear, smell, taste, and feel what is happening.

Tell the events in a logical order. Your reader needs to be able to follow along with the **sequence of events**. Explaining what happened out of order makes your story confusing. Be sure to introduce your characters and setting early in the story. Then, you can begin building conflict. Use transitions like *before*, *after*, and *meanwhile* to tell when things happen in your story.

Think about the **pacing** of your story. If you want to keep your readers in suspense, you would use short sentences to slow down the pace.

> **Examples:** The man crept slowly down the dark hallway.
> The violent storm dragged on for days.

If your story is more upbeat and fast-paced, you can combine actions in longer sentences to make the reader feel rushed.

Examples: She scrambled about the house, yelling for her daughters to wake up.

The boys enjoyed the carnival so much that four hours felt like ten minutes.

Once you have an order, you can write your story. Then, you can add details to make your story even more interesting. Try this for yourself. Make up an exciting character or an imaginary setting. Think about what descriptive words and details you could add to your story that will make it fun to read. Add some **dialogue** to your story. This can make your story more exciting as well. Show your characters' actions and describe their appearance. And remember that figurative language helps you say things in exciting, new ways (To read more about parts of a story, review chapter 6.).

CHAPTER 10 SUMMARY

The **writing process** uses steps to make writing easier. It includes **brainstorming, planning, drafting, revising, editing,** and **publishing**.

Brainstorming means coming up with ideas for your writing.

Freewriting is a form of brainstorming in which you write as much as you can about your topic.

Clustering is a way of organizing your ideas using a cluster map. **Outlining** helps you organize your ideas by writing out main ideas and supporting details.

Details make your writing more interesting. **Concrete details** are facts, and **sensory details** appeal to the senses. Sensory details are very much like **imagery**.

Similes are comparisons using *like* or *as*. **Metaphors** are comparisons without *like* or *as*. **Personification** describes an object or idea as if it were a person.

Dialogue refers to the words that characters say to one another.

Editing is looking for and fixing small errors like punctuation and spelling mistakes. **Peer editing** allows you to catch more errors than editing alone.

The **author's purpose** is the reason for writing a text. You may be asked to write to give an opinion, to inform or explain, or to tell a story.

Persuasive writing tells your opinions and gets others to agree with you.

Expository writing gives information about a topic.

Narrative writing is the term used for story writing. Narratives often use elements of **plot**. These include **exposition, rising action, climax, falling action,** and **resolution**.

For additional practice, please see Chapter 10 Test located in the Teacher Guide.

Chapter 11
Research

This chapter covers DOK levels 1–3 and the following fifth grade strands and standards, please see page x):

Reading Literature 1, 2
Reading Informational Text 1, 2
Writing 7, 8, 9, 10

In this chapter...

- You will demonstrate the ability to locate and evaluate relevant sources for a variety of research tasks.
- You will use multiple sources in order to research a topic and will synthesize information based on multiple sources.
- You will take proper notes during the research process and use time management skills to plan projects effectively.

One important reason to build your reading skills is so that you can conduct **research**.

Research might sound scary, but you already do it every day. If you want to order a pizza, you have to find out which restaurant delivers. You also need to see a menu and find out what kinds of pizza they make. Yes, that's research! If you want to buy a new video game, you have to see where it is sold. You also might search for the electronics store that has the best price. You just did more research! Let's take a look at some research skills you will need.

11.1 SELECTING AND USING SOURCES

Whether you're looking for sources online or off, it's good to know what kinds of sources to seek. The source you select depends on your purpose. You might be looking for information to use in your own life, like the examples given above. Or you might be doing a short **research project** for school and need to find the best information.

TYPES OF SOURCES

You should know how to make sense of various research sources. You can find a world of information in the many **print sources** available. These are resources you can hold in your hands and read. They include books and magazines. You can find many of them in the library.

Other sources are called nonprint resources. Some of these resources involve information you get from electronic sources. These include online databases and computer networks. Libraries have computers with their own databases. Nowadays, many print resources like books and magazines also have online versions called **digital sources**. But nonprint resources also include people you can interview and artifacts you can examine.

You can even use your own experiences as research. Everything you have read and done in your life gives you facts. Maybe you need to write a report on one of the fifty states. You can always choose to write about the state you live in, but perhaps you have visited another state on vacation or some other trip. You can use what you already learned about that state in your report!

Print Sources	
Source	**Description**
Almanacs	An **almanac** is a book of data and facts about a variety of topics, organized like an encyclopedia. An almanac is a good source to use if you want the basic history and statistics of a city, state, or country.
Artifacts	An **artifact** is a tool or object that tells something about a period of time. For example, an arrowhead is an artifact of early life on the North American continent. The pyramids are artifacts of times of the pharaohs in Egypt.
Atlases	An **atlas** is a book of maps. It also has other facts about countries or regions of the world.
Encyclopedias	**Encyclopedias** are reference books. They have articles on many subjects. There are entries for important people, places, historical events, and so on. Articles are arranged alphabetically. There are also encyclopedias about specific topics, like medicine and art.
Magazines	**Magazines** are periodicals containing articles and ads. This makes them a good place to get a variety of current information. A magazine usually focuses on a specific area of interest. There are magazines for entertainment, business, sports, and so on.
Newspapers	**Newspapers** contain news stories, articles about local and world events, and sections for special interests. News reports present facts, statistics, and quotes from people involved in stories. They also contain opinion-based writing, like editorials and reviews.

Digital Sources	
Databases	A **database** is an online collection of articles and journals on certain subjects. The authors of the articles have done vast amounts of research on the topics. Most articles in a database have been reviewed so you can know that they are factual and okay to use.
Electronic Card Catalogs	By using a **library catalog**, you can find good resources. A library catalog is an alphabetical listing of books and other materials in a library. Most catalogs are on library computer networks. Items are listed at least three ways in a catalog: once by author, once by title, and once by subject.
Technology/ Internet	Today, one of the most commonly used resources is the Internet. It includes **computer networks** and websites. Today, you can access many print sources online. You can even watch television shows online. The Internet is an invaluable tool. It is usually the first place people go to look for information. But you need to evaluate sources carefully. Keep in mind that anyone can place information onto the World Wide Web.

INTERNET SAFETY

Remember to be safe when you are searching the Internet for sources. Here are some guidelines to follow:

- Never give out personal information, like your name, address, phone number, or school name.

- Don't post a picture of yourself online without your parents' permission.

- If you come across content that is inappropriate or makes you feel uncomfortable, tell a parent or teacher.

Be aware that people on chat pages and message boards are not always who they say they are. Do not respond to people who ask you to share personal information.

WHICH IS THE BEST SOURCE?

Once you find your sources, you have to **pick the best sources** to use. Some will be better for your topic than others. You must make sure the sources you find have **relevant information** for your topic. If a source is relevant, that means it is appropriate to use.

The **purpose of your research** will also tell you what kinds of sources you need. Are you researching to learn more? An encyclopedia or an Internet site might be best. Are you trying to support an argument? A government website filled with statistics might help you. Opinion pieces might show you the different sides of the argument. Are you researching to write a report? Objective sources will be better than opinion sources.

As you review each source, ask yourself some questions:

- Who wrote this? Is the author an expert?

- Does it answer my questions?

- Does it give me interesting facts I can use?

- Do I understand it all?

- Can I verify this information in another source?

If you can answer *yes* to all of these questions, you likely have a good source!

Practice 1: Selecting and Using Sources

W 7, 8 (DOK 2, 3)

Read the text. Then, answer the questions that follow.

Koalas

The koala is a cute animal that looks like a teddy bear. But it is not really a bear. The koala is a marsupial. That means it has a pouch like a kangaroo. Marsupials are a large animal group whose young are born in an immature state. The koala mother carries the babies in her pouch until they grow. Like kangaroo babies, koala babies are called joeys.

Koalas are native to Australia. They live together in groups, just like people. The slow-moving koalas mainly stay up in the trees. This keeps them away from most predators and close to their food.

The Aborigines in Australia have known about the koala for thousands of years. But when Europeans arrived on the continent, it took eleven years for them to spot the first koala! This is because the animal's camouflage is so effective. January 1789 is the date of the first known record of a European seeing a koala. On an expedition to the Blue Mountains, explorer John Price wrote about seeing a sloth-like animal that the Aborigines called a *cullawine*. Some people suppose this Aborigine word was turned into the word *koala*.

Koalas are herbivores. That means they eat no meat, only plants. They feast on the leaves of the eucalyptus (YOO-kuh-LIP-tuhs) trees in which they live. An adult koala eats about a pound and a half of leaves every day. Then the koala spends five hours, mostly at night, chewing the leaves into a soft paste. The koala has a slow metabolism and spends most of the day sleeping.

Raising koala babies in captivity had once been considered impossible. But thanks to many years of research, koalas are now successfully bred in captivity. Koalas can live up to about eighteen years in captivity. No one really knows how long they live in the wild since they are so hard to observe.

---

1   Where most likely would a student find this information about koalas?

   A) on a map of Australia   C) in an encyclopedia

   B) in an almanac   D) in a newspaper

2   Say a student was to present facts about the koala in class. Which nonprint resource could **best** be used with this print source to help the audience understand koalas?

   A) an actual eucalyptus leaf from a nearby plant shop

   B) videos of koalas eating and climbing trees

   C) an audio of a person talking about visiting Australia

   D) pictures of the koala habitat at a nearby zoo

3 What would be the **best** way to find out more about Aborigines?

A) Find a book about Australia in the library.

B) Search for John Price's journal on the Internet.

C) Look at a map of the Australian continent.

D) Read an almanac published in the year 1789.

4 Look at the following web searches about koalas.

Google   koalas

Web   Images   Maps   Shopping   News   More ⌄   Search tools

About 4,160,000 results (0.26 seconds)

Exotic Pets for Sale!
Find animals like koala bears, wallabies, snow leaopards, etc.,
on sale for low...
www.rareanimalpets.com

Koala Kiddie Playground
Come to Koala Kiddie Playground for tons of fun for all ages!
www.koalakiddieplayground.com

Save the Koala Habitats
SaveKoalas.net is a nonprofit organization that raises money to
save koalas' natural...
http://www.savekoalas.net/

Facts about Koalas: Habitat
In this section of facts about koalas, learn more about where
koalas live...
http://www.factsaboutkoalas.org/

Which Internet search would give the **most** relevant information for someone writing a report on koala habitats? Give a reason for your answer.

_____

_____

5 Your teacher has asked you to write a paper arguing whether or not a koala would make a good pet. Find **three** sources, either print or online, that you could use to write this paper. List each source and explain why they would help you with this assignment.

Source 1:

_____

_____

_____

Source 2:

_____

_____

_____

Source 3:

_____

_____

_____

11.2 MAKE A LIST OF YOUR SOURCES

When you write a report, you must give credit. Even if you paraphrase information, it is important to cite the original authors. **Citing** a source means that you tell where you got the information right after it appears in your writing. There are many reasons for citing your sources. First, it helps show that you did your research. It shows exactly where you found your information, so your readers know they can trust your writing. Your readers may even want to find more information about your topic, and providing sources helps them do that.

Citing sources also ensures that the people who created the sources you use get credit for their work. If you work very hard on something, you don't want others to take the credit for it. Failing to cite your sources is like stealing ideas. Your readers will assume that all the ideas are your own, so it is important to tell them, by citing, when you borrow information or ideas from others.

One of the most important reasons to cite sources is to avoid **plagiarism**. Plagiarism is a form of cheating that happens when one writer uses another person's ideas without giving credit. Sometimes, plagiarism involves copying parts of other people's work without giving credit. Sometimes plagiarism can be accidental, like when you borrow someone else's words or ideas and forget to use quotation marks or cite your source. No matter how plagiarism happens, it is a very serious offense. If you plagiarize, you may fail your assignment. More importantly, plagiarism makes people think they cannot trust your work. Always take careful notes, use quotation marks for other people's words, and make sure to cite each source you use.

You must write your citation in a specific way to help your readers find your source. You must cite sources in two places. First, you write a citation after the information in your report. This citation is put in parentheses and usually includes the author's name, the title of the resource, or a page number. Sometimes you won't see an author's name listed on a source. This can be the case with information from a website. In that case, you just cite the website's name. Then, when you are finished with your report, be sure to **provide a list of sources**. Often, this list of sources is called a bibliography or works cited page.

Ask your teacher about the format to use for this list. Most likely, it will be something like this:

1   List the **author**'s last name, followed by a comma. Then, list the first name, followed by a period. (When there is no author, the title of the source appears first.)

   Example: Robinson, Michael.

2   Next, list the **title** of the work. If it is a short work, like a poem, story, or article, put it in quotation marks. If it is a long work, like a whole magazine, a book, or a website, put it in italics (If you are writing by hand on a report or a test, underline the title.). Put a period after the title.

   Example: *Space Exploration.*

3   Then, list the **publication** information. This includes the city of publication, followed by a colon, then the publisher's name and a comma. After the comma, put the latest copyright date (You can find all this on the copyright page.). Then include the final period, and you're done! Next, put the **medium of publication**. That means write "Print" if your source is in hard copy, or "Web" if the source is a website. Finally, include the final period.

   Example: London: DK Children, 2011. Print.

4   For a website, include the name of the author (if there is one). Next, write the name of the article and the name of the website. This is usually found at the top of the home page. Next, include the date the article was created (day first, then abbreviated month, then year). Then, add the medium of publication (Web) and the date you looked at the site. Finally, put in the whole **web address** between brackets that look like this < > (Note: Including the web address is now optional. Ask your teacher whether or not to include it when citing your sources.).

   Example: "Origins of Baseball." *Wikipedia.* 10 Dec. 2011. Web. 13 Jan. 2013.
   <http://en.wikipedia.org/wiki/History_of_baseball>.

Here are the sources the author of the koala article on page 197 used for her research. They are listed using the format you just read about.

Works Cited List

"Koala." *Wikipedia.* 12 May 2009. Web. 30 Sept. 2013. <http://en.wikipedia.org/wiki/ Koala>.

"Marsupials." *Explore.com.* 10 May 2009. Web. 28 Sept. 2013. <http://42explore.com/ marsupial.htm>.

Sharp, Ann, and Philip Wright. *The Koala Book.* Hong Kong: Pelican, 1985. Print.

Do you see what else the author has done with this list? It is in alphabetical order. The first entry is an article titled "Koalas," which starts with a K. Next comes the article "Marsupials." Then comes an author's name, Sharp. When you make a list, be sure to put the sources in ABC order by whichever comes first—the author's last name or the title.

Practice 2: Listing Your Sources

W 8 (DOK 2, 3)

Read this article from the website *Geology for Kids* and the questions that follow.

Mechanical Weathering
by Linda Smith

Mechanical weathering is a process where rocks are physically broken into smaller pieces by wind, water, ice, or heat. Examples of this type of weathering are everywhere. For example, the Grand Canyon is a channel cut through rock by the powerfully surging waters of the Colorado River over a period of many millions of years. Freezing and thawing cycles also weather rock mechanically. If you ever travel up the East Coast to a northern state like New Jersey or New York, you find that the roads become bumpier. This is because the winters are colder up north. Why should that matter? Water gets into the cracks and crevices of the concrete and asphalt that roads are made of (concrete and asphalt are just processed rock). When the water freezes, it expands. The ice crystals push against the solid rock, weakening its structure. When it warms up again, the ice crystals melt and the pressure is released—but the rock structure is weakened even more. Each time the rock freezes and thaws, it cracks a little more. Finally, the road is broken down into rubble.

---

1   A student is using this source to write a report. Read this paragraph from his report and the question that follows.

> One of the many ways rocks break down into dirt is through mechanical weathering. This is a process where rocks are physically broken into smaller pieces by wind, water, ice, or heat. Running water from rivers breaks down rocks by flowing over them. Water that freezes inside cracks of rocks also breaks rocks.

Did this student successfully avoid plagiarism? If so, how? If not, how can he fix it?

_____

_____

_____

2   What is the correct citation for this website article?

A) Smith, Linda. "Mechanical Weathering." *Geology for Kids*. 3 May 2010. Web. 7 Oct. 2013. <http://www.geologyforkids.com/Mechanical_Weathering>.

B) Linda Smith. "Mechanical Weathering." *Geology for Kids*. 3 May 2010. Web. 7 Oct. 2013. <http://www.geologyforkids.com/Mechanical_Weathering>.

C) Smith, Linda. Web. "Mechanical Weathering." *Geology for Kids*. 3 May 2010. 7 Oct. 2013. <http://www.geologyforkids.com/Mechanical_Weathering>.

D) <http://www.geologyforkids.com/Mechanical_Weathering>. Smith, Linda. "Mechanical "Weathering." *Geology for Kids*. 3 May 2010. Web. 7 Oct. 2013.

11.3 EXAMINING YOUR SOURCES

So once you find a source, what do you do with it? You figure out how you can use it the best. What you learn from sources helps you know your topic. Your papers and reports can mention what you found out. In this section, we'll talk about how to examine your sources. This includes how to take notes and organize your facts.

You use sources to find relevant facts for reports and essays. You can also use sources to prepare yourself for class discussions.

TAKE NOTES

When you read sources, you can't remember all the facts they give you. A good way to hang on to the facts you need is to **take notes**. Use a journal or note cards to jot down any information you might want to use. **Summarize** the main points of the story or article and write the summary in your own words. Keep in mind that your notes serve as a reminder for you of what you read or heard. Only you will use your notes, so they do not need to be written in complete sentences or even complete words. You can **paraphrase** what the author says or even use abbreviations or symbols if you want. Make sure you jot down key words and phrases that you might want to use later. The more you practice, the easier it will be to take good notes.

You may also need to note other facts about your sources. Be sure to write down the title of each source. Also, write down the author, publisher, and year it was published. You will need these facts when you cite and list your sources. The next section will show you how to do this.

There are a few different ways to take notes that help you stay organized. **Outlines** are a way to organize your notes by writing out ideas using topics and subtopics. Outlines are very useful in that they can easily be adapted into reports.

> **Example:** I. Introduction—I love playing baseball.
>
> > A. It's a fun game.
> >
> > B. Anyone can play.
> >
> > C. It brings people together.
>
> II. Many fun parts
>
> > A. You get to run a lot.
> >
> > B. You can work on your aim.
> >
> > C. You hit the ball with a bat.
>
> III. Easy for anyone
>
> > A. Many different roles to play
> >
> > B. Everyone gets a chance to hit the ball.
>
> IV. Builds teamwork
>
> > A. You have to watch what your team members do.
> >
> > B. You can only win if you work together.
> >
> > C. Even if you don't win, you have fun.
>
> V. Conclusion

Another way to keep your notes organized is to take Cornell notes. With this style of note taking, you divide your paper into three squares like the image below. Use the large right square to take notes like normal. Then, when you have finished, write your main ideas and key questions in the left box. Finally, summarize the source in the bottom box. This method of note taking helps you pull out the most important ideas from the source.

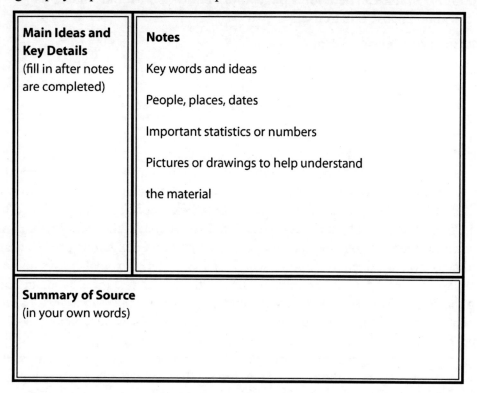

A similar method is four-square note taking. In this method, you divide your paper into four squares. Each square holds a different type of information: main ideas, key details, vocabulary, and questions. You can use the questions to guide you in your further research. A single source usually will not answer all your questions, but it may show you where the holes in your information are.

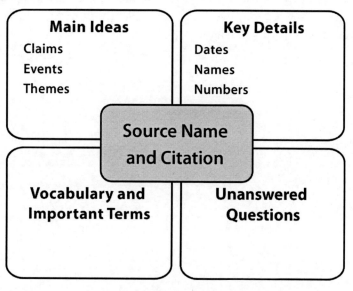

Practice 3: Examining Your Sources

W 7, 8 (DOK 1–3)

A. Read the text below, and take notes using one of the methods you have learned about in this section. A blank Cornell notes page and a blank four-square notes page are provided for you. Choose one to use.

Letter Ascribed to Amerigo Vespucci

Amerigo Vespucci was an Italian explorer. He was the first person to realize that Christopher Columbus had discovered America, not Asia. America is named for Vespucci. This letter is thought to be written by Amerigo Vespucci, though scholars disagree.

We anchored with our ships at a distance of a league and a half from the shore. We got out the boats, and, filled with armed men, we pulled them to the shore. Before we arrived we had seen many men walking along the beach, at which we were much pleased... and they showed fear of us, I believe because we were dressed and of a different stature. They all fled to a hill, and, in spite of all the signs of peace and friendship that we made, they would not come to … us. As night was coming on, and the ship was anchored in a dangerous place, off an open unsheltered coast, we arranged to … go in search of some port or bay where we could make our ships secure. We sailed along the coast to the north, always in sight of land, and the people went along the beach. After two days … we found a very secure place for the ships, and we anchored at a distance of half a league from the land, where we saw very many people. We went on shore in the boats on the same day, and forty men … landed. The natives were still shy of us, and we could not give them sufficient confidence to … come and speak with us. That day we worked so hard with this object by giving them our things, such as bells, looking-glasses, and other trifles, that some of them took courage and came to treat with us. Having established a friendly understanding, as the night was approaching we took leave of them, and returned on board. Next day, at dawn, we saw that there were an immense number of people on the beach, and that they had their women and children with them. We went on shore, and found that they all came laden with their food supplies … Before we arrived on shore, many of them swam out to receive us at a cross-bow shot's distance; for they are great swimmers, and they showed as much confidence as if we had been … with them for a long time; and we were pleased at seeing their feelings of security.

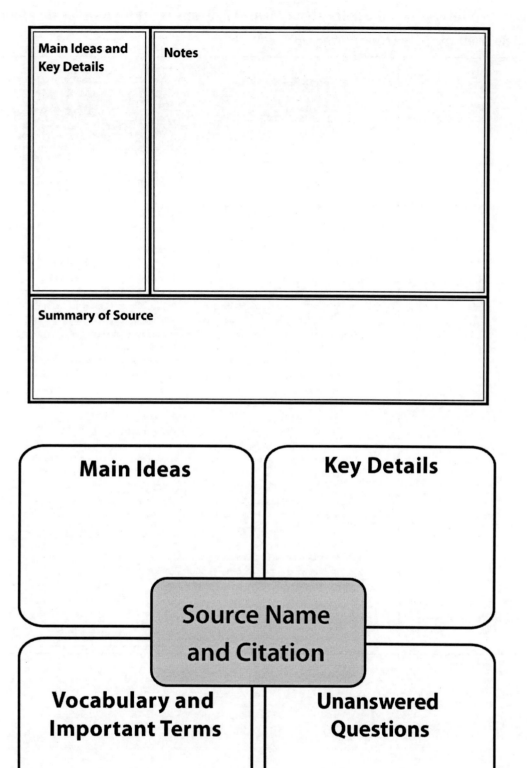

B. Read the sources and take notes about them. Then, answer the questions that follow.

1. Article from the Magazine, *History for Kids*

Notes	

History for Kids

The Golden Spike
by Johnny Jameson

The two great locomotives stood head to head, magnificent symbols of progress, as the final yards of track were laid. Hundreds of people gathered around to witness the historic event. For the first time, a railroad line had been completed that joined America's east and west coasts. The scene was Promontory Summit, Utah Territory, in 1869. The leaders of two railroad lines pounded a golden spike into a wooden tie. It was the last spike connecting the two lines of track that had met at last.

How it was done

One railroad company began laying tracks in Sacramento, California, and headed east. The other company had started laying track in Council Bluffs, Iowa, heading westward. These tracks connected with the railroads that already spanned as far as the east coast. The meeting of the two sets of tracks in Promontory Summit, Utah, changed our land forever.

Travel time

Before the railroad, any people from the east who wanted to travel to California's gold fields had two choices. They could board a ship and sail around Cape Horn, the southernmost part of South America, and then sail back up along the west coast. Or they could travel by wagon some two thousand miles across wide plains, treacherous mountains, and deadly deserts. Both trips took months and were very dangerous. The new railroad reduced travel time to less than a week.

What it meant

Because of the transcontinental railroad, for the first time our country was united by a rapid form of transit from the east coast to the west coast. The railroad allowed the further settling of the West. And it symbolized the end of the "Western Frontier."

 |

2. Copyright Page from the Book *Rails Across the Nation*

Notes	
	RAILS ACROSS THE NATION
	Published by
	Cahill Publishing
	627 W. 43rd Street
	New York, NY 10036
	Library of Congress Publication Data
	Jason Listor
	Rails Across the Nation
	Copyright © 2007 by Jason Listor
	All rights reserved. No part of this book may be reproduced or transmitted in any form or by any means, electronic or mechanical, without the written permission of the publisher.
	Book design by Roberta Talley
	Manufactured in the United States of America
	October 2007
	ii

3. Page from the Website Transportation.com

Notes	
	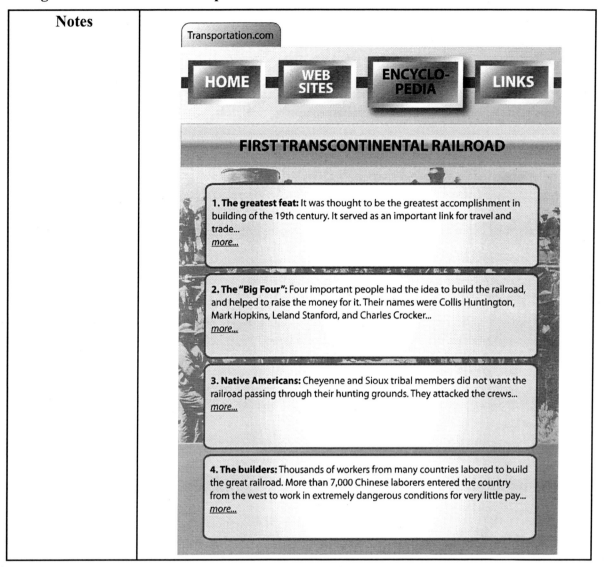

1 On the menu of the website Transportation.com, which entry would give you the **best** information about the people who developed the idea for the railroad?

A) The greatest feat   C) Native Americans

B) The "Big Four"   D) The builders

2 To find a brief summary of the importance of the transcontinental railroad, which source would be **most** helpful? Explain your answer.

_____

_____

_____

3 Jonathan took notes on the article "The Golden Spike" in the *History for Kids* magazine.

> First Transcontinental Railroad Construction
> Two railroad companies laid the tracks
> - Majority of laborers were immigrants
> - _____

What fact goes in the blank above?

A) Golden spike connected two rails   C) Ships sailed around Cape Horn

B) End of the "western frontier"   D) Trip by wagon two thousand miles long

4 Write the correct bibliographic entry for the book *Rails Across the Nation*.

_____

_____

_____

5 Read these sentences from a student's report on the Transcontinental Railroad.

> The new Transcontinental Railroad made travel to the west much easier. Before the railroad, trips out west took months and were very dangerous. The new railroad reduced travel time to less than a week.

Has this student successfully avoided plagiarism? Why or why not? If not, how could the student fix the problem?

_____

_____

_____

11.4 USING SOURCES

Now that you have found and examined your sources, you need to know how to use them properly. When you know the best way to use a source, your writing will be much stronger.

EVIDENCE FROM LITERATURE

Sometimes you will be asked to use a piece of literature to **support** your ideas. You might be asked to compare or contrast characters or events in a story. You will need to **draw evidence** from the story to help support your essay.

For example, read this text and the following prompt.

Excerpt from *The Adventures of Joel Pepper*
by Margaret Sidney

It was snowing tiny flakes when Joel's eyes popped open, and the small, feathery things whirled against the little paned window, as if they would very much like to come in.

"Dave—Dave!" cried Joel, poking him, "get up—it's snowing!"

David's eyes flew quite wide at that, and he sat up at once. "Oh, Joel," he squealed, as he watched the flakes, "ain't they pretty!"

"Um! I guess so," said Joel, springing into his clothes; "they're nice for snowballs and to slide on, anyway."

David reached over for one blue woolen stocking on the floor by the side of the bed, and sat quite still with it in his hand, regarding the snowy whirl.

Based on the text, how are David and Joel alike, and how are they different? Use your inference skills to tell what kind of character each boy is. Give specific details from the text.

If you had to answer this prompt, you would use the text to answer the question. Your response might look something like this.

Both boys like the snow. The author describes how David "squealed" about how pretty the snow is. Joel thinks the snow is good for "snowballs and to slide on." That shows that they are glad for different reasons. It is not clear but maybe David has never seen the snow before. He watches the snow very closely. Joel just gets up fast and throws his clothes on. On the other hand, David "sat quite still" to watch the snow. Perhaps snow is not as exciting to David anymore.

Notice how the student uses quotations and paraphrases from the text to support her answer.

EVIDENCE FROM INFORMATIONAL TEXTS

Other times you will need to use informational sources in your research. You will need to show how an author uses **reasons and evidence** to support his points.

Here is an example of an informational report. The student who wrote it states an opinion.

Why Ban Books?

Why do people censor books? It makes no sense. Censorship is a tool that does not achieve its goals for many reasons.

First, censorship just makes a controversial book more popular. It makes the book more desirable to those who may not have noticed it otherwise. Think about it: a book somebody tells you not to read is much more tempting than one that is allowed!

Also, in trying to protect children, those who support censorship are actually harming them. They are blocking knowledge that could help kids to make the right decisions later in real life.

Eventually, all kids will have to learn to make their own decisions. It is better for students to be taught that they can make positive choices about what they read. They need to make these choices, but adults can help them learn why and how.

Before banning a book, people should consider the long-term effects. People who ban books from schools and libraries teach children by example. But it is the wrong example. They teach that just a few people can read these books and decide about them for everyone else.

Do you see how he backs up his ideas with evidence? This is a great way to persuade readers.

USING MULTIPLE SOURCES

Different types of sources give you different types of information to use in your work. For example, a textbook can tell you the facts about a war, but an interview with a soldier who was there can give you firsthand details that a textbook could not. You should choose the types of sources you use based on the type of information you need. Most of the time, it is helpful to use a variety of source types to give you a fuller picture of your topic.

Similarly, it is useful to use **multiple accounts** on your topic. Because each person experiences things in a particular way, no single person can tell you everything about a topic or event. Think of a family holiday, for example. You might experience a lot of anticipation for the event. You might feel like you have to wait forever for the festivities to begin. Your parents, on the other hand, probably experience a lot of preparation for the event. They may feel as if time goes by too quickly to get everything done. If you have very young siblings, they may not even know that something exciting is about to happen. All these experiences are true and valid even though they are different. Looking at your topic from multiple perspectives can help you get a better sense of what really happened.

Practice 4: Using Multiple Sources

W 7, 8, 9 (DOK 3)

The Wong family recently took a vacation to Hawaii. Each member of the family kept a journal about his or her experience on the trip. Read the journal entries about entering the hotel lobby. Then, draw a picture of the lobby using information from the journal entries.

Mr. Wong's Journal

> June 12—Reached the hotel today. Four rows of palm trees like the ones at home cut straight down the lobby. The row closest to the right wall leads to the registration desk. The room is large, with high ceilings, but the palm trees hang a bit low. I had to brush them out of my face as I walked in to register our room. They look nice enough, but they should raise them up higher. Nothing worse than a palm branch in the face.

Mrs. Wong's Journal

> June 12—We finally made it from the airport to the hotel. It's a nice place, and I think we made a good hotel choice. There is a lot of natural light, probably good for the palm trees. The hotel is not quite as ornate as the ones I sometimes visit for work. But the carved arches leading off the back wall toward the rooms are magnificent. The gold and green painted carvings are of vines, leaves, and fruits arching across like a tropical arbor. I can smell the water from the spa every time I enter the lobby. I'll be following that smell off to the left this evening. A hot tub is the perfect cure for travel tension.

Mike Wong's Journal

> June 12—This hotel is gonna be amazing! I walked in, and just past the spa-looking area on the left was an arcade! They have all the coolest games in there. They have the hunting game where you try and hunt a deer and the game with the space invasion you have to stop. It's got all these black lights and neon lights, and it just looks like I could go in there and never come out. They even have some awesome vending machines. Seriously, I could live in that place. I just need to get mom to give me some quarters.

Kelly Wong's Journal

June 12—Dear diary, I'm so excited. The hotel has the best elevators. They're right next to the big arches. The front is glass. You can see everything! And the elevators go so fast! I hope our room is on the top floor. That way I can ride them all the way to the top!

Susie Wong's Blog

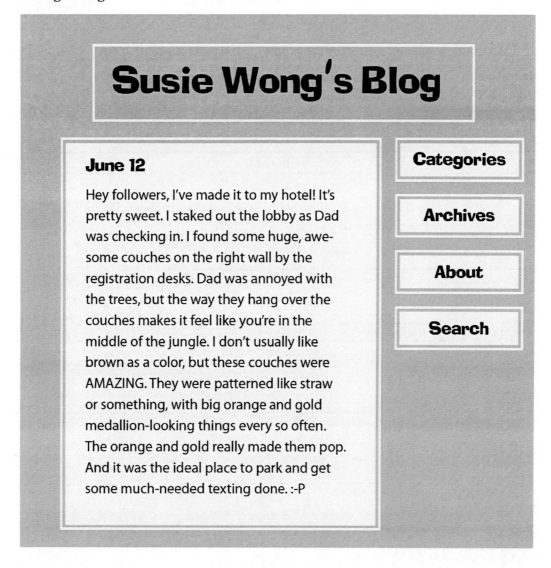

Susie Wong's Blog

June 12

Hey followers, I've made it to my hotel! It's pretty sweet. I staked out the lobby as Dad was checking in. I found some huge, awesome couches on the right wall by the registration desks. Dad was annoyed with the trees, but the way they hang over the couches makes it feel like you're in the middle of the jungle. I don't usually like brown as a color, but these couches were AMAZING. They were patterned like straw or something, with big orange and gold medallion-looking things every so often. The orange and gold really made them pop. And it was the ideal place to park and get some much-needed texting done. :-P

Categories

Archives

About

Search

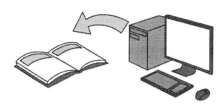

Research Connection

You have decided to plan a dream vacation for your family. Your fantasy budget for hotel, excursions, and airfare is $5000. Use the Internet to plan your dream trip. Include an itinerary of what your family will do each day and how much everything costs. Also, be sure to keep track of your sources. Once you have completed the research, design a brochure to show your family how exciting and affordable the trip will be!

Itinerary	
Day 1	Arrival Time: Activities:
Day 2	Activities:
Day 3	Activities:
Day 4	Activities:
Day 5	Activities: Departure Time:

Works Cited

Source 1: _____

_____

Source 2: _____

_____

Source 3: _____

_____

Source 4: _____

_____

Source 5: _____

_____

11.5 PACING

Many times when you do research, you will be preparing a large project. This means that you will not be able to research properly in a single sitting. You will have to do research, take notes, and prepare your final project over many days or even weeks. Because completing a project takes so long, you must plan your time wisely. Planning your project over a period of time is called **pacing**.

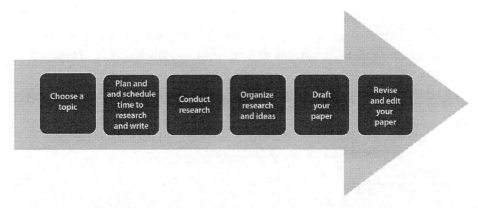

Generally, you should plan to use one third of your time to do research. The other two thirds of your time should be spent writing and revising. If you spend too much time researching, you may not have time to write and revise. If you spend too little time on research, you might find that you don't have all the information you need. Sometimes you may feel like you can put off work until the last minute, but that is not a good way to work. You may become very stressed, or your work may not be very good. It is best to begin working early.

One way to make your work easier is to break it up into chunks. Write down your due date and figure out how much time you have. Use a calendar to write down when you need to have each part complete. Look at the example pacing calendar.

October–November

Sunday	Monday	Tuesday	Wednesday	Thursday	Friday	Saturday
		Oct. 16	17	18	19	20
				RESEARCH FOR PAPER →→→		
21	22	23	24	25	26	27
	RESEARCH FOR PAPER →→→			WRITE ROUGH DRAFT →→→		
28	29	30	31	Nov. 1	2	3
WRITE ROUGH DRAFT →→→		ROUGH DRAFT DUE		EDIT AND REVISE PAPER →→→		
4	5	6	7	8	9	10
		EDIT AND REVISE PAPER →→→				
11	12	13				
EDIT AND REVISE →→→		FINAL DRAFT DUE				

Do you see how this student divided his work into pieces? This can make large projects feel more manageable.

Practice 5: Pacing

W 10 (DOK 2)

Your science teacher has given you three weeks to complete a science fair project. Using the blank calendar and list of due dates below, plan out the project. Remember to divide your project into smaller chunks.

Important Dates:

Assignment Given: April 2   Final Project Due: April 23

April 2014						
Sunday	Monday	Tuesday	Wednesday	Thursday	Friday	Saturday
		1	2	3	4	5
6	7	8	9	10	11	12
13	14	15	16	17	18	19
20	21	22	23	24	25	26
27	28	29	30			

Chapter 11 Summary

Looking for facts is called **research**. Research consists of **selecting** and **using sources.**

Print sources include books, magazines, brochures, and so on. You can use the library catalog to find certain books.

Digital sources include websites containing facts you need that you can find online. They can also include CDs, DVDs, and other digital media.

You need to be able to **pick the best sources** to use for your topic. These depend on the **purpose of your research.** You find out which sources are best by **examining sources.**

When you find appropriate sources, a good way to keep track of the facts you need is to **take notes.** You might use **outlining, Cornell notes,** or **four-square notes.**

Citing a source means that you tell your reader where you got the information. At the end of your report, you should always include a **list of sources** you used. Failing to cite your sources or using others' work as your own is called **plagiarism.**

Sometimes you will be asked to use a **literary source** to **support** your ideas. You will need to **draw evidence** from the story to help support your essay.

Other times you will need to show how an author of an **informational source** uses **reasons and evidence** to support his or her points.

Using multiple sources helps you understand a topic more fully.

Pacing allows you to divide your projects into manageable chunks.

For additional practice, please see Chapter 11 Test located in the Teacher Guide.

Chapter 12
Speaking and Listening

 This chapter covers DOK levels 1–3 and the following fifth grade strand and standards (for full standards, please see page x):

Speaking and Listening 1, 2, 3, 4, 5, 6
Reading Foundational Skills 4

In this chapter…

- You will actively participate in group discussions and follow group discussion rules.

- You will listen respectfully and actively to speakers in order to determine main ideas and supportive reasoning of ideas from speakers.

- You will use multimedia in order to enhance your oral presentations.

As you have learned, there are certain rules in English to follow that help you read and write the language correctly. However, words are not only meant to be read silently. They can also be spoken aloud and listened to. In this chapter, you will learn the best ways of speaking and listening.

12.1 CLASSROOM DISCUSSION

Often, you may be asked to read stories or other texts ahead of time that you will discuss later in class. You may be asked to talk about these texts with your teacher, classmates, or a small group. **Class discussion** helps you understand what you read. You can hear the views and opinions of other students, some of which might be different from your own views. You can ask and answer questions among yourselves as you discuss a topic. This also gives you a chance to express your ideas clearly.

PREPARATION

It is important to know how to **prepare for discussions**. Here are a few things that you can do to prepare.

READING THE REQUIRED MATERIAL

The first step is to **read the required material** that your teacher assigned. You need to read it carefully and slowly. This will help you make sure you understand what you read. Taking notes, asking questions, and rereading are all strategies that can help you comprehend what you are reading.

RESEARCHING THE TOPIC

You can find out more about a topic by doing some **research** (You read about how to do research in chapter 11.). For example, say you are reading a book about gorillas. You can look up *gorillas* in an encyclopedia to learn even more about them, or perhaps your city has a zoo with a primate exhibit that you can visit. You can even do research when reading a story. You could find out more information about the author or the setting. This will help you **explore ideas** that may come up in your class discussion. It might even change your first opinions of the text.

TAKING NOTES

As you read and research, you can **take notes**. Make some notes about these items:

- Main idea of the text
- Details that support the main idea
- Answers to questions you ask yourself
- Ideas you have about the meaning of the text
- Questions you still have after reading

It is also a good idea to **summarize** what you read. This means putting the main points of a text in your own words. This will help ensure that you have understood what you read. For more information about taking notes, review chapter 11.

FOLLOWING THE RULES OF DISCUSSION

There are some **rules of discussion** that everyone should follow. These rules may be set by your teacher or by the class. They allow a group to work well together. Each group member has a role to play, and following set rules helps each member do his or her part. Having rules helps a discussion go smoothly without anyone being rude or hurting other classmates' feelings. This ensures that everyone gets a chance to talk.

Rules for discussion might look like this:

1. Talk to others in a respectful way. Raise your hand, and wait for your turn.

2. Listen attentively to others. Make eye contact, and pay attention to what each speaker is saying.

3. Speak one at a time. Do not talk while others are speaking.

4. Stay on the topic. Only speak about the text you are discussing.

5. If someone asks a question, try to answer it before someone else asks another question.

6. Explain your ideas in a way others will understand.

7. If you make a comment about the topic, make sure it is not simply repeating what someone else has already said. Take the opinion and add something to it or even respectfully disagree with it.

Remember, if someone's opinion is different from yours, it is okay. Not everyone will see the same things when reading a text. As long as you discuss your opinions properly and politely, it is all right to disagree.

Practice 1: Following the Rules of Discussion

SL 1 (DOK 2)

Go to the website below to watch a video of students participating in a class discussion.

http://americanbookcompany.com/media/class-discussion

Some students follow the rules of discussion while some don't. On the chart below, take notes about how students follow or fail to follow the rules of discussion. Then, in a group or as a class, discuss how the students in the video could follow the rules of discussion better.

Examples of Following the Rules of Discussion	Examples of Not Following the Rules of Discussion

12.2 LISTENING

When a person gives a report in class, be sure to listen closely. Look at the speaker. You should pay attention so you can understand the topic.

LISTENING COMPREHENSION

In school, you will spend time listening to others speak or read aloud. When you listen, think about what you hear. **Summarize** the main points and supporting details of what the speaker says or reads. You need to listen carefully to do that. You might need to take notes, too. Just as with reading, if you paraphrase what the speaker says, it will help you understand what you heard.

If there is a part you do not understand, make a note about it on paper or keep track of it in your head. You will usually have a chance to ask your questions at the end of the speech.

IDENTIFYING THE SPEAKER'S SUPPORT

Sometimes a speaker will try to persuade you to share an opinion. Listen carefully to the speech to hear the speaker's claims. Each claim should have **support through reasons and evidence**. Say your friend is trying to convince you to pick up the discarded plastic bottles and aluminum cans around the school to recycle them. Some good reasons she could give are that there is always trash on the floors or that recycling is good for the environment. Those are solid pieces of evidence that support her point. But if she said that you would not be popular if you did not help her, then that would not be good support for her cause.

ASKING QUESTIONS

Asking questions about a speech can help you understand it better. Afterward, you can ask the speaker a question about the topic. But be sure it is really about the topic! Also, it might turn out that another student in class has an answer to your question. In turn, you might be able to answer questions that others ask.

In a class discussion, you can add what you know. When all students share, each one gets to know the topic better. Talking about a speech or report is like any other class discussion. Remember to wait until it is your turn to talk.

Practice 2: Listening

SL 1, 2, 3 (DOK 2, 3)

Go to the website below to watch a presentation. Then, answer the questions that follow.

Tricks of the Trade
http://americanbookcompany.com/media/tricks-of-the-trade

1   Why are famous people used in commercials?

   A) They want to improve people's lives.

   B) They help convince people to buy things.

   C) They help to raise the quality of products.

   D) They want to entertain people.

2 What sentence from the text is the **best** support for the point that companies spend a lot of time and money to get your attention?

A) They make their product the star of the advertisement.

B) How many advertisements do you think you see a day?

C) All of these are examples of how advertisements can be misleading.

D) These are all forms of media, and they all contain advertisements.

3 What is **one** question you should ask yourself when you see an advertisement?

_____

_____

_____

4 What is the **best** summary of this text?

_____

_____

_____

12.3 SPEAKING

Sometimes you will need to give a report in class. When you give a report, it is important for you to know your **purpose for speaking**.

PURPOSE FOR SPEAKING

Just like in writing, your speaking has a purpose. Sometimes you might speak to **inform** your listeners about a topic. You speak about something you want others to know more about. Other times you might speak to **voice your opinion**. In that case, you would explain your opinions using reasons and evidence. You might also have to **persuade** your listeners to share your opinions. You would explain why your reasons and evidence mean your listeners should agree with you. Sometimes you might speak simply to **entertain** your listeners. You might tell about an interesting experience or a funny story. (For more information about purpose, review chapter 10.)

Other people will speak to you as well. Most days, your teacher probably speaks in front of the class. Even when others give presentations or speeches, you will have the opportunity to speak to **ask questions** or **learn more** about a topic. You can ask questions to strengthen your understanding. You can clarify unfamiliar concepts. You can ask how to find more information on a topic. In all these instances, it is important to use the speaking skills you are learning.

GIVING A PRESENTATION

If you need to give a report, be sure to do your research first. You should know as much as possible about your topic. You might not include all your research in your speech. But members of your audience may ask you questions about your topic afterward. This way, you will have the information you need to answer them.

When you are speaking out loud, give your ideas in a **logical order**. Tell them in a way that those listening to you can follow easily. Be sure to give enough details that support your main points. Describe the people, places, and events carefully.

Whatever you are speaking about, you will want to do these things:

1. Stay on the topic.

2. Include only appropriate facts and descriptive details.

3. Speak clearly and at a good pace—not too slowly, and not too quickly.

4. Use complete sentences.

5. Make eye contact with your audience.

6. Try not to move around or fidget.

7. After your speech, answer questions from the audience.

USING APPROPRIATE LANGUAGE

The language you should use is determined by your purpose and audience. Sometimes it is acceptable to use **informal language** in your speaking. This is usually appropriate for group discussions. In group discussions, you will probably speak the same way you normally speak. You don't have to make sure every word is precise as long as your listeners understand you.

However, when you give a presentation, you should use **formal language**. You should not use slang, like *cool* or *dunno*. You should avoid general terms like *stuff* and *things*. You should also avoid filler words, like *um* and *you know*.

Practice 3: Analyzing a Presentation

SL 2, 4, 6 (DOK 2, 3)

A. Shel Silverstein's silly poetry is meant to be read aloud. Visit WatchKnowLearn at the website below to listen to a poem. Then, answer the following questions.

http://www.watchknowlearn.org/Video.aspx?VideoID=48878#

From Shel Silverstein: Poems and Drawings; originally appeared in *Where the Sidewalk Ends* by Shel Silverstein. Copyright © 2003 by HarperCollins Children's Books.

1 How does the speaker's voice enhance the experience of hearing the poem?

_____

_____

_____

2 How does the illustration enhance the poem?

_____

_____

B. Choose another Shel Silverstein poem. Practice reading it aloud with emotion. Then, record yourself reading it and listen to it two to three times. Write a paragraph about your performance and the strengths and weaknesses of your poetry reading.

_____

_____

_____

ADDING MULTIMEDIA COMPONENTS

In school, you might use an **audio recording** to enhance your presentation. Audio resources can be mp3s, CDs, audiotapes, or even old-fashioned record albums. If you are giving a biography of a famous composer, you might use a sound recording of one of his or her musical works. Whenever you use an audio recording, it must go with your report. If you use a sound clip that has nothing to do with your project, the attention of your audience will wander off the topic, and your main idea or theme will be lost.

When you present, you can use **visual displays**, too. They can help you clearly express your topic and ideas. Graphs, posters, charts, and graphics can be used along with your speech. Graphs and charts are useful to present data and facts. Pictures and posters can help illustrate a story. You can use graphics printed out on paper or show graphics on a computer.

Look at these visual aids from a presentation about an animal shelter. Notice how the visual aid with the image gives greater force to the words.

She needs a home.

You need a friend.

It's a win-win.

Do you see how appropriate multimedia can improve your reports and presentations? The second visual aid is a much stronger choice than the first.

Practice 4: Speaking

SL 4, 5, 6 (DOK 1, 2)

Read and then answer the questions.

1   Marnie is writing a report about how certain types of fish swim upstream when they are ready to have babies. She wants to use a visual to support her speech. Which of the following would be the **best** visual for Marnie to use?

A)

Where Do Fish Swim Upstream?	
Hayes Creek	Yes
Little South Stream	Yes
McGill Pond	No
Lake Chutney	No

C)

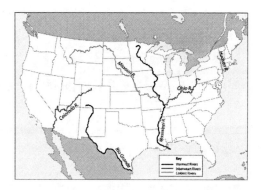

B)

Average Daily Fish Consumption

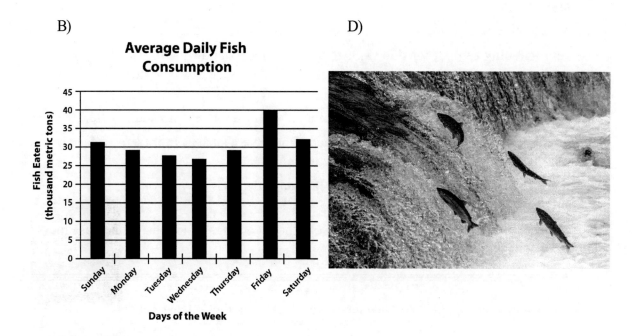

D)

2 Marnie is giving her report to her class. Her teacher will also be in attendance. What kind of language should she use in her report?

_____

_____

3 When presenting a report, what should you do?

A) Have a study partner come up with you and speak, too.

B) Ask your classmates as many questions as you can.

C) Talk about anything that comes to mind.

D) Stay on the topic of your report.

4 Barry is giving a report about his trip to Washington, DC. Which point is **not** appropriate for him to add to his speech?

A) which monuments he saw

B) what he wore on the airplane

C) when his trip to the capital was

D) what happened on his trip

CHAPTER 12 SUMMARY

Classroom discussion helps you understand what you read.

Prepare for discussion when you come to class. **Read the required text** before the discussion. **Research** the topic. **Take notes** about what you learn. **Paraphrase** or **summarize** what you read.

Follow the **rules of discussion**, such as waiting for your turn to speak.

Use your **listening comprehension** skills to help you understand what the speaker says. Listen closely to **identify the speaker's support**. Good presentations provide **reasons and evidence** to support points.

Asking questions that are relevant to the presentation helps you understand it better.

You might be asked to write or speak for different purposes, such as to **inform**, **voice an opinion**, **persuade listeners**, **entertain**, or **learn more**.

Whether to use **formal English** or **informal language** depends on your purpose as well as your audience.

Use appropriate **multimedia** components, like audio recordings or visuals, to increase the impact of your presentation.

For additional practice, please see Chapter 12 Test located in the Teacher Guide.

Post Test

"Typhoid Mary" Mallon

In 1906, several cases of typhoid fever broke out in Oyster Bay, New York, alarming public health officials. Typhoid fever was a deadly virus back then. People were understandably scared of getting sick. The study of diseases and the ways they are spread was a new science. Back then, the causes of sickness were looked upon with superstition and fear.

George Soper, a researcher sent to track the source of the sickness, was surprised to see a typhoid outbreak in the home of a rich banker. People assumed typhoid was a disease of the lower classes. They knew it was caused by poor sanitation and careless personal hygiene. But in this case, six members of a wealthy family had caught typhoid fever. What could have caused this to happen? Soper had to investigate a life-or-death mystery.

He found that the family's cook had left her job right after the family members got sick. Mary Mallon, a poor immigrant from Ireland, worked as a cook for many different families. George Soper found that six other families she cooked for had caught typhoid fever; in all, Mary had infected twenty-two people.

After tracking Mary Mallon to a rich Manhattan household, Soper went to her kitchen and confronted her with the evidence. When he asked her permission to collect medical samples from her, Mary flew into a rage and chased him out. Soper came back with police and a female doctor and had Mary placed under arrest—but not before the stout woman put up a fight!

At the jail, Mary was examined by doctors. Although she appeared healthy, Mary Mallon was full of typhoid germs. An organ in her body, called her gallbladder, made the germs all the time. Mary was lazy and rebellious and would not wash her hands, so when she touched the food, she passed the germs on to the people who ate her cooking. Sometimes she took care of people she cooked for who got sick; often these people got even sicker while she cared for them. When the whole family grew sick, Mary simply quit working for them and would find another job with a new family. Thus, it would begin all over again.

The doctors told her it would help if she had her gallbladder taken out, but the headstrong Mary refused. Knowing she was a danger to the public, the doctors sent Mary to a hospital on an island in the East River, where she would be isolated. She was placed in quarantine to keep her from infecting others.

It was big news. Everyone found out about Mary; the newspapers called her "Typhoid Mary." Mary felt wronged. She was healthy, she said fiercely. She was being kept in the hospital for something she didn't do. She sued to be released. A kindly judge who didn't know much about the disease let Mary out after making her promise never to work as a cook again. Mary agreed, and she soon disappeared.

Five years later, typhoid fever hit the nurses at a hospital in New York City, and twenty-five of them got sick. Two of them died. Doctors narrowed it down to Mary Brown, the sharp-tongued hospital cook, whom the nurses had called "Typhoid Mary" as a joke. A little questioning soon showed that they were right: It was Mary Mallon!

In 1915, there were few jobs for a middle-aged immigrant woman to do; a cook made more money than a maid. So Mary Mallon had changed her name to Mary Brown and went right back to cooking for a large number of people, and in a hospital, too. People didn't accept her excuses, though—she had been told that she could spread a deadly disease with every meal she served.

She was sent back to the lonely island, where a one-room cottage had been built to be her permanent home. Mary lived out the rest of her life there, in sight of New York City, with a dog for a companion. She was bitter and miserable, sure that she was being falsely imprisoned. She felt healthy, so the doctors had to be wrong. But no matter how healthy Mary felt, her body was full of typhoid germs.

Mary Mallon spent over half her life on the island until she died of a stroke in 1938. Even so, her reputation followed her. Perhaps because he remembered her as "Typhoid Mary," the doctor who wrote the last report made a mistake; he wrote that she died from typhoid fever.

---

1 Read these sentences and the directions that follow.

RI.5.4
DOK 2

> The doctors told her it would help if she had her gallbladder taken out, but the headstrong Mary refused. Knowing she was a danger to the public, the doctors sent Mary to a hospital on an island in the East River, where she would be isolated. She was placed <u>in quarantine</u> to keep her from infecting others.

This question has two parts. First, answer part A. Then, answer part B.

Part A

If you are put <u>in quarantine</u>, what does this mean?

A) You made an A on your test and your parents congratulated you.

B) You're sick and must be kept away from others.

C) Your mom got mad and grounded you for a week.

D) You found buried treasure in your backyard.

Part B

Underline **two** phrases that help you understand the meaning of <u>in quarantine</u>.

2 Which sentence from the text **best** supports the point that Mary Mallon was a danger to the public?

RI.5.8
DOK 3

A) A kindly judge who didn't know much about the disease let Mary out after making her promise never to work as a cook again.

B) People didn't accept her excuses, though—she had been told that she could spread a deadly disease with every meal she served.

C) But in this case, six members of a wealthy family had caught typhoid fever.

D) She was being kept in the hospital for something she didn't do.

E) But no matter how healthy Mary felt, her body was full of typhoid germs.

3 This historical text uses chronological order to relate events in the order they happened. What organizational pattern would a scientific text on typhoid fever **most likely** use?

RI.5.5
DOK 2

_____

_____

_____

4 How would the account of Mary Mallon's life **most likely** be different if Mary Mallon wrote it herself? Select **all** that apply.

RI.5.6
DOK 3

A) She would deny any blame for the typhoid outbreaks.

B) She would provide recipes for her favorite meals.

C) She would give no details about her past.

D) She would explain her motivations and thoughts.

E) She would describe Soper as a close friend.

5 Read this sentence from the text and the question that follows.

RI.5.1
DOK 3

  Mary was lazy and rebellious and would not wash her hands.

Based on the author's use of language in this sentence, what can you infer about his attitude toward Mary Mallon?

_____

_____

_____

6 Read the timeline and the question that follows.

RI.5.7
DOK 3

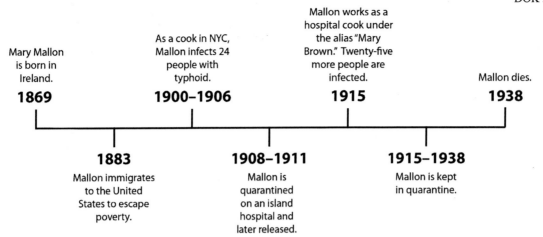

Based on the timeline and the information in the text, when did George Soper conduct his investigation of Mary Mallon?

A) between 1900 and 1906

C) between 1911 and 1915

B) between 1906 and 1908

D) between 1915 and 1938

7 Why did Mary constantly seek new jobs as a cook?

RI.5.3
DOK 2

A) She had a real flair for cooking great meals for people.

B) She was saving money for a long vacation someday.

C) She wanted to spite George Soper and the doctors.

D) She had few job options and made the most money as a cook.

E) She couldn't be a maid because she was allergic to dust.

Lunchtime Trouble

Characters:

Dad

Zack, a ten-year-old boy

Melody, Zack's thirteen-year-old sister

Scene: *Driving down the road in the family mini-van, Dad, Zack, and Melody are deciding where to get lunch.*

Dad (*smiling at Zack and Melody*): So, what do you guys feel like having for lunch? I thought that new deli that just opened might be good.

Zack (*looking eager and excited*): I want to go to Biggie Burger! They have a new burger. I heard about it on television. It has fifty percent more meat. Can we go there, Dad?

Melody (*cringing and sticking out her tongue as if gagging*): Zack, that stuff is bad for you. Dad, I can't eat there. I'm trying to stay fit for the school dance team auditions next month. Let's go someplace where I can get a salad or a healthy sandwich.

Zack (*trying to convince his sister*): You can get a toy there, too—one of the action figures from that new film *Danger Valley*.

Melody (*not convinced*): Zack, a toy can't make up for the yucky stuff some fast-food places put in their food—stuff like sugar, artificial flavoring, fat, and chemicals. I can't eat that if I want to do well in the auditions. I feel tired and sluggish after I eat stuff like that. I need to be careful about the things I eat so I can feel my best.

Dad (*looking at Melody approvingly*): I'm glad you're thinking more about good nutrition, Melody. You seem to know a lot about it. Where did you learn all this?

Melody: Oh, our dance teacher, Mrs. Fritz. She talked to us about nutrition one day, and I got really interested. I started looking at the list of ingredients on food labels and read some articles in health magazines and looked on the Internet for information about nutrition.

Zack (*looking a little surprised*): Yeah, but you used to love junk food. Aren't you going to eat it anymore?

Melody: I'll still eat it sometimes. A little bit isn't bad. I like guilty snacks as much as the next person. But it just makes me feel all full and bloated. I figure if I eat healthy most of the time, I can eat treats occasionally.

Dad: That sounds like a good plan to follow. Everything in moderation. I'm sure you'll be ready for the auditions, and you'll do great. But we still need to figure out where we're going to eat.

Zack (*pointing out the window*): Dad, that deli you were talking about is just up ahead. I'm sure they have salads, and I can get a turkey sandwich.

Dad (*surprised*): What? You don't want to go to Biggie Burger anymore?

Zack (*shrugging his shoulders and smiling*): A sandwich just sounds better to me now. Besides, I want to be ready for our biking trip next week. Maybe I'll even beat Melody in a race.

Melody (*laughing*): Fat chance!

8 What does the adage "Everything in moderation" mean?

L.5.5
DOK 2

A) Too much of anything is bad for you.

B) People should never eat junk food.

C) If you like something, you shouldn't have it.

D) If a food tastes good, it must be unhealthy.

9 What can you infer based on the text? RL.5.1
DOK 2

A) Heavy junk food can make a person feel sluggish.

B) Boys like junk food while girls prefer healthy salads.

C) Turkey sandwiches are the best for a quick lunch.

D) Sports can make people more conscious about diet.

10 Read this part of the text and the directions that follow. RL.5.3
DOK 3

Zack (*looking eager and excited*): I want to go to Biggie Burger! They have a new burger. I heard about it on television. It has fifty percent more meat. Can we go there, Dad?

Melody (*cringing and sticking out her tongue as if gagging*): Zack, that stuff is bad for you. Dad, I can't eat there. I'm trying to stay fit for the school dance team auditions next month. Let's go someplace where I can get a salad or a healthy sandwich.

This question has two parts. First, answer part A. Then, answer part B.

Part A

Compared to Zack, how does Melody **most likely** feel about going to Biggie Burger?

A) nervous

B) excited

C) disgusted

D) angry

Part B

Underline the phrase that **best** reveals how Melody feels.

11 How would seeing a movie adaptation of the text **most** enhance the story? RL.5.7
DOK 3

A) You could see how fast the mini-van is driving.

B) You could hear the emotion in the characters' voices.

C) You could see what kind of toys Biggie Burger has.

D) You could hear the music playing on the radio.

12 What **most** reveals that this text is a drama? RL.5.5
DOK 2

A) The text teaches about a topic in an unbiased way.

B) The action builds to a mysterious climax that readers must solve.

C) There are stanzas rather than paragraphs of narration and dialogue.

D) There are stage directions for the actions of the characters.

13 What technique does the author use to show his point of view? RL.5.6
DOK 3

A) The author scares readers into healthy eating while teaching about fast food.

B) The author paints a picture of a happy family while relating an everyday event.

C) The author informs readers about nutrition while entertaining with a fun scene.

D) The author focuses attention on world hunger while telling an amusing story.

14 This question has two parts. First, answer part A. Then, answer part B.

RL.5.1
DOK 3

Part A

How does Zack **most likely** feel about his big sister?

A) He wishes she hadn't come along on this ride.

B) He teases her, but he listens to what she says.

C) He is tired of her trying to impress their dad.

D) He loves her, but her food lecture annoys him.

Part B

Explain how you chose your answer for part A, supporting your answer with details from the text.

_____

_____

15 How would the author of the text **most likely** respond to the idea that people should never eat burgers or fries? Explain your answer using details from the text.

RL.5.6
DOK 3

_____

_____

_____

Read and answer the following questions.

16 This question contains two parts. First, answer part A. Then, answer part B.

W.5.2
DOK 2

Part A

James is writing an informational essay about mockingbirds. Read this paragraph from his essay and the directions that follow.

Mockingbirds are common and popular birds in the eastern and southern regions of the United States. In fact, it's the state bird of Arkansas, Florida, Mississippi, Tennessee, and Texas. Their nickname is "mockers" because they can mimic other birds, mammals, and insects with song and sounds. There's a Mother Goose rhyme about mockingbirds and a famous book called *To Kill a Mockingbird*. Mockingbirds often live close to human homes, nesting in ornamental hedges and eating berries.

Underline the sentence that does **not** relate to James's topic and should be removed.

Part B

Explain why the sentence you underlined does **not** belong in the rest of the paragraph.

_____

_____

_____

17 A student is writing a persuasive letter to his parents. Read the letter and the directions that follow.

W.5.1
DOK 2

> All the other kids in my class have at least one pet. Dogs are the cutest and sweetest animals. My friends say their dogs are loyal and friendly. Having a dog teaches kids responsibility. There's nothing I want more than a dog. You wouldn't have to take care of it; I'd do all the work. Dogs protect their owners and home. I want to be a veterinarian when I grow up, and taking care of a dog would be good practice.

The paragraph does not have a logical order. Rewrite the paragraph, stating an opinion and creating a clear organizational structure.

_____

_____

_____

_____

18 Stanley is writing an essay about what to do during a school fire drill. Read this paragraph from his essay and the directions that follow.

L.5.1, L.5.2
DOK 1

> Do you know what to do when the fire alarm goes off at school? First of all stay calm. You're teacher will give instructions on what to do. Stay quiet and walking in a single-file line. Follow your classroom's emergency exit plan. When you leave the school building, remain quiet and wait for instructions from the teacher or principal.

Rewrite **three** sentences from the paragraph that contain errors in grammar.

_____

_____

_____

19 Anya is writing about the bird species for science class. She has decided that the underlined words are not precise enough for her audience. Read this paragraph from her essay and the directions that follow.

W.5.2
DOK 1

> Birds are vertebrates that have feathers. Some examples of birds are crows, finches, ducks, penguins, parrots and ostriches. Birds have a beak or bill, two wings, and two legs and claws. The shape of a bird's wings, beak, and claws often help people know the bird's <u>place of residence</u> and diet.

Rewrite the last sentence, replacing the underlined words with a more precise term.

_____

_____

20 Trianthony is writing a report about the history of immigration in the United States. Read the paragraph from his report and the directions that follow.

L.5.2
DOK 1

> From 1850 to 1900, the United States had a boom in immigration. In the East, most new arrivals came from Europe. The West Coast had more immigrants from China because Chinese people saw an opportunity to make money building railway lines. Immigrants had many different reasons for coming to the United States: to seek a better life and to escape hardships like famine or persecution. Immigration increased so much that by the 1880s, almost 80 percent of New Yorkers were foriegn born.

A sentence in Trianthony's report contains a spelling error. Rewrite the sentence, correcting the **one** spelling error.

_____

_____

_____

21 Sophie is writing an informational essay about the new walking program at her school. Read the paragraph from her essay and the question that follows.

W.5.2
DOK 2

> Our school is dedicated to improving students' health, so it introduced a walking program. Daily physical activity will help students and teachers alike stay in shape. Sitting still all day is not good for your health, and our recess has been cut down to just thirty minutes. Our school sought another solution to help students stay active. The walking program takes place right after school before clubs and sports practices start. There is a track we use, and the school is clearing a path through the woods by the school for a more scenic trail. Participants record their walking progress each day of the week by wearing pedometers. Each month we will announce the people with the most steps walked.

Sophie wants to add more detail to her essay. Which of the following sentences would be **best** to add to her paragraph? Select **all** that apply.

A) Walking can get kind of boring unless the scenery is pretty.

B) At the mall, people tend to take the escalator instead of walking up the stairs.

C) Just a brisk thirty-minute walk a day can help people control their weight.

D) Our basketball court and sports equipment are in need of repair too.

E) Health experts recommend walking at least 10,000 steps a day.

F) A pedometer is a useful tool for measuring the number of steps you take.

22 Jacob is writing a narrative about a special memory. His teacher suggested he
add dialogue to improve the narrative. Read these paragraphs from his narrative
and the directions that follow.

W.5.3
DOK 2

One of my fondest memories of childhood is summer at Gran's. Those were days of
endless discovery for me. There was always something new and interesting for me, be
it gardening with Gran or rummaging through her quilt-patch box. She didn't mind
lying on the grass and staring up at the clouds, either. That was one of my favorite
ways to pass the time even though some people might call it a waste of time.

Gran pointed to one cloud and said it resembled an elephant. Those brought good luck.
I studied the cloud that hung above us and listened as Gran pointed out the trunk, tail,
and feet in the fluffy-animal cloud. Her voice was like an old woolen blanket, rough
and scratchy, yet warm and soothing.

Rewrite the underlined sentences, adding dialogue to the narrative.

_____

_____

_____

23 Pam is writing a narrative about a pen pal. However, her draft lacks a
transition between paragraphs. Read her story and the directions that follow.

W.5.3
DOK 2

"Listen up, kids," said our teacher one morning. "We are going to be
writing letters to pen pals in Tokyo, Japan. In your letters, you can talk about your
family, your favorite hobbies, and anything else that you find interesting. Yes, you can
even include poems or drawings."

I was very pleased with the results. My teacher helped us address our letters properly. I hoped that my pen pal, Satsuki, would have lots of cool things to write back. It
would be two weeks before our teacher said, "Guess what, kids? Your pen pals have
written back!"

Write **at least one** transition sentence that logically connects the two paragraphs and is
consistent with the tone of the narrative.

_____

_____

_____

Listen to the presentation, and answer the questions that follow.

After Apple-Picking
by Robert Frost

http://americanbookcompany.com/media/after-apple-picking

24 What **best** summarizes the main idea of this poem?

SL.5.2
DOK 2

A) Humans should sleep as peacefully as the woodchuck.

C) Apples are a healthy fruit with the power to heal.

B) The more fruit there is, the more money one will make.

D) Apple-picking is a rewarding but tiring experience.

25 What happens to apples that are dropped on the ground?

SL.5.1
DOK 1

A) They get thrown away.

C) Cider is made from them.

B) Someone eats them.

D) They are left for the animals.

26 This question has two parts. First, answer part A. Then, answer part B.

SL.5.4
DOK 2

Part A

Read this line from the presentation.

There were ten thousand thousand fruit to touch,

Which type of figurative language does the speaker use in this line?

A) hyperbole

C) metaphor

B) simile

D) personification

Part B

What effect does this example of figurative language have on the meaning of the poem? Explain your answer.

_____

_____

27 In the presentation, the narrator says he skimmed "a pane of glass" from a drinking trough in the morning. What does the narrator mean by this?

SL.5.3
DOK 2

A) Someone had dropped a drinking glass into the trough, and it broke.

B) Winter is coming, and a thin sheet of ice had formed on the water.

C) Through the water, he read words written on the bottom of the trough.

D) He was looking through a window and seeing the trough outside.

Listen to the presentation, and answer the questions that follow.

Harriet Tubman
http://americanbookcompany.com/media/harriet-tubman

28 How did the Underground Railroad get its name? Name **at least three** details from the presentation that explain how it was similar to a railroad.

SL.5.3
DOK 2

_____

_____

_____

29 Which sentences from the presentation **best** support the idea that Harriet Tubman was a determined woman? Select **all** that apply.

SL.5.3
DOK 3

A) Tubman, an African American woman, was an escaped slave herself.

B) She became an important abolitionist (a person who opposes slavery).

C) Sometimes Tubman and her passengers experienced great hardships.

D) Once on the journey, Tubman made sure no person would ever turn back from the challenges.

E) "You must go on or die," she would tell everyone.

30 Which multimedia display would be the best choice to enhance this presentation? SL.5.5
DOK 3

A) a map showing the routes of the Underground Railroad

B) a video of a train pulling into a train station

C) an audio clip of an African American spiritual

D) a timeline showing the chronology of the Civil War

SL.5.6
DOK 2

31 Which sentence is **not** appropriate for a formal presentation on Harriet Tubman?

A) Using the Underground Railroad, Tubman guided them on the perilous journey to freedom.

B) The Underground Railroad was not an actual railroad that ran beneath the earth.

C) "Stations" connected the slave states of the South to northern states and to Canada.

D) Her followers knew she meant business and wouldn't put up with any of that tomfoolery.

Read and answer the following questions.

32 Ruthie is researching famous explorers. She types the key words *Marco Polo* into an online search engine. Which of the online sources below looks **most** relevant to her research assignment?

W.5.8
DOK 2

A) **Learn Marco Polo**

www.funkidspoolgames.com

Learn about the best pool games you can play this summer! Includes instructions for Marco Polo, Sharks and Minnows, Categories, and more! Toys included …

B) **Marco Polo Biography – Smart History for Kids**

www.smarthistorykids.com/marco-polo

A famous Venetian explorer, Marco Polo was born in 1254. He set sail for Asia at the young age of 17 and continued his travels …

C) **Marco Polo Italian Restaurant**

www.marcopoloitalianrestaurant.com

Delicious Italian meals and a family-friendly atmosphere. View our menu and hours. Call 770-555-8395 to make reservations for parties of 8 or more …

D) **Annual Marco Polo Jubilee**

www.marcopolojubilee.com

Come celebrate the friendship between Chinese Americans and Italian Americans. All are welcome at the 8th annual Marco Polo Jubilee which takes place Oct. 3 …

33 Nathaniel is researching the protection of endangered species for a report. Read these sources from his research and the question that follows.

W.5.7
DOK 2

Source 1

Many people appreciate animals for their beauty, strength, fierceness, or cuteness. But why else do people try to save endangered species? Animals actually have numerous benefits to people and the planet itself. Animals are vital to the world's ecosystems. They provide food, transport, protection, and assistance to humans. Saving endangered species keeps the planet's life in balance.

Source 2

Everyone should make an effort to save the planet's endangered giant pandas! There are many animals that are in danger of dying out. Once they're gone, they're gone forever! Don't let this happen to a cute animal like the giant panda. These are people's favorite animals at zoos. Pandas deserve to have a long and healthy existence. Contribute today to a wildlife preservation organization!

Which source provides the **most** useful facts for Nathaniel's essay? Explain your answer.

_____

_____

_____

34 Alexis is writing an informational essay about Judy Blume. Read this paragraph from her essay and the question that follows.

W.5.8
DOK 2

Judy Blume is a well-known American children's author. She was born in 1938 in New Jersey and graduated from college with a teaching degree. She started writing children's books when her own children started preschool. Some of her best-known books are *Tales of a Fourth Grade Nothing*, *Otherwise Known as Sheila the Great*, and *Blubber*, which were published in the 1970s. Judy Blume has won many literary awards.

Which of the following books will provide the **most** useful information for Alexis's essay?

A) *Tales of a Fourth Grade Nothing*

B) *Children's Authors: Judy Blume*

C) *A Treasury of Children's Literature*

D) *Famous Authors of the 1970s*

35 Mariah is researching O horizons for a science report. Read these sources and the question that follows.

W.5.7
DOK 2

Source 1

Location	Amount of dead plant material each year
Meadow	122 kg
Pine forest	129 kg
Desert	59 kg
Deciduous forest	203 kg

Source 2

Soil is enriched by both **organic matter** and **inorganic matter**. Organic matter results from the decay of living things like plants; inorganic matter results from the decay of nonliving things like rocks. These ongoing processes continue to develop the soil until, at some point, the soil can be called **mature.** Maturity is reached more quickly in hot, wet climates than in cold, dry climates. Mature soil has four layers, called **horizons**.

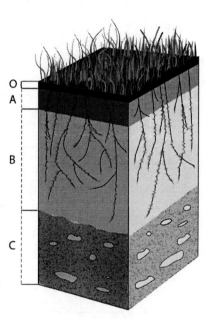

At the very top, above the soil line, is the **O horizon**. What do you think that "O" stands for? Organic! The O horizon is the organic layer, where plants live. It is most commonly found in forest areas. Just below that is the **A horizon**. This layer, also called topsoil, contains organic matter, including decaying plants and plant roots. The A horizon is very rich in nutrients, so it is also the home of many insects, worms and burrowing animals.

Next comes the **B horizon**, which contains clays and mineral deposits that have not yet been weathered. This layer is called the **subsoil**. The structure of the subsoil will be gradually broken up by seeping water and intruding plant roots. The nutrients in this layer will be gradually incorporated into the A horizon as plant roots absorb them.

Below that is the **C horizon**, containing weathered bedrock. This horizon is mostly isolated from the soil formation process. It is called the **substratum**.

Based on the information in the sources, which location would **most likely** have the deepest O horizon?

A) a meadow

B) a pine forest

C) a desert

D) a deciduous forest

W.5.9
DOK 3

36 Tim is researching Sherman's march to the sea. Read the sources and the question that follows.

Source 1

In 1864, Ulysses S. Grant's most trusted general, William T. Sherman, marched into Georgia. He knew Atlanta, the capital of Georgia, was an important railroad hub. If Sherman took Atlanta, the South would not be able to ship supplies and soldiers where they were needed. Despite its best efforts, the Confederate Army was unable to stop Sherman. He took over Atlanta in September. As a result, more Northerners supported Lincoln, and he was reelected. Before Sherman's Atlanta campaign, some Northerners wanted to replace Lincoln with someone who would negotiate with the South and stop the war. Sherman's success renewed the North's confidence that it could win the Civil War.

Source 2

That Union general, Sherman, is destroying our state! News spread quickly when he took Atlanta two months ago. Not only did he beat the Confederate forces, but he burned the great city! Now he's marching southeast toward the sea, toward our Savannah home, and destroying everything in his path. Buildings, rail lines, factories, bridges … he's wiping them all out. I've never seen our town so scared. The leaders are talking about surrendering should he arrive at our city. At this point, I don't care who wins the war. I just want the fighting and devastation to end.

How do the authors' different perspectives affect how they describe the event? Explain your answer using details from the texts.

_____

_____

_____

Performance Task

Your class is practicing making speeches in preparation for a speech-giving contest. Because some students have expressed nervousness about speaking in public, your teacher has asked you to research this phobia and ways to cope with it. Below are four sources you have found in your research.

After you have looked over the sources, you will answer some questions. Take a look at the sources and the questions. Remember, you'll need to scan every source to gain information to answer the questions and write a narrative essay.

In Part 2, you will write your essay using information from the sources.

Steps to Follow:

In order to plan and write your article, you will do the following:

1.   Examine four sources.

2.   Make notes about the information from the sources.

3.   Answer three questions about the sources.

Directions for Beginning:

Now you will study the different sources. Take notes because you may want to refer to them while writing your narrative. You will be allowed to come back to any of the sources as many times as you like.

Research Questions:

After studying all of the resources, use the rest of your time in Part 1 to answer three questions about them. Your answers will be scored. Also, your answers will help you think about what you have researched, which should help you in your writing assignment.

Part 1

Source #1

A short story about a student's fear of public speaking

Dexter's Dilemma

Dexter was furious with himself. At first, when Ms. Rosenthal had made the assignment, Dexter thought it would be great: he was a whiz at science, and the chance to do a science project was a dream come true. He had gone home that very Friday afternoon, mapped out a plan, and begun work the next day. After three weeks of conducting the experiment, he was finished. The next step was to prepare a report and presentation, and Dexter did this with the same dedication as when he had started the assignment. In the end, Dexter's report was well written. He also had a nicely decorated poster that showed off all of the diligent planning.

There was just one problem, and it was a huge one. This problem was the reason that he sat chin in hand, elbows on table, thinking about what in the world he was going to do. Poor Dexter had been working so hard on his project that he had forgotten the most difficult part—the presentation. The presentation part would be the worst because Dexter had a fear of speaking in front of others; the worst was when he had to get up in front of his classmates.

Sitting there, wondering how it would go tomorrow in class, Dexter couldn't help but feel apprehensive. He could only imagine the worst; in his mind's eye, he could picture himself standing at the front of the room and facing his giggling classmates. They would stare back at him blankly, and he would begin to sweat and shudder. They would stare. He would stand there, mute and feeling ridiculous, for what would seem like an eternity before Ms. Rosenthal would give him her disappointed look and ask him to take a seat.

He thought he was the only one afraid to give a speech. Then, his mom gave him a book about public speaking, and he found out he was not alone. Knowing that he wasn't alone in his fear of public speaking, Dexter felt slightly better. He read the book carefully for advice on how to conquer his fear.

That evening, Dexter started practicing his presentation. First, he stood in front of his bathroom mirror and watched his body language and facial expressions as he spoke. He relaxed his shoulders and made an effort not to fidget with his hands. He practiced staring straight ahead, not looking down at his notes. Tomorrow, he would have to make eye contact with his audience.

Next, Dexter recorded himself speaking. He played it back and realized he was talking too fast; in some parts, he would mumble when he became nervous. Dexter practiced his presentation again and again, making an effort to slow down. He recorded himself a second time. This time, he spoke at an even rate, and his words were easier to understand. Dexter started to feel more confident.

Finally, he called his mom and dad into the living room and asked if he could give his presentation in front of them. They sat on the couch and listened attentively. Even his little sister, Maggie, stopped playing with her toys and joined them. Dexter took a deep breath and presented his report. His parents smiled at him and seemed interested in what he had to say. As he went on, Dexter became more at ease. He spoke with expression and excitement. When he finished, his mom, dad, and Maggie clapped and told him he did a great job. Dexter grinned.

As he went to bed, Dexter imagined how the presentation would go tomorrow. He still felt a little nervous, but he told himself that he'd do well. If he kept a positive attitude, he was sure to succeed!

Source #2

An article about the fear of public speaking

The Fear of Public Speaking
by Regina Butters

What is your greatest phobia? Roller coasters? Spiders? Aliens or vampires? What about speaking in front of others? Perhaps public speaking comes easily for you, but for many, it is as scary as jumping from an airplane or walking a tightrope. According to national surveys, Americans fear public speaking just as much or more than major fears like flying in airplanes or terrorist attacks. In fact, it has been reported that for some, the idea of speaking publicly is even scarier than death!

When faced with the task of public speaking, some people instantly panic. Anxiety symptoms might include butterflies in the stomach, sweaty palms, shortness of breath, and a loss of concentration. In cases where people actually get to the speaking part, their voices might be altered—higher, whinier, and shakier. In some cases, people might find themselves frozen stiff and struck mute in front of an audience. For some, even the anticipation of the task of public speaking can cause such a reaction.

This common fear is a widespread issue. But there is advice for those people who face this phobia. Here are some ways that experts say people can combat this fear of speaking in front of others:

- **Prepare adequately.** Often, if you are well prepared, you will have the confidence necessary to deliver a successful presentation.

- **Take deep breaths.** Taking deep breaths prior to the presentation will slow down your heart rate and help to relax you.

- **Use your imagination.** Pretending that you are alone or that you are speaking in front of the mirror at home can often help make the task of public speaking easier to bear.

- **Find a focal point.** Sometimes it is easier to focus on a point in the room. Speaking to this point rather than to an audience can help you to maintain focus and concentration.

- **Cut yourself some slack**. No one is perfect. So in public speaking, why strive for perfection? Remember to be realistic and simply do your best.

Post Test

As you're giving your speech, remember the following dos and don'ts.

Dos	Don'ts
<ul><li>show enthusiasm for your topic</li><li>make eye contact with the audience</li><li>tell an appropriate joke or story relevant to the speech topic</li><li>answer questions as best you can (it's okay to say, "I don't know")</li></ul>	<ul><li>touch your hair or face excessively</li><li>say filler words like *uh* and *you know*</li><li>read from your note cards word for word</li><li>mumble or talk too fast</li><li>pace or sway side to side</li></ul>

Source #3

The King's Speech

"There are two types of speakers: those that are nervous and those that are liars." – Mark Twain

The fear of public speaking is such a common phobia that even celebrities and great leaders struggle with it. One such person was King George VI, the ruler of Britain during World War II. George VI's story of overcoming this fear was featured in the award-winning film *The King's Speech*.

George VI was born Prince Albert (nicknamed Bertie by his family), the son of the Prince of Wales. His father later became King George V. Prince Albert grew up with a stammer. He was a shy person, and his stutter made him hesitant to speak in front of other people. It was especially hard when he had to give speeches.

In 1936, Prince Albert's older brother Edward took over the throne. But Edward didn't want to be the king. He abdicated (gave up the position of king) later that same year. Prince Albert was next in line for the throne. He was reluctant to take the position, but he didn't have much choice. Europe was heading into war. Britain needed a strong leader.

As the new king, George VI had to address the people over the radio. He was terrified that his stammer would make it impossible for him to get through the speech. He would get stuck on a word, unable to say it, and become more and more anxious. He began seeing a speech therapist named Lionel Logue.

Logue gave George VI speech exercises to practice to help with his stammer. He also counseled the king on how to deal with his speech anxiety. When George VI gave his radio broadcast, alone in a room with just a microphone, Logue stayed with him and silently coached him through the speech.

George VI was able to conquer his fear of speaking. He spoke slowly but clearly and deliberately. His people were inspired by his strong, passionate words. They knew he would lead them through the war. George VI and Logue remained good friends.

A website listing the most common phobias among Americans

Source #4

A website listing the most common phobias among Americans

WHAT ARE WE SCARED OF?

THE MOST COMMON PHOBIAS IN AMERICA

Snakes? Why did it have to be snakes? According to a recent Gallup poll, Americans have a great fear of the slithering creatures, followed closely by public speaking. Phobias, or irrational fears, are common among children and adults. Here's a breakdown of the most common phobias Americans have.

Phobia	Definition	% of Americans who reported the fear
1. Ophidiophobia (oh-fid-ee-oh-foh-bee-uh)	fear of snakes	56
2. Glossophobia (gloss-oh-foh-bee-uh)	fear of public speaking	45
3. Acrophobia (ak-ruh-foh-bee-uh)	fear of heights	41
4. Claustrophobia (klaw-struh-foh-bee-uh)	fear of tight spaces	36
5. Arachnophobia (uh-rak-nuh-foh-bee-uh)	fear of spiders	34
6. Musophobia (moo-so-foh-bee-uh)	fear of mice	26
7. Trypanophobia (trip-an-oh-foh-bee-uh)	fear of getting shots	21
8. Aerophobia (air-uh-foh-bee-uh)	fear of flying	20
9. Astraphobia (as-truh-foh-bee-uh)	fear of thunder and lightning	17
10. Latrophobia (lah-tro-foh-bee-uh)	fear of doctors	12
11. Enochlophobia (ee-knock-low-foh-bee-uh)	fear of crowds	11
12. Cynophobia (sigh-nuh-foh-bee-uh)	fear of dogs	10
13. Achluophobia (ak-lew-oh-foh-bee-uh)	fear of the dark	8

Did the fact that there are thirteen phobias listed make you nervous? You might have Triskaidekaphobia (tris-kay-dek-uh-foh-bee-uh)—a superstitious fear of the unlucky number thirteen!

Source: http://www.gallup.com/poll/1891/snakes-top-list-americans-fears.aspx

Notes

What are phobias?	
Why do people fear public speaking?	
How do people cope with phobias?	
How do people prepare for public speaking?	
What makes an effective speech?	

37 Compare and contrast Dexter's and King George VI's stories. Why were they afraid, and how did they cope with their fear? Use information from **at least three** sources in your answer.

W.5.9
DOK 4

_____

_____

_____

38 What conclusions can you make based on the information in the sources? Select **all** that apply.

W.5.7
DOK 4

A) The fear of public speaking is a widespread issue.

B) Practicing a speech beforehand is a useful strategy.

C) The fear of public speaking is the most common phobia.

D) If people are afraid to give speeches, they should avoid it.

E) Nervousness causes physical symptoms as well as mental ones.

F) There is nothing to be done to cope with glossophobia.

G) Speaking quickly during a speech makes you sound more confident.

39 Watch this video of a person giving a speech, and then answer the question.

W.5.8
DOK 4

http://americanbookcompany.com/media/performance-task-speech

Evaluate the speaker's presentation. Based on the information in the sources, name **at least three** suggestions for improving the speech.

_____

_____

_____

Part 2

You will now have time to review your notes and sources. Use this time efficiently to plan, draft, and revise your essay. You may use your notes and refer to the sources. Remember, you may also use the answers you wrote to questions in Part 1, but you cannot change those answers. Now read your assignment. Review the information about how your essay will be scored. Then, begin your work.

Your Assignment

Your assignment is to write a narrative essay about a time you had to prepare for speaking in public. What lessons can you take from other people who had to deal with a fear of public speaking? Use facts and details from the sources you have researched to give your narrative essay real facts and examples. The audience for your essay will be your teacher and classmates.

REMEMBER: A well-written narrative essay:

- has a clear plot
- is well-organized and stays on the topic
- has a beginning, middle, and end
- uses transitions
- uses details from the sources to support your plot
- develops events and characters clearly
- uses clear language
- follows rules of writing (spelling, punctuation, and grammar)

Planning

Use this plot diagram to help plan your narrative. Don't forget to review your notes from part 1.

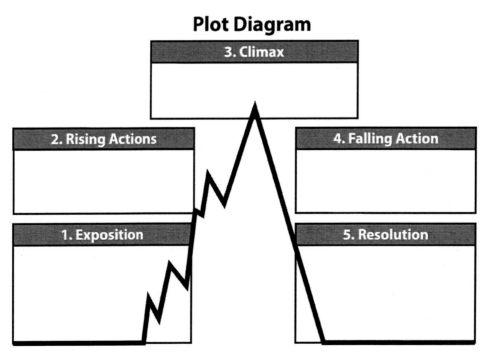

Plot Diagram

Copyright © American Book Company

Now, begin work on your essay. Manage your time carefully so that you can do the following:

- plan your essay

- write your essay

- revise and edit for a final draft

Writing Checklist Questions

☐ Did I respond to the prompt?

☐ Is my main idea clear?

☐ Do my details all support the main idea?

☐ Did I make the best word choices?

☐ Are my points all in a logical order?

☐ Are all my sentences complete?

☐ Are there any errors in usage, grammar, punctuation, and spelling?

---

40 For Part 2, you are being asked to write a narrative essay that is several paragraphs long. Use your own paper for this assignment. Remember to check your notes and your prewriting and planning as you write, then revise and edit your essay.

W.5.3–10
DOK 4

End of Test

Index